DISCARDED

IN THE DARK BACKWARD

IN THE DARK BACKWARD

By
HENRY W. NEVINSON

"In the dark Backward and Abysm of Time."
The Tempest, Act I, Scene 2.

Essay Index Reprint Series

 BOOKS FOR LIBRARIES PRESS
FREEPORT, NEW YORK

First Published 1934
Reprinted 1970

STANDARD BOOK NUMBER:
8369-1621-2

LIBRARY OF CONGRESS CATALOG CARD NUMBER:
72-111854

PRINTED IN THE UNITED STATES OF AMERICA

CONTENTS

SCENE	I.	"TROY WAS": *How, being at Helles in the Dardanelles, I saw from the S.S. "River Clyde" the fall of Troy and the fate of the captives* . . . pp.	1–12
SCENE	II.	BACK TO NATURE: *How, being in the Syrian desert beside the Euphrates, I saw the King of Babylon return from the Wilderness* . . . . pp.	13–23
SCENE	III.	A HAPPY WARRIOR: *How, in coasting along the Black Sea, I saw Xenophon with the Ten Thousand reach Trebizond* . . . . . pp.	24–57
SCENE	IV.	"MY SERPENT OF OLD NILE": *How, being in Epirus during a Greek retreat, I beheld the Battle of Actium.* . pp.	58–70
SCENE	V.	VIA DOLOROSA: *How, being in Jerusalem, I saw the Roman soldiers and a rabble of Jews leading Christ to Calvary* . . . . . pp.	71–84
SCENE	VI.	THE GODS DEPART: *How, on landing at Spalato, I heard the Emperor Diocletian discussing the world and saw him witnessing a martyrdom of Christians.* pp.	85–108
SCENE	VII.	ST. CRISPIN'S DAY: *How, being with my colleagues at Rollancourt, I witnessed the Battle of Agincourt* . . pp.	109–121
SCENE	VIII.	THE ABBEY OF JOY: *How, being at Chinon, I saw Joan of Arc, and dwelt in the Abbey of Thélème* . . pp.	122–136

CONTENTS

SCENE IX. "NOT WITHOUT HONOUR": *How, walking in Aldersgate, I met Milton and accompanied him to his home* . pp. 137–145

SCENE X. "KING OF ALL HIELAND HAIRTS": *How, being at my ancestral home in Westmorland, I saw Prince Charlie and his Highlanders advance and retreat* pp. 146–160

SCENE XI. REVENANT: *How, being at a performance of "Samson" in Wales, I heard the composer conduct* . . . pp. 161–169

SCENE XII. "L'HOMME": *How, leading a running party of students at Jena, I witnessed the battle, and the intrusion into Goethe's house at Weimar* . . . pp. 170–183

SCENE XIII. "THE PILGRIM OF ETERNITY": *How, being at Newstead Abbey, I felt the presence of Byron, whose heroic end I witnessed on my way through Ætolia* . . pp. 184–202

SCENE XIV. "DAILY SELF-SURPAST": *How, while exposing the slave-trade in Angola, I witnessed Livingstone's noblest sacrifice* . . . . . pp. 203–221

SCENE XV. THE RED SULTAN: *How, being in Macedonia, I witnessed the misrule of Abdul Hamid, and in the Bosphorus followed his subsequent fate* . . . . pp. 222–237

SCENE XVI. ON THE OCEAN WAVE: *How, in passing the icebergs off Newfoundland, I beheld the drowning of Mr. Jones* . pp. 238–248

SCENE XVII. DISSOLVING VIEWS: *How, in travelling over the sites of the Great War at various times, I witnessed scenes in which I had then been present* . . . pp. 249–272

INDEX . . . . . pp. 273–276

INTRODUCTION

FROM boyhood up I have lived a double life, but I do not use the phrase in the sense of amorous relationships concealed under an appearance of respectable behaviour. My double life has implied living in two different ages at the same time. One is called the present, and the other the past, but the two are so closely united that the difference becomes of small account. In the following chapters I have chosen only those events in the past which were present with me in a few definite scenes of my own life. But in many other parts of the world I have been conscious of what happened there in a different age, sometimes remote, and sometimes only a few years away.

Naturally, this sense of a double life is felt most keenly among the relics of Greece and Rome, and among the surviving churches, ruined abbeys, and castles of England, for there the suggestion of past ages is at once vivid. " You have an unerring nose for castles," said a friend who used to accompany my wanderings from Harlech to Bamborough, and from Dover to Carlisle. Certainly I have delighted in discovering for myself Ludlow, Chepstow, Bodiam, Lewes, Shrewsbury, the Peak, the Tower, Ashby-de-la-Zouch, and about a dozen more. So also I have delighted in our great cathedrals of Durham, York, Lincoln, Ely, Peterborough, Norwich, Rochester, Chichester, Winchester, Exeter, Hereford, and a few

INTRODUCTION

others; and in our abbeys of Fountains, Rievaulx, Tintern, Canterbury, Newstead, Ulverscroft, Shap, and many more; all of them beautiful, as ancient work is. But to me their beauty was not the chief attraction. That has been the visions rising from the dark backward and abysm of time, for in those visions I have lived as vividly as in the present hours, which are themselves transitory, rushing every moment into the same dark backward.

At any minute and in any place this consciousness of being, not in two places, but in two times at the same time, may come upon us. In ordinary scenes and on ordinary days or nights it may come. It is not an uncommon visitation, and perhaps it befalls most of us. In his lyric called "The Memory of Earth" the Irish poet "A. E." (George Russell) has given it expression:

> "In the wet dusk silver sweet,
> Down the violet-scented ways,
> As I moved with quiet feet
> I was met by mighty days.
>
> On the hedge the hanging dew
> Glassed the eve and stars and skies;
> While I gazed a madness grew
> Into thundered battle cries.
>
> Where the hawthorn glimmered white
> Flashed the spear and fell the stroke—
> Ah, what faces pale and bright
> Where the dazzling battle broke.
>
> There a hero-hearted queen
> With young beauty lit the van;
> Gone! the darkness flowed between
> All the ancient wars of man." [1]

Or the vision may be reversed, and in the midst of thundering battle cries and the dazzling battle one may

[1] From *The Earth Breath and Other Poems*, by A. E. (1897).

INTRODUCTION

become conscious of the same scene as it appeared in distant and quiet times. During " the troubles " in Dublin, for instance, while I was in the midst of the bombardment and burning of the Four Courts, and the whole city was crackling with deadly conflict, I felt myself equally present with Swift in St. Patrick's Deanery just across the Liffey while he was writing the *Drapier's Letters* or *Gulliver*, or even when he was tramping to and fro for many hours a day in his large room, his memory quite gone, his noble indignation, his courageous passion for freedom, and his superb intelligence—all quite gone, and the populace, in terror or derision, peering at him through the tall iron railings, or even being admitted into the house by his servants to stare at him for a small fee :

" Down Marlborough's cheeks the streams of dotage flow,
  And Swift expires a driveller and a show."

More pitiable even than one of his own Struldbrugs Swift was to know the wretchedness of those who cannot die.

Birds and beasts and insects are said to inherit a " race memory ", and it is hard to discover any other cause for the " instinct " which urges bees and ants and termites to live under a monotonous and tyrannical communism, birds to migrate, and lemmings to process towards mass-suicide in the ocean. But these creatures appear to have no personal consciousness of time past beyond the compass of their own lives, and to have no backward vision is to live only a single life when it might be multiple. I can imagine that the Pilgrim Fathers, on first landing on their unexplored continent unripened by memories, may have found existence rather crude, and to our First Parents even Paradise may have appeared dull until they fell into a memorable error.

INTRODUCTION

Time purifies all things, as Euripides said of the sea, and space, which is time's sister, also possesses a purifying power. It is a miracle of space that atrocious smells are subdued by a few hundred yards of open air, and I am told that our rivers and streams, which are the natural receptacles of civilization's dye-works and sewage, run themselves so clear within ten miles that they cease to steam with poison-gas and can be drunk without much risk of death. So the visions of the past are purified by time, and lose much of their horror. Haggard fear is shed, and the element of filth can be recalled only with effort. Hunger, thirst, and exhaustion can be recalled, but they no longer torment ourselves. The cruelty of the past may be realized with almost unendurable anguish, but even the old delight in cruelty, that peculiar characteristic of mankind, has in some modern races been slightly appeased. I suppose that is the greatest change which has come about in man's immemorial history, for physical evolution and mechanical inventions are trivial in comparison. Other motives to pleasure, such as love, ambition, and the exercise of faculty, hold good. The preference of virtue to vice remains as astounding as ever. But the infliction of cruelty for pleasure is no longer so widely prized.

I have not learnt why it is that a scene of distant time or place will suddenly intrude itself upon the mind without any traceable connection with the present scene or occupation. But the visions of the past described in the following chapters, running in order of date from Troy to the Great War, have been suggested by imagination or ancient records only where the events actually took place. The bare fact that the past is gone for ever is one of the innumerable marvels among which we live, all equally overwhelm-

INTRODUCTION

ing in mystery so inexplicable that I sometimes think I shall burst with wonder—explode, as Sir James Jeans tells us the Universe once exploded, and I only wish he would tell us what the Universe was like before the explosion. That left the earth, he says, spinning as a smaller speck in space than the tiniest mote in a sunbeam. He also tells us that we may travel so far through time that all human history will shrink to a tick of the clock, and a man's life to less than the twinkling of an eye. Since that is so, an inborn capacity for living a double life in the tick of a clock seems hardly worth mentioning, so inconceivably vast is the mystery which surrounds us. Here is an exploded Universe for space; here are incalculable ages for time; and here is the meanest flower that blows. How can we contain ourselves? How continue without some solution to our amazement? It is difficult to imagine that all this process of universal movement, with its Milky Ways and stardust, its birds, beasts, and man slowly developing an inexplicable brain, moves along its course without some sort of a purpose. George Meredith, a man of acutely sceptical mind, once told me he agreed that it was difficult.

H. W. N.

London,
  1934.

IN THE DARK BACKWARD,

SCENE I

"TROY WAS"

How, being at Helles in the Dardanelles, I saw from the S.S. "River Clyde" the fall of Troy and the fate of the captives

ONE summer evening in 1915 I was staying on the *River Clyde*, which still lay aground off V Beach, with Cape Helles on one side and the old Turkish castle of Seddel Bahr on the other. Between them stretched a low and curving cliff, terraced like the seats of a theatre, which had been the scene of slaughter and incredible courage on the previous April 25th. The battered ship was now in command of my friend Lieutenant Cather, R.N., a man of chivalrous self-forgetfulness, as shown when, after his ship sank, he handed his life-belt to a drowning sailor. To me the *River Clyde* was often a haven of rest, as being one of the safest spots on the Gallipoli Peninsula. For the Turks had no desire to destroy the ship since her funnel was useful for sighting their four big guns camouflaged on the Asiatic side across the Hellespont, when they wished to throw shells over Cape Helles to burst upon W Beach, where most of the ammunition and supplies were landed.

So there I once was at sunset, looking forward to a

"TROY WAS"

night of comparative peace, as I climbed out to the top deck through heaped-up sandbags and scattered sand. To one of the ship's officers who met me I said, " I'm just going to have another look at the view," and he answered, " I'm dead sick of the view." For in moments of crisis or periods of prolonged anxiety, no beauty of any kind, human, artistic, or natural, has any soothing effect. It remains unnoticed or irritating, and no poet exposed to danger or monotony would take the smallest interest in mountain heights or the triumphs of architecture.

But I had not been chained for weeks, like the officer, to the *River Clyde*, and so I climbed to the deck, and looked again across the deep strait of the Hellespont, always swirling downward at six knots an hour, as it pours the water of Russian and Turkish rivers into the Ægean.

Opposite me, between the fortified promontory of Kum Kali, which the French had briefly occupied on the day of the Landings, and the grey and battered village of Eren Keui, where the rocky coast begins to rise again, lay a fairly open stretch of country, almost to be called a plain. Along the shore ran a narrow line of white and sandy beach, and across the open ground towards the Kum Kali headland I could trace small watercourses marked by low bushes and reeds, green among the prevailing grey of rocky and desert land. In the middle of the plain, about half a mile from the thin watercourses, rose a hill or large mound with rugged summit and steeply scarped sides, apparently a citadel. As well it might be, for it was Troy.

Those thin green lines of streams nearly dry were all that remained of the Rivers Simois and Scamander, once capable of divinity. That barren open land was the windy Trojan plain. That white and sandy beach was the shore where the fleet of the invading Greeks was hauled up for ten years to dry and rot, without a drink of salt water. As I looked I wondered how all those gallant ships could lie along that narrow beach. For over eleven hundred were gathered there from all parts of Greece and the Greek islands. They were laid up in double lines, it is true, one line farther from the water than the other, but still over a thousand ships make a large fleet, and some of them carried over a hundred men. Striking an average, the Greek army must have counted about a million, and though they bought wine from Lemnos, it was hard to imagine how such a host was supplied for ten years with the first necessity of food. Who ravaged the surrounding villages of Asia? Who drove in the flocks and herds, the slaughter, dissection, and cooking of which the poet describes with such minute satisfaction? Even the purchased wine they used queerly, strowing grated cheese upon it, and mixing it all up with a handful of ground barley, as the Scots fortify water by an admixture of oatmeal.

Greeks and Trojans appear to have sprung from the same stock, for they understood one another perfectly, except that among the Trojans there were some Carians who spoke an unknown tongue. The auxiliary gods on both sides, though violently opposed, were also familiar with each other, but did not hesitate to trick, lie, and use dissimulation, especially in the matter of sexual affection, though they were closely related, boasting descent, one and all, from the great Ocean who surrounds the earth. Zeus, the king of gods, uneasily endeavoured to hold an even balance between the rival parties of divinity, but to demonstrate his power in disputed cases he assured both gods and goddesses that they could not move him from heaven with a chain of gold, whereas he could draw them all up and leave them dangling from a peak of Olympus. Indeed, he had shown an example of his omnipotence when he took his own wife Hera, tied two anvils to her feet and bound her hands with golden cords to a summit in heaven, so that she hung suspended in space, discovering the disadvantages of immortality.

The deeds of bloodshed committed upon that plain between the white beach and the castellated hill were what journalists within my memory would have called "phenomenal". With evident relish the poetic historian dwells upon the nature of the fatal wounds, and gloats over the copious black blood that flowed from dying men as darkness covered their eyes and they fell to the ground with a thud, their armour clanking upon them. A spear, he tells us, went clean through the thigh, breaking the bone and severing the sinews where they are thickest. A spear passed right through the throat. A sword pierced the neck after the man had been taken alive, entangled in the crowd. A sword slashed below the ear so deep that nothing was left to hold the head on but a shred of skin. A spear ran through the mouth right into the brain, smashing the teeth and bones. A spear ran through the right jaw, so that the man was hooked out of his chariot like a fish from the sea. A big stone struck the helmet so hard that the brains were smashed to a pulp inside. A spear struck the midriff that runs around the heart. A spear pierced the chest close to the nipple, and was drawn out with all the blood and the soul. A sword split a head clean in two halves. A spear pierced the helmet, scattering the brain so that the man did not care about fighting any more. A spear drove right through the middle of the back, so that the point came out at the navel, and the man fell holding his bowels in his hands. A spear lamed a man at the knee, and a sword finished him off. While one clasped the knees in supplication, the other drove a sword right through into the liver, and the black blood spouted out. A spear ran into one ear and came out at the other. The blow of a sword severed the head, and the marrow oozed from the backbone. A spear pierced the belly at the middle, and the consequences are what might be expected. A frequent parting word spoken by the victor to the dead was, "Now you will be of more service to vultures than to your wife."

When Achilles, roused at last from his sullen withdrawal to his tent, met Hector, the noblest character in the story, he drove his spear through the thick part of the neck, not severing the windpipe, and when that chivalrous hero implored him by his life and knees not to suffer the dogs to devour his body but to send it home to the city, Achilles answered, " Dog, don't talk to me about knees or home. I only wish I could cut you in pieces and eat you raw! But nothing shall save you from the dogs and vultures. They will eat you up every scrap." He drew the spear from the neck and stripped the armour. Then all the Greeks came running up, and each plunged his spear into the dead body, saying, " It is easier to deal with Hector now than when he was trying to set our ships on fire." And all the time Hector's wife Andromache was warming the water for her husband's bath, as she always did when he had gone to the battle, just as a miner's wife prepares the bath when her husband is coming out of the pit. And afterwards lovely Helen herself lamented for Hector, who was the only man,

"TROY WAS"

except old King Priam, his father, who had always been polite to her ever since she ran away with Paris and caused the ten years' war.

These scenes of savagery, inculcated into our youth by our public-school education, fill the greater part of the narrative, and are described in episodes loosely connected. It seemed to me remarkable that the Greek poet or poets who stitched them together into this puzzling work, which ranks among the few immortal poems of the world, should have described the Greeks as rather more brutal and ruthless than the Trojans, among whom signs of pity and human kindliness are occasionally to be discerned and horror is not unmitigated. It is true that the metaphors with which the succession of bloodthirsty incidents is frequently relieved are derived from the stormy movement of clouds and tempests such as smote us on Gallipoli during our campaign, or from the natural savagery of bulls, wild boars, and lions, which must then have existed in large numbers throughout Western Asia, as we see from the Assyrian sculptures. But amidst all the monotonous accounts of bloodshed, severed limbs, and writhing bowels we find interspersed little glimpses of a beautiful and peaceful manner of life which any age might envy. A wealthy house is described as being supplied with fine and convenient furniture such as Hephæstos, who fell from heaven right down upon the island of Lemnos, the base of our Gallipoli fleet, used to construct of bronze and precious metals —tripods that ran of themselves on golden wheels, drinking cups, armlets, brooches and golden chains. It is true he was a god, and worked chiefly for deities, but the Greeks, like all mankind, imagined heaven only as a celestial counterpart of the very best they knew on earth, and the poet's pictures of divine residences were only records of what he had known in earthly palaces, like the Cretan, raised to a celestial power.

I read once again of the Shield that Hephæstos himself made for Achilles at the petition of the sea-nymph Thetis. Besides the representation of the earth, the sea, and the skies, shining with the principal stars under the names we still know them by, he wrought in metal various scenes of common life— weddings with music and dancing, the women watching from their house-doors, since a wedding is a most interesting event to all women ; and next a judgment hall, with elderly men giving just decision in a quarrel ; and then peasants ploughing with oxen, and at the end of each furrow given a large cup of wine to drink, as our peasants still are given cider, " sometimes a pint, sometimes a quart, sometimes a gallon, and sometimes a lot", as one of them has said ; and next came the reapers in a large cornfield, reaping with sickles, and followed by the binders of the swathes, while women were roasting a large ox, and stirring gruel for their dinner, and the landlord looked on in silence, happy as an English squire might be to see other people at work for him ; and next there came a picture of vintage, young men and maidens carrying the grapes in baskets, while a boy cheered them on with a lyre, singing the vintage song ; and here were herds of cattle, driven by four herdsmen and nine dogs to the water meadow, though a big lion is represented as seizing the foremost bull, and dragging him away, while the dogs kept at a safe distance, barking ; and here was a flock of sheep, feeding in a mountain glen, and last there came a village green on which young men and maidens were dancing hand in hand ; the girls wore linen dresses, and the youths wore home-spun shirts, a little oiled to preserve the skin; the girls had wreaths of flowers, and the youths had golden daggers hanging from silver baldrics, while a musician played or sang to them with a lyre, and two acrobats or clowns performed their tricks. It was a scene just like one of our folk-dance festivals, when men and women dance to the ancient music and the hobby-horse gambols around.

Then I read how, when a deputation came to Achilles, most ruthless and implacable of the Greeks, urging him to cease sulking about the pretty girl whom Agamemnon the King had taken from him, they found him singing to the lyre, recounting the deeds of ancient heroes. That was a sign of grace, but still more remarkable in those or any times was his obstinate refusal of a heavy bribe to renew his valiant deeds in the war. He was offered in the King's name seven new tripods, ten talents of gold, twenty iron cooking-pots, twelve race-horses, seven skilled and beautiful needlewomen, the particularly pretty girl over whom the quarrel had arisen, and (after Troy should have fallen) as much gold and bronze as he liked, twenty Trojan women, the most beautiful next to Helen, and when they got back to Argos one of the King's own daughters with a big dowry, together with seven rich and substantial towns. It was a considerable inducement even in the reckoning of women alone; for a really beautiful and useful woman was estimated at a hundred head of cattle and a herd of a thousand sheep mixed with goats. Yet Achilles refused, and the petitioners went away disappointed, like a railway deputation who had hinted wealth to a British Minister of Transport.

But while I was thus turning the leaves of the Greek Scriptures, the sun had set and across the black water of the strait and the darkened plain where these events had happened, I could hear singing and the sound of sacred dances, rising from the fortified hill beyond. The people of Troy were rejoicing in happy relief from their prolonged and daily anxiety and loss. Peace had come at last, and the hosts of Greek armies had departed in their ships. Now all could go to rest in the joyful security that we know when trumpets sound the armistice. In the quiet homes, husbands hung upon the walls their swords and spears since there would be no use for them again for ever, and all sank peacefully to sleep, husbands lying with wives, and the children sleeping within reach.

But then indeed arose a tumult of shouting and battle-cries and the dull thud of swords striking upon bare flesh. Men who had stood the ten years' siege fell in blood beside their beds, their bodies pierced, their limbs hewn off by Greeks who gave no quarter. Wives, mothers, and girls ran naked and shrieking down every familiar lane, not knowing where to turn. Bloodstained and lustful men rushed after them or sprang from every corner. Refuge in the temples was no help. From the very altars they were dragged by the hair for ravishment or death. Upon the roof where Hector's wife used to carry their little boy to visit the old King, in the palace, Greek soldiers now stormed, waving their spears in triumph and shouting victory. At the consecrated altar of the highest temple a noble Greek took the old King himself by the hair, plunged his sword up to the hilt into his side, and cut off the royal head. The night was given up to massacre and lust, and the hearts of Heaven's Queen and the Virgin of Athens were sated with a triumph long deferred.

Slowly the night of death and terror passed, and the

"'TROY WAS'"

dawn began to shed brown light from behind Mount Ida and the Asian Olympus. Near the beach I saw shadowy forms of soldiers moving about over the ground where the bones of so many heroes of both races now lay together, indistinguishable. They were busy round the huts, their shelter for so many weary years, now to be left for ever. From the huts down to the ships they were herding like droves of cattle the Trojan women whom they had captured alive as concubines and slaves-of-all-work. Hungry, naked, and crying miserably to each other, the women dragged themselves along, urged forward by curses and the points of spears. With them came Cassandra, crazily shouting the marriage song, and with the same maddened breath muttering the future doom of him, the king of men, who had chosen her for his pleasure. And out between rows of soldiers, bawdily mocking, came lovely Helen, the cause of all this woe, lovely and unperturbed, excusing her dubious past with specious lies, anxious now only to return in peace to her own husband's royal bed in far-off Sparta. And before her stumbled the aged Queen, Priam's lawful wife, mother of Hector and Paris and so many noble sons and daughters, now chosen as a domestic servant for Ulysses. For the great and noble women were separately chosen for the lords of Greece. And beside her came Hector's own wife, so dear, so attentive to all her hero's wants and pleasures, and in her arms she carried their little son, called the City's Lord.

Then down upon her marched a platoon of soldiers under command of a sergeant, disciplined to overcome his own kindly nature so as to be fit for war. He ordered his men to drag the child from the mother's arms and carry him away. For he was to be flung to death from the height of the captured city's walls, lest Hector's son should grow to be his father's like. It was done, and the shattered little body, first washed of his blood in the river, was brought back to the women and the aged Queen. So they, with unavailing lamentations, wrapped him in fine linen and laid him in the earth beside the shore, never again to delight his mother's heart with his prettier ways than any child but Hector's could have.

As I listened to their wailings, I suddenly saw under the increasing light of the day a redder glare kindling upon that hill in the middle of the open ground. Volumes of smoke poured upwards, black at first but turning brilliant red and orange as long tongues of flame shot flickering in the sky. Against that light the black walls of the city stood revealed. High towers in the centre showed like dark columns in the fiery glow. Yellow flames burst from the windows of the lofty palace—from the windows of those fifty bedchambers, the promise of so fertile a dynasty. Walls built by the gods themselves—walls that had withstood the assaults of all those years—crumbled away into dust under the heat. Sinister forms of the spirits and gods who had hated Troy appeared hovering in the tumultuous smoke and stalking among the very flames. The whole city's hill melted down into a mass of glowing and shapeless ruin. As when loads of craggy ironstone are flung into a smelting furnace, and through a hole at the base the ore comes pouring out into a trough ready to receive it, and lies there sparkling and glowing like the sun, too hot and too bright for anyone to touch or look at it; so the ancient city of Troy glowed, a molten mass of red-hot stones—stones that once were walls and towers and palaces and the secluded dwellings of the Trojan race.

"TROY WAS"

Louder and more distinct than the crash of the falling towers came the successive booms of the four Turkish guns camouflaged upon the Asiatic shore a little to our left of that white and haunted line of beach. One after another the big shells screamed over my head, to burst crashing upon W Beach among the loads of supplies and the sheltered offices of transport. The last shell rushed over me with a scream more highly pitched, and at a speed as though to overtake the other three. "That's the one the French call '*Marie pressée*,'" said the naval officer, who had now come on deck beside me. "Let's climb over the cliff to W Beach and see what damage she has done." So we climbed together and saw.

SCENE II

BACK TO NATURE

How, being in the Syrian desert beside the Euphrates, I saw the King of Babylon return from the Wilderness

AS I drove through the Syrian desert from Tripoli through Homs on my way to Baghdad I had to pass through the rows of orange columns and arcades which mark the site of Palmyra, the city of the noble-hearted queen Zenobia, who dared to stand against the power of Rome nearly seventeen centuries ago. Her city, among the beautiful relics of which a few Arab huts and a wretched khan now seek shelter from the sun, has been superb in splendour, and amid the sandstone cliffs and desert spaces one came upon it as a miracle. But where, I wondered, was water for so magnificent a place? One small well for the villagers was evident in the middle of an open square, but that was all. I drove on, regretfully leaving so strange a memorial of an almost forgotten age and woman, but as I entered upon the flat desert that extends almost to the Euphrates, I looked south and there lay a vast sheet of brilliant water, the edge not more than a mile or two away, and here and there it was fringed with palm trees and bushes, wavering in the steamy heat.

" Plenty of water there for all the queens of the

BACK TO NATURE

world to drink and wash in," I thought, and asked the driver to turn aside so that I might swim out into the lake and be cool.

"It is a mirage," he objected.

"Why is it there?" I asked, unable to believe him.

"By God's will," he answered; "it is always there."

We drove on. That night the November rains began and turned the hard-caked surface of the desert to liquid slush into which the cars sank deep, especially the cars that were heavy with mails for the British in Baghdad. Day after day, from dawn till late evening we toiled. We hauled, we dug, we laid down stones for the wheels to bite on, but four nights and days were spent in mud before the Euphrates came in sight, and then, at the fort of Ramadi, we were held up again by the news that a torrent of rain made the track to the bridge at Felujah impassable. So there I walked along the bank of the ancient and famous river, which was sweeping down its course in streaks of blue and brown, like any other powerful river that had a source far away among mountains.

It was noon again, and as I sat in the shade by the river bank, hoping that by next morning the track would be dry enough for movement, I looked south down the water and thought of that great city through the centre of which it once had flowed. As in a mirage I saw the city rise, not far away. In reality it was about fifty miles, but it looked much nearer. I saw vast walls standing there, over three hundred feet high (high as St. Paul's dome at the Golden Gallery); seventy-five feet thick, so that chariots could pass each other along the top, leaving an ample margin on each side; and the wall facing me was fourteen miles long, the other three sides that made up the square of the city being also fourteen miles long, so that the area inside must have been three times the size of London County. Twenty-five brazen gates through each of the four walls gave entrance to the city, and down through the centre flowed the Euphrates. The river was fenced by walls on either bank, and twenty-five gates faced each other on either side, leading to interior streets set square as in an American city, so that no one could lose his way. Ferry-boats plied from bank to bank, and at one point stood the stone piles of a bridge, across which wooden planks were thrown by day, but removed by night.

Round the outer walls ran an enormous trench or moat, from which the clay had been dug to make the unnumbered bricks required for the building of the walls. The bricks were cemented with boiling bitumen or asphalt, perhaps brought from the Mosul district of the modern oil wells. The moat was kept full of water from the overflow of the Euphrates, and, for further defence, another great wall with moat had been constructed at the narrowest part between that river and the Tigris, starting somewhere near the Felujah bridge which I was so anxious to reach. From the city itself rose vast edifices, between which the river ran. On the left bank stood the main palace of the King, rising in terrace on terrace supported upon arcaded arches, and on each terrace gardens were laid out with shady trees and flowering plants. On the opposite side of the city, rising to a still greater height, stood the eight towers built over the vast temple of the supreme god, Bel, whose statue of solid gold gleamed in their midst. In various parts of the city were scattered the shrines of four thousand other gods, each with his appropriate name, and the gloomy lurking-places of the seven devils who habitually haunt mankind. The common houses along the city streets were three or four stories high, and so vast was the space within the walls that room was found for large gardens and even cultivated fields. Hanging in quivering air, like the mirage of Palmyra's lake, I saw before me the ancient wonder of the world, the greatest of all cities under heaven.

But Babylon lay uneasy. The sentinels upon the two-hundred-and-fifty towers of the outer wall waited in vain for the daily watchword. Now and then they could see a four-horse chariot driving along the top of the walls, as along the edge of a precipice high above the level of the moat, but no watchword came from the palace. In the temple of Bel the priests climbed from tier to tier of its pyramid, and circled in agitation round the golden statue that rose from the summit. From every quarter of the city's area astrologers, magicians, and soothsayers came hurrying to the temple up the streets and by the bridge or the ferries from across the river. In the shady terraces of the Hanging Gardens loiterers sat whispering together. Within the royal palace itself was a silence of awe. In the women's chambers the royal wives and concubines cowered together in vague alarm. At their doors huge Ethiopians with drawn swords stood dumbly waiting.

In the Council Chamber silent figures gathered one by one. There came the princes, the governors, the captains, the judges, the treasurers, the counsellors, the sheriffs, and the rulers of surrounding districts. Silent, in white robes, they took their places upon their seats of sandalwood and ivory. But the great golden throne stood empty. He who had raised the city from the dust to glory ; who had surrounded her with lofty walls for her protection, and devised the gardens for her delight ; who had built the palace for his habitation, and the temple for the golden image of Bel ; who had gathered gold for splendour, and made silver to be of no account ; who had conquered the world up to the confines of ocean and the ancient river of Egypt, and had brought line upon line of the heathen to be his slaves ; he for whom they continually prayed that he might live for ever—Nebuchadnezzar the King, the King of Kings, had disappeared in the night.

That morning his ivory bedstead, covered with purple silks and cloth of gold, was found empty and unused. Above the pillow still hung the golden crown, one huge emerald shining in its front. Beside the bed lay the golden sceptre, one great diamond gleaming on its top. Suspended upon the image of a god, the royal robes stood ready, lustrous with gold thread and white silk and purple dye. But the royal chamber was empty. Wives and concubines had not seen him. Savage Ethiopians could say no word. The King was gone, and his city, " The Marvel of Mankind ", sat desolate and amazed.

And I saw in the mirage that far away beyond the Tigris, among the mountains that confine the Persian race, the King Nebuchadnezzar had found a deep cavern, looking over the wide Mesopotamian plains, and there he took shelter from the heat and from rain and wind, and from the ways of men. Below his feet the surface of the world lay extended, and above the world rose the hollow dome of the sky, the marching-place of the sun from dawn till evening.

And when the sun had set, gradually the dome was filled with radiant stars of gold and silver and blood, moving in silence upon their way, and marshalled in order like all the armies of the world. Beyond calculation of numbers they were, and some hung down from the dome, and others retired so far into the depths of space that no eye could follow them into their secret homes. And sometimes a thin moon vanished into the sunset, but night by night she grew larger till she was round as the diamond on the King's sceptre. Then she waned smaller and smaller again, till she hung above the sunrise thin as a bow but reversed, and then she vanished again.

And, beholding the ways of the sun and the moon and the stars, and how alternate darkness and light moved across the face of the earth below him, and upon the mountains where he made his lair, Nebuchadnezzar stretched out his hands to the sky and cried aloud: "Lo! I am he that did build Babylon, that great city, the habitation of the gods, the marvel of mankind. By my own might and for my own majesty did I build it that my glory should fill the world for ever. Likewise I subdued the kingdoms of the earth up to the confines of ocean, and brought multitudes of the heathen into captivity to be my slaves. But this mountain is more lofty than the temple of Bel, and that plain is wider than the compass of my city's walls, and those stars are more numerous than the hosts with which I subdued the world, or than the slaves that I led into captivity. The sun is brighter than the gold of my golden image, and the moon brighter than the silver of the high priest's throne, nor can rubies and diamonds surpass the stars that turn with the dome of heaven or wander here and there at will.

"What glory, therefore, has the King of Kings? What is the subjugation of the world that it should be accounted of? Or what the pleasure of riches that we should seek after it with such solicitude? The generations of mankind are like the leaves that are swept away by the wind in autumn and are forgotten. An ant-heap counts more inhabitants than Babylon, and a swarm of bees labour with finer industry than all my slaves. What glory, therefore, has the King of Kings? In a few years he shall be as though he had not been, but the earth shall bear again as she bore before he reigned, and the sun and moon shall shine, and the stars go upon their appointed ways."

So Nebuchadnezzar abode in the cavern, drinking the dew and the rain that gathered in the rock-pools, and eating wild grasses and toadstools and the grains of pulse that he took at night from the cultivated fields out upon the plain. And often at night he heard the lions which he used to hunt in safety from his chariot, growling with satisfaction after they had devoured their prey. And wild animals and birds came and held intercourse with him according to their several tongues. So the King remained in the wilderness until seven seasons were fulfilled.

But there came a day when the watchers upon the towers of Babylon perceived a strange figure approaching the eastern gates. The hair of his head hung loose around his shoulders, and his uncombed beard descended to his navel. His brown body was covered with hairy fur, and his nails were long and sharp as an eagle's talons. And when he knocked at a brazen gate, the keepers of it said to each other, "Doubtless this is a holy maniac," and they let him in. But he said to them, "I am Nebuchadnezzar, the King of Kings, and I have come to teach my people the truth." And they laughed him to scorn, saying, "That is what all the holy maniacs say."

But one ran to the palace, where the princes and the governors and the captains and the judges and the treasurers and the counsellors and the sheriffs and all the rulers of provinces had made their habitation, together with the astrologers and the magicians and the soothsayers, and he told them, " Here is another maniac boasting himself to be Nebuchadnezzar, the King of Kings."

Then the princes and the governors and the captains and the judges and the treasurers and the counsellors and the sheriffs and the rulers of provinces, together with the astrologers and the magicians and the soothsayers, ran with speed to the gate, and when even the last of them had come up with the rest, they set the holy maniac in their midst, and he answered them, saying, " I am Nebuchadnezzar, the King of Kings, and by this you shall know me. In the crown that hangs above my bed is an emerald as large as a crocodile's egg, and on the summit of my sceptre is a diamond like the morning star for brightness."

Then all the princes and the governors and the rest of the royal Court, together with the astrologers and the other divine attendants upon the will of the gods, fell upon their faces, crying : " This is indeed the King of Kings ! " And they did obeisance to Nebuchadnezzar as he stood naked and shaggy in their midst. Also they sent for the players upon cornets and flutes and harps and sackbuts and psalteries and dulcimers and all kinds of music, and, setting the King in the forefront of the procession, they escorted him up to the royal palace. And all the multitude of Babylon ran together and shouted : " It is the King of Kings ! Our King has returned to us alive ! "

And in the royal chambers of the palace the handmaidens led him to the marble bath, and they washed him and poured perfumes upon him, and sheared his hair and beard and pared his nails and anointed his head. And they laid him upon the royal couch covered with purple silk and cloth of gold. Then they set wine before him and delicate meats, and so they served him until the evening, nor did the sweet sounds of the cornet, the flute, the harp, the sackbut, and the rest of the royal orchestra ever cease.

But when the sun had gone down and Nebuchadnezzar had eaten and drunk his fill, he lay upon the bed to which he was accustomed in former times, and he gazed up at the purple ceiling that was painted with yellow stars, and he looked at the emerald shining in his crown and at the diamond upon the top of his sceptre. And the chamber was filled with sweet fragrance, and the air was still, nor could rain or wind or snow penetrate within the walls and roofs. And the King's heart was comforted that no longer was a desert cave his home, nor grasses and wild locusts his sustenance, but the peace of security wrapped him round. And as he fell asleep he said to himself: " Great indeed is Babylon which I have built, and great is the majesty in which I am established. But where now is Nineveh, that great city? And where is Assurbanipal, who also was the King of Kings? But the starry heavens remain, and the sun runs his course, and month by month the moon fades and is restored. Beside the spaces of heaven, Babylon is not seen, and beside the multitudes that time sweeps away my majesty is as a grain of dust, and myself no man at all."

And at sunrise next morning Nebuchadnezzar sent trumpeters throughout the city to call together all the Chaldæan priests and astrologers and soothsayers, and when they had come into the palace, he said to them : " Gold is not so bright as the sun, nor silver so radiant as the moon, nor are the black places where the seven devils dwell so dark as is the night. Therefore I command that you pull down the golden image of Bel which I caused to be made, and that you destroy the silver shrines of the four thousand gods, and fill up the dark holes where the seven devils have dwelt. And I command that my people shall cease to bring offerings to the altars of the gods or to present gifts to the priests, astrologers and soothsayers. But all the people alike shall fall in worship before the sun and the moon and the stars of night, and shall kiss the surface of the earth upon which we live and which feeds us from one flying moment to another as the generations of mankind pass away and are no more seen."

Then the Chaldæan priests and the astrologers and the monthly prognosticators and the soothsayers and all the attendants at the four thousand temples bowed themselves to the ground and cried with one voice : " O King, live for ever. It shall be done even as thou hast commanded." And they went away to the base of the temple of Bel on the other side of the river. There they took counsel together with great tumult, rending their robes and crying one to another : " Who is this that would destroy the golden image that is the marvel of all the nations of the world from the Nile to the Persian Gulf ? Who is this outcast that would stir the wrath of all the gods of heaven and earth against us, and let the seven devils loose upon our wives and children ? Who is this savage that would deprive us holy men of the offerings that rich and poor suppliants bring us of their own free will for the protection of our prayers and our services to the gods ? Doubtless he has imbibed the heresy of the barbarian Persians who dwell beyond the mountains where he had his cave. For they have no gods like those who bless the land of Babylon, but worship only light and flames that have no substance, but shift and flicker like the river mist. Let him die the death."

And with one accord they cried, " Great is Bel ! Great is the god of Babylon ! " And so they continued crying unto the evening.

But that night three of the priests entered the chamber where the King of Kings lay asleep, having the crown above his head and the sceptre beside him ; and in the morning Nebuchadnezzar was no more than the handful of perishing dust which he had known himself to be. But fourteen years later the Persian Cyrus came marching with speed across the eastern mountains, and entered the city by way of the river course which he had drained till it was dry. Then the Wonder of the World began to crumble until it amounted to no more than a few large heaps of miscellaneous rubbish, as anyone who passes down the Euphrates may now see upon his way.

On the November morning after the mirage had vanished, I was able to reach the bridge at Felujah, and so ran across the narrow space of the remaining desert and came to the Stanley Maude bridge over the Tigris, and to Baghdad, which itself was once a great and famous city but now was fading away in mud which surged up to the belly of any horse.

SCENE III

A HAPPY WARRIOR

How, in coasting along the Black Sea, I saw Xenophon with the Ten Thousand reach Trebizond

ON January the 5th, 1907, I was sailing down the Black Sea from the valley of the Phasis and the southern Caucasus, where the Russians had been slaughtering the ancient people of Georgia and devastating their villages, as is the Russian way whether the Government is by Tsar or Soviet. I was on a French boat, and the Swiss lady on board, being apprehensive of sea-sickness, kept on murmuring, " Ça va balancer. Ça va balancer ! " until in despair she retired to a sofa in her cabin for rest. But even there she was not secure, for a flying fish, hotly pursued by porpoises, fled through the porthole into the refuge of her bosom. Even there it found no resting-place ; for, aroused by the chilly shock, she rushed into the salon, to the delight of all spectators, all lovely in cool attire as she was, leaving the intrusive fish to languish alone.

By evening she had recovered enough to sit for dinner next the Captain, while I was at the other end of the table beside her husband, a harmless man. While he was thoughtfully sprinkling salt on his salad, I was startled by the lady's sudden shriek : " Aristide ! Aristide ! " " Heavens ! " I thought to myself, "what can have happened? Has she swallowed a slug? Or has the Captain under the table—— Well, one knows what Frenchmen are." "Aristide! Aristide!" she cried again. "Quelle imprudence! C'est déjà salé!"

The ship came to anchor at the various little ports along the Turkish shore, and for a day and night we lay off Trebizond, while Turkish labourers slung clusters of goats into the hold, each goat being tied by a thin rope round a hind-leg; and sacks of maize had also to be loaded. Little white houses with green blinds and verandahs could be seen piled up the mountain-side, which divides into steep ravines. That morning the cliffs were enveloped in a thin haze. So was the ruin of a Crusaders' castle, and on a flat promontory an old Turkish fort, armed with antiquated guns, was only just visible.

With the exclamatory Swiss lady, her husband, and an American missionary returning from a vain attempt to extend Christianity among the Moslems of Samarcand, I went ashore and lunched with a charming Swiss family half-way up the steep. In the afternoon we drove far inland among the hills, and, leaving the carriage, I hastened forward till at last I reached a high point commanding the half-hidden site of the town, with its castle, the ruffled surface of the Euxine, stepmother of sailors, and far away across the sea to the north-east the crests of the frosty Caucasus, to which Prometheus was clamped.

What was the French steamer doing here? Or the Swiss lady and her husband? Or the Turkish labourers, the Turkish fort, the Crusaders' castle, the comfortable white houses with verandahs and green blinds? For me all had vanished like the stuff of dreams, and around me I felt only an eager crowd of young Athenians and other sons of Greece—the remnants of ten thousand. And in their midst, just at my side, stood the Athenian knight who had led them to safety through unknown lands, all the devious ways from the plains of Babylon.

I regarded him with envious admiration, for the life of few men on earth has been more enviable. His tall and powerful form had been suppled by youthful exercises, and beautified by recent hardships. The expression of his face showed military resolution animated by habitual thoughtfulness and quick perception of nature's life and every side of human interest. He appeared to stand somewhere in those most active and adventurous years of man, half-way between thirty and forty, but open-air activity and self-control had left him so young that many believed him still to be only thirty-one, and his modest but quietly self-confident bearing seemed to prove them right. In any case, he had lived through thirty years of a century during which the human intellect reached its highest development in every form of art, speech, and thought, and, without conscious effort, had received the finest civilization as the natural endowment of his mind.

For he was born upon the slopes of Pentelicon, from which they had recently quarried the marble for rebuilding the city after the Persian invaders had burnt it, temples and all. Among the ravines and woods of the mountain-side the boy gained an accurate knowledge of wild animals, and an active sympathy with horses and dogs while hunting through the oleander bushes and sweet-smelling herbs that abound among the rocky clefts, even in dry weather. Not many miles away he could see the square rock of the Acropolis gleaming with the rising or just-completed temples to house the protecting gods of the city and the ancestral heroes—the temple of Erechtheus and Poseidon, the temple of the Virgin Athene, that triumph of the world's architecture, and the entrance gates, up the rocky steps to which the solemn processions of priests, priestesses, and mounted youths like himself climbed on the festivals of the gods. And beyond the temples lay the purple sea, with the pointed island of Ægina in the centre of the view, the low and heroic island of Salamis on the right, and on the left the long, empurpled mass of heath-covered Hymettus.

If he was born two or three years before the outbreak of the long and disastrous war with the Spartans and other less civilized States of Greece, the boy grew up in the brief years of the city's highest power and beauty. When the war began and the enemy poured into the surrounding country, destroying crops and burning villages according to the custom of war, he was hurried with the rest of the family into the city to live under the protection of her walls, three of which almost made her an island by connecting her with the sea-ports. It is even possible that as a growing child he may have heard Pericles deliver that speech over the fallen which remains the highest example of patriotic eloquence, and the noblest tribute to a city's greatness.

But like a stroke of heaven's irony, a hideous plague followed immediately, and the people, crowded into the ramshackle and stifling huts of refugees, died in hundreds, losing in the presence of imminent death all regard for the customary distinctions between good and evil. Years of tragic misery and almost alternate success and disaster in the war passed on, until the Athenians attempted an invasion of the northern country dominated by Thebans, whose watchword was always "As our Fathers have told us". We know that Socrates was present in the consequent defeat at Delium, Apollo's shrine near the Bœotian coast (424); for Alcibiades, who was also present there, has described his sturdy courage. An old legend tells that Xenophon was present, too, and was even defended from death by the unyielding philosopher. The legend is probably false, for in that case the boy must have been about seventeen or eighteen, and a common assumption that he was born at the beginning of the war in 431 cannot be true.

So it is unlikely that his rescue at Delium first introduced Xenophon to Socrates, but at all events Socrates was attracted to the youth just when he was emerging into manhood. He was good-looking, and modest, having gained that distinctive Athenian quality of modesty in the course of the ordinary education; amorous, too, for Socrates warned him with special emphasis of the danger of love, telling him that even a kiss may instil a poison worse than an insect's bite, and love may act as a poison even at a distance, which no insect can. There is a pretty story handed on by tradition to a gossip of later times, that Socrates, meeting Xenophon in a narrow lane, barred the way with his staff and asked him where he could buy this, that, or the other, to which the youth readily replied. But when Socrates, as his manner was, asked him where he could get the noblest quality of mind, and saw the youth hesitating to reply, he said, "Follow me", and so the attractive youth became his disciple, and listened so carefully to his definitions of the ordinary virtues, and his advice upon everyday behaviour, that in his mature years he wrote his recollections down without falsifying his master's character as a humorous and perpetual critic of life.

A HAPPY WARRIOR

The word that Socrates used for "the noblest quality" often had a touch of irony in it, as our word "culture" is coming to have—a touch of Quixoticism or the behaviour of the superior person or "the perfect gentleman". But Xenophon did not perceive that hint of a smile, and by modesty, self-control, and wholehearted devotion to the matter in hand he strove to obtain the quality of "The Beautiful-and-Good" in all the affairs of common life. Socrates also anxiously impressed upon his youthful mind respect for the established gods and for the country's accepted laws—a respect which he himself observed carefully, though with the irony involved in his nature.

But the youth received a still higher form of mental education in the theatre of Athens, where the solemn tragedies of Æschylus were perhaps still being enacted, with a religious awe due to the originator of divine and personal drama ; and where the plays of Sophocles and Euripides were succeeding each other, to the applause of a critical audience, sitting as judges day by day. With Euripides he would certainly be well acquainted, since the ironic playwright was, like himself, a friend and disciple of Socrates. And besides, their contemporary, Aristophanes, was bringing the criticism of laughter to bear upon all the habits and political interests of the people, especially upon their misguided enthusiasm for the prolonged and miserable war. It must have been an exhilarating moment for Xenophon if he was present when, during the burlesque attack upon the philosopher in "The Clouds", his master stood up in the audience to show who was the object of the joke.

While the noblest of all tragedies and the keenest of satires were being written and acted, the war continued with a ferocity that might seem incredible if we had not known war. The years were marked by the extermination of the gallant town of Platæa, the internecine cruelties of political parties in Corcyra, the massacre of the Mytileneans (partially saved by a spasm of mercy among the Athenian people), and the tragedy of Melos, where the Athenians murdered all the grown males and sold the women and children into slavery. In reading the narrative of these cruelties, we must often wonder how or why the human race has survived. For no kind of bird or beast is so cruel, even the cat practising cruelty only to keep her powers alert ; and our wonder is increased because these appalling events undoubtedly occurred during the century when the intellect and artistic genius of mankind reached the highest point in human history.

We may next imagine Xenophon as a young man somewhere about twenty (in 415) watching the great Athenian fleet of one hundred ships setting out from the port, amid cheers, songs, and the outpouring of wine, for the invasion of Sicily—a scene similar to the gallant starting of our own fleet from the great harbour of Lemnos, bent on the invasion of Gallipoli in 1915. One against another the Greek triremes raced as far as Ægina in the exhilaration of the enterprise, and on that island coast the boy Plato, then about thirteen, may have watched and cheered as he saw them pass—pass to the lingering doom of two hopeless years, the swaying battle in the Syracusan harbour, the horror of the stone-quarries, and the pitiful end.

Bit by bit the control of Athens over islands and her outposts near the Asiatic shores dissolved ; her own boasted democracy was swept away by violence, and was never fully restored ; her brave efforts to regain the command of the sea resulted in victories counterbalanced by loss; the influence of the Persian satraps of the western provinces was felt, especially when Cyrus, the King's younger son, was appointed to the three main provinces of the centre and south. Ten years after the beginning of the attempt upon Sicily, Lysander, for the second time in actual command of the Spartan fleet, caught the Athenian ships lying at ease off the stretch of flattish shore just south of Gallipoli, and captured all but a few of the one-hundred-and-eighty. News of this overwhelming disaster reached Athens one evening, and that night, says Xenophon in his narrative of the time, no one slept. Lysander, blockading the routes of supply, advanced very slowly, leaving starvation to do the work. But in March, 404, he sailed into the Piræus, occupied the city, and destroyed the Long Walls between her and the ports. His sailors cheered as the massive fragments fell, and hired concubines added to the gaiety with dances and flutes. So the war of twenty-seven years between the two most highly civilized peoples of the world ended in the destruction of the more civilized. It was evident that intellect and the immortal arts were no present help against military and naval strength.

There was no room for culture or philosophy under the subsequent bloodthirsty tyranny of the Thirty, established by the hostile advice of Lysander. Socrates, already suspected as having been the only one in authority who opposed the execution of the generals after the naval engagement at Arginusæ, incurred further displeasure by being the only one of five who refused obedience to the Thirty's unjust command to arrest an innocent Athenian in Salamis, and he was then ordered to give up his method of dialectics for the exploration of truth by conversations with youths and friends like Xenophon. But in less than a year the tyranny of the Thirty was overthrown in a sharp civil war, though at their call Lysander with Spartan troops again entered the city. Thrasybulus and other citizens exiled by the Thirty then set up a new form of government, and new laws were adopted. That date (403) marks the end of Athenian glory in the material world. Under the new control the position of the followers of Socrates was no better, and it was this government that a few years later (399 B.C.) caused Socrates himself to drink the soothing poison of hemlock as a witness to those unwritten and eternal Laws of God to which Antigone appealed.

What was a man like Xenophon, clear-sighted and active by nature, to do as the splendid city sank in the midst of shifting chaos and uncertainty? We do not know whether he served in the cavalry as one of the "Knights", or on which side he may have served, though he would probably be with Thrasybulus against the Thirty. He may have taken part in some handicraft with Socrates, who always extolled manual work, and found his own tranquillity and satisfaction in sculpture. When civil strife was not actually raging, he might roam about the city, taking pleasure, like Aristophanes, in watching the country people bringing in their goods to market and discussing quality and price, as market people always have done. Thus he acquired knowledge that he was long afterwards to use in his *Guide to Women on Housekeeping*. And besides, there were the disputations with his master and other friends about practical points of behaviour. But mere conversation, as in a modern Club, cannot satisfy anyone who longs for action, and a sudden joy must have come to him with a letter from a young Bœotian friend, Proxenus, inviting him to join a considerable force of Greeks and Persians which the young Satrap Cyrus was gathering round Sardis, the magnificent city of Lydia. Xenophon asked his master's advice, and Socrates, with his accustomed irony, told him he ought surely to consult Apollo at Delphi; for the oracle could be depended upon, since, in answer to an inquirer, as to who was the wisest man in Greece, it had replied that no one was wiser than Socrates.

But Xenophon's mind was already made up. The purpose of Cyrus was quite unknown; perhaps it was only to suppress troublesome bandits in a southern province. No matter. The chance of activity, adventure, and the exploration of a fabulous empire was attractive. The journey from Athens to Delphi, with an easterly breeze down the Gulf of Corinth, would take only about three days, and when Xenophon arrived he did not ask the priestess on her tripod over the sacred steam whether he should go, but to what gods he should sacrifice before he went. Apollo, through the lips of the inspired woman, gave the due answer, and Xenophon returned to his master full of joyful confidence. Socrates reproached him for not asking the direct question, but as the thing was done, advised him to make sacrifice to the gods specified by the oracle. Having performed the appointed sacrifices, Xenophon set sail with the exultation of release. He was never to see his master again, for less than two years later Socrates, a man notorious for self-restraint and religious observance, was executed for impiety and the corruption of youth.

Xenophon's own account of what followed is so attractive a story that I cannot help summarizing it. He must have reached his young friend Proxenus in

February, 401 B.C.; for the main force started early in March, and to reach Sardis Xenophon would have some three days' journey after landing at Ephesus, the city of the many-breasted goddess, more than four hundred years later well known to St. Paul. By calling in the Greek troops that had been assembled at various points for some months previously, Cyrus mustered about thirteen thousand men of light and heavy arms (increased by a subsequent addition to over fourteen thousand), besides a host of Persians said to number one hundred thousand. Xenophon, as a volunteer without office, would naturally attach himself to Proxenus, who brought two thousand men under his own command.

We do not hear how Cyrus proposed to feed so large a host advancing through a sparsely inhabited country, partly mountainous, but the troops for the most part " lived on the country ", plundering the villages, or buying eatables with their pay, the army chests being largely supplemented by the generosity of a Cilician queen, passionately attached to Cyrus, as the rumour went. During the devious advance through Asia, by way of Iconium, (the Konia of Turkish times), the Taurus mountains, to Tarsus, some four centuries later to be the birthplace of St. Paul, past Issus, where nearly seventy years later Alexander was to overthrow the Persian Empire, round the bay of Alexandretta, north-east to the Euphrates (which the army could there ford on foot) and down the famous river's left bank to a point near the present bridge at Felujah— through all this rapid and toilsome advance Xenophon kept a regular diary of the distances covered, and the duration of the pauses for rest.

The time extended from early March to early September, and the distance must have been something over one-thousand-five-hundred miles. The longest pauses were at Celænæ and Tarsus, making about seven weeks together. The delay at Tarsus was partly due to a mutiny of the Greek troops against their commanding officer Clearchus, a rough Spartan officer, desperately fond of fighting for its own sake, and exiled from his own city for disobeying orders. He was so unpopular that some of his own men hounded and pelted him in the camp, for they rightly surmised that as no notice was taken of the supposed bandits in Pisidia, the real object of the whole campaign was an attack upon the Persian King himself. Nevertheless, when Clearchus had wept for a long time in their presence, as was the established habit of Greeks, and had also secured a rise in their pay to about thirty shillings a month, the mutiny subsided and only a few took the opportunity of sailing home.

After crossing the Euphrates breast-high, the host pushed on down the left bank, and entered the Syrian desert, where they disturbed herds of wild asses, swifter than horses, and ostriches which escaped with striding legs and wings spread out like sails. I doubt if the ass or the ostrich is now found there, but the antelopes or little gazelles and bustards mentioned by Xenophon still abound. Mud abounds, too, and into it the transport wagons sank so deep that Cyrus called upon his Persian officers and princes to lend a hand in hauling and pushing. They at once complied, plunging into the slimy clay in all their fine costumes and ornaments, throwing only their scarlet cloaks aside. Travellers in that desert can realize the scene. For the surface is not sand, but a kind of marl which dries and cracks in summer, and is turned into sticky mud at the first rains, usually falling in November. The advance of Cyrus was in late August or early September, so that Xenophon's account of the mud is hard to understand, unless the weight of the transport broke through the sun-dried surface into underlying slime that never dries. Certainly in crossing the desert I found it impossible to drive cars over that surface, though it looked hard enough. But that was in November, and the rains had just begun.

Along the river's left bank the host pushed rapidly southward, hoping to gain the advantage of surprise. But there could be no surprise. King Artaxerxes had in fact ordered a broad and deep trench to be dug between the Euphrates and the Tigris to obstruct their approach, and it is unaccountable that he left it undefended. He even left a narrow space open beside the river. Through this gap the Greeks under Clearchus, and we must suppose the whole mixed army, passed unopposed. The advance then followed the river to the point where it most nearly approaches the Tigris, just past the present bridge at Felujah, a few miles below Baghdad, and nearly opposite the ruins of Ctesiphon, well known to our army in 1916. As the line formed up, Cyrus kept the Greeks on his right flank, knowing that Greeks were far superior soldiers to Persians, and he attributed their superiority to their freedom. Xenophon, who would be with the brigade under Proxenus, tells us that Cyrus in his address to the Greeks called upon them to prove themselves worthy of their freedom—" freedom which he valued far above all his own possessions ". It was a remarkable utterance for a son of the Persian dynasty, and would be even more remarkable in the mouth of any European ruler or oligarch in 1933.

As the great trench was undefended, Cyrus expected no further opposition, and the diversified host proceeded slowly in loose order—about thirteen thousand

A HAPPY WARRIOR

Greeks, light and heavy infantry, on the right flank, their own left being under Menon, an effeminate general, very inferior to the fighting Clearchus, though probably more popular with the men. In the centre marched the mass of Persians, with twenty chariots fitted with projecting scythes. On the afternoon of the third day's march, one of Cyrus's staff, galloping hard on a sweated horse, brought the news that the Great King's army was advancing in battle order, and presently a white cloud of dust was seen on the wide horizon. The cloud turned black as it rose and spread over the plain. For the King's army was estimated at about a million and a quarter, with two hundred chariots armed with scythes, and six thousand cavalry as a vanguard concentrated round the King himself.

Cyrus hastily clamped his armour on, and hastily restored his line to order, riding along the front to see that all was straight. As he passed, Xenophon, acting as *aide* to Proxenus, rode up to inquire if he had further commands, and Cyrus, pulling up, informed him that the omens were favourable, and hearing a murmur along the line, he was told by Xenophon the Greeks were repeating one to another the watchword " Zeus the Saviour and Victory ". Cyrus said it was a good watchword, and rode away. Xenophon never saw him again.

Thus on the level and narrow plain between the two famous rivers, only about thirty-five miles north of Babylon, the greatest city in the world, of which hardly a ruin now is left, the hosts of the West and East faced each other, and gradually drew closer. Both sides glittered with steel—swords, spears, and breastplates. The Persian archers had wicker shields which they set in the ground as a fence. The

Egyptian foot serving under the King used long wooden shields covering the whole body. A conflict of such vast numbers gathered on one small spot was sure in those days to be bloody with death. Armed with arrows, spear, or sword, a man was compelled to kill or be killed or run away, exposing his back to the sword or spear of the pursuer. In a battle like this of Cunaxa (Xenophon does not mention the since accepted name) there was no cover, and the slaughter would probably be greater than on any single day of a modern engagement.

Just before the fronts closed Cyrus asked Clearchus to transfer his Greeks to the centre where he was himself with a bodyguard of horse ; but Clearchus refused, being unwilling to change position in the very front of the approaching enemy and to deprive his right flank of the river's protection. As a soldier he was right to refuse, but if only he had obeyed, the course of history might have been altered. For if Cyrus, supported by Greeks, had then become the Great King, Alexander's invasion of Persia seventy years later might have failed.

When the Persian front, silently advancing, had come within striking distance of about half a mile (the Athenians charged over an even longer distance at Marathon), Clearchus called upon his Greeks, and they charged at the double, shouting or singing their pæan. Except for the Satrap Tissaphernes with a body of horse, the Persians did not even await the onset of Hellenic swords, but ran back in confusion, making their slaughter an easy matter. The King, confused by crowds in the centre, did not perceive this retreat on his left, but commanded the host on his right to swarm round the exposed left flank of the Persians under Cyrus with his superior numbers. He thus exposed his own centre except for the body of mounted guards immediately around him, and Cyrus, perceiving the danger to his left flank, impetuously but wisely ordered his own guard to charge at this weak spot in the enemy's line. The charge cleared away most of the King's six thousand horse, leaving him deserted by all but a few personal friends. Unhappily, Cyrus, riding full tilt into their midst, caught sight of his brother, and, impassioned with the fratricidal hatred common among Oriental princes near the throne, he shouted "There he is!" and flung his spear, which pierced his brother's breast, but with only a slight wound. He himself was at once cut down and beheaded by the handful still protecting the King. So died this young, generous, and daring Persian, a man of attractive nature, his mother's favourite son, a queen's chosen lover, and to Xenophon an inspiring ideal of modesty, generosity, and adventurous action. Xenophon, in his summary of his qualities, especially notices his knowledge of horses, and his skill in hunting. Indeed, he was a man after Xenophon's own heart, and was the embodiment of the knightly virtues which he attributed in his *Cyropædia* to the elder Cyrus, who had conquered Babylon about a hundred and thirty years before.

Unaware of their leader's fate, Clearchus with Xenophon, Proxenus, and the main Greek force continued the pursuit of the runaway Persians for three miles, but on turning about they found the army's left wing had been destroyed, or had treacherously gone over to the King's Persian host, which was now again drawn up in line threatening the Greeks from their rear. Clearchus twice beat them off, and the Greeks reached their camp without much loss, but only to find it pillaged and robbed of food. They had received no rations all that hard day, and the Persians had proved themselves better at pillage than at fighting. The Greeks, however, killed many of them in the camp, and rescued one of Cyrus's mistresses, who had escaped by flinging off her outer garment. The other, a woman of great beauty and intelligence, was carried off for the entertainment of her lover's brother in Babylon.

Next morning the Greek soldiers, being reduced to starvation, killed many of the transport animals and roasted the meat on fires made with the arrows, wicker shields and long wooden shields left by the enemy in their flight. But hearing now that Cyrus was dead, they were at a loss what next to do. Tissaphernes as commandant of the Persians in the army had nominally succeeded Cyrus, but he rejected a proposal to take over the claim to the kingship, and, indeed, he was already in league with the King himself. He pointed out to the Greeks that their only safety lay in retreat, but return by the way they had come was impossible, for the army on its advance had eaten up the country like locusts and all would starve. He then offered to guide them to another route by which they might possibly escape.

The position was critical, all the worse because Clearchus had now to be on guard against the Persians in his own army as well as against the King's host, never far removed. But food was, as always, the first necessity, and Clearchus followed a lead, first through some devastated villages, and then through a rich district providing plenty of food for purchase. So, after prolonged discussion with Tissaphernes, who represented the King, they passed through the great Median Wall, said to run for seventy miles at a height of one hundred feet for the protection of the approach to Babylon, until at last they reached the Tigris, opposite the site of the ruins at Ctesiphon, and some forty miles north of Kut-el-Amara, now famous for its prolonged and disastrous siege under General Charles Townshend. In spite of warnings, the army crossed the river on a long bridge of boats in safety, and turned north, having the Tigris on their left and keeping close to the river bank. Thus they must have passed through the future site of Baghdad, home of *The Arabian Nights*, now a dilapidated city of mud, and pushing steadily along the river bank, after plundering some villages that belonged to the mother of the King and Cyrus, they reached the Zabatas (the Greater Zab), a broad tributary of the Tigris.

Here a terrible disaster befell them. For Clearchus, having noticed continual bickerings between the Persian troops in the van and the Greeks who kept about three miles behind them, went to Tissaphernes to warn him of the danger. He was received with the utmost courtesy, was entertained to a fine banquet, and requested to return next day with other generals for a discussion. He chose five, among them being Xenophon's friend Proxenus, a thoughtful and promising man of thirty, a favourite with all, but too sympathetic, Xenophon considered, with the common soldiers. Menon from Thessaly was another, an effeminate and treacherous creature, for whom Xenophon had a special contempt, intelligible to students of Greek morality. On entering the Satrap's tent all five were captured, and sent back to the King, who beheaded four, saving Menon for other purposes, but putting him to death by torture a year later. Clearchus, as Commander-in-Chief of the Greeks, prided himself upon being a rude, rough soldier, as indeed he was, feared and hated by his men, who none the less obeyed and trusted him. Xenophon thought him a great general, and especially praised his skill in raising supplies. It may seem strange that a man of his experience should be caught by a common trick of Oriental treachery. But he was a typical example of the military mind.

The news that their five generals had been captured was brought to the Greeks by an Arcadian, who galloped over, holding back his bowels with his hand, for he was wounded. The situation was indeed desperate. They were in the midst of a hostile country inhabited by unknown and savage tribes, deserts behind them, high mountains in front; no guide, no compass, no provisions, and at nearest more than a thousand miles from any city of their own race; no mounted force, no means of crossing the wide rivers. Sick for home, sleepless and, careless of food, they lay down as they were in the open.

Then came Xenophon's opportunity. He here introduces himself with a well-educated man's modesty: "There was in the army an Athenian named Xenophon, who had come, not in any military capacity, but simply at the suggestion of his old friend Proxenus." As he was dozing off, he says, a vivid dream roused him, and, like the Homeric heroes, he took much account of dreams; for, being beyond the control of conscious reason, they must be messages from God. He called up the officers, first those of the Proxenus brigade, and then of the whole Greek army, to a midnight council, and addressed them with daring good sense. In his narrative he quotes his speech in full, and it is long. But he seems to have kept a diary throughout the campaign, and probably took notes of all that was said. Besides, we must remember that Athenians were accustomed to public

A HAPPY WARRIOR

speaking, and all educated Greeks from infancy learnt Homer by heart, as the English once learnt the Bible, so that their memories were strengthened. His fear was that the Greek force might surrender without fighting, and the main point of his speech was the invariable truth that the better part of discretion is valour ; that people who save their lives lose them ; that it is not numbers that win in war, but courage and discipline. This he proved by reference to the victories of Marathon and Salamis. As to the want of cavalry, the Persians were largely occupied in clinging round their horses' necks for fear of falling off, and so were no match for the steady sword ; if the Greeks submitted, the Great King would perhaps allow them to settle on the land, in hopes of getting rid of the trouble they caused ; but in that case, what with making love to the fine Syrian and Persian women, and always having plenty to eat and drink, they would sink to the level of the Lotus-eaters and forget their far-off homes, to which he called upon them to struggle on. To suit this occasion of extreme peril, Xenophon tells us he had put on his very best uniform, much as the Spartans carefully combed their hair at Thermopylæ, and as Falkland always put on a clean shirt before going into action. Xenophon admitted he was young (which perhaps shows that my estimate of about thirty-five may have been rather too high), and that he had not come as an officer, but only as the friend of Proxenus. But in true Athenian fashion he put the resolution to the vote, and it was carried unanimously by show of hands. So, too, was his proposal that they should elect five generals in place of the five treacherously carried away. Five were elected, Xenophon himself taking the place of Proxenus. His final proposal was the wisest of all, but the hardest to accept. It was to burn all the wagons, tents, and every ounce of superfluous kit so as not to allow the baggage-train to become their general. Every student of war knows how necessary, though harsh, that order may be. It was, for instance, a disputed question whether it would not have been wiser for Sir George White to abandon all the mass of stores in Ladysmith, and march out before he was surrounded, thus liberating Buller from the long and costly business of relief. On evacuating the Dardanelles, on the other hand, all the stores were burnt while the men came away with very small loss.

It is remarkable how all the other officers respected Xenophon's opinion, mainly because he was an Athenian, though young and untried. All wagons, tents and superfluous belongings were at sunrise collected in the open square of the camp and burnt. Rejecting all proposals of surrender or union with Persian troops treacherously friendly, the force then crossed the Zab—a difficult task, for it was one hundred yards broad near its meeting with the Tigris—and on the other side of the river Xenophon's proposal to advance in hollow square, with the pack-animals and remaining stores of food in the centre, was adopted. He chose the rear rank of the square for his command, and the rear of a retreating square is the post of danger. The pursuit by Persian horse and archers was, indeed, so harassing that Xenophon had to command his men to turn about and charge to free themselves from attack. It was a dangerous movement leaving the rear of the square open and delaying the advance ; so that Xenophon had to apologize to the general Cheirosophus, commanding the front, his excuse being that he could no longer stand the losses among his men without requital.

A HAPPY WARRIOR

To protect his men from similar attacks, which became more threatening a day or two later, Xenophon patched up a body of fifty men which he called his cavalry, mounting them upon any horses that were left, and even upon the poorest baggage-animals. Having noticed also that the Persian archers and slingers outranged his own, he called upon some Rhodians to serve with their powerful plaited slings and leaden bullets, while his archers picked up the Persian arrows and shot them back, both lead and arrows never failing to hit someone when discharged into the thick of the enemy. By these means the forces of Tissaphernes and a Greek deserter Mithridates, though continually reinforced, were repulsed with loss or held in check. Keeping the Tigris still on their left, the Greeks then advanced through the enormous ruins of two deserted cities, probably both formerly included in the huge city of Nineveh, which had been captured and destroyed by Medes and Persians more than two centuries earlier.

Xenophon speaks of city walls one hundred feet high and twenty-five feet broad on the top. It would be interesting to know whether he found the big Assyrian bulls with human heads still there in position, but he makes no mention of them, and they were left for Layard to discover in the middle of the nineteenth century. Nor did he know that at Mosul, a little way farther up on the other side of the river, lay the future oil wells which we have compelled the Turks to surrender to Iraq.

As the plain was now narrowing to the foot-hills of a high mountain range, the army had no longer space to advance in hollow square, because at every bridge or narrow part of the road the sides of the square crowded together in confusion. So Xenophon and the

A HAPPY WARRIOR

other generals agreed to divide the army into companies, some of which on each side cast off and, wheeling outwards, waited to fall in at the rear. Even among the hills the enemy continued to hang upon the march, causing such loss that the Greeks had to rest at times while the army surgeons looked after the wounded. They were even compelled to make a forced night march, so as to outdistance the enemy, who always retired about eight miles at night for fear of surprise. The Greeks thus left a gap of some sixteen miles behind them, but none the less, the enemy caught up in a day or two and occupied a high position in front, threatening the advance. Being asked his advice by the senior general, Xenophon replied that he detected a still higher point commanding the enemy's position, and volunteered to lead a storming party to occupy it. As he rode up the hillside, one of his men complained it was all very well for an officer on horseback to be in such a hurry, but the men on foot had to carry their armour. Whereupon, Xenophon dismounted, took the man's heavy shield and began climbing up on foot, until his men so set upon the " grouser " with blows and stones that Xenophon had to restore the shield to him and remount. By avoiding frontal attack the threatening summit was thus cleared, and the army proceeded.

They soon came to a spot where the mountains approached so steeply and close down to the Tigris, which was there too deep for fording, that they could no longer follow its course. A soldier from Rhodes offered to make a bridge supported on inflated skins over the river, but a crowd of horsemen was seen on the other side, ready to prevent such an attempt. The generals consulted prisoners about the possible routes, and were told that the road west across the river led to Ionia (a blessed word !) ; the road south to Babylon they knew already ; to the east a road went to Susa and Ecbatana, where no one wanted to go ; and the road north would lead into Armenia, but it was terribly difficult, passing through the mountainous territory of the Kurds, a savage and unconquered people, who had lately swallowed up a vast army sent by the King and never heard of since. The generals decided to fight their way through this savage country, Cheirosophus leading with the light-armed, and Xenophon following in the rear with the heavy infantry.

The passage through these wild and unknown mountains was unusually difficult, for the Kurds (Carducians) displayed the savage and implacable temper that has distinguished them to the present day. Though the Greeks had orders to treat them as friends, and not to plunder anything but the needful provisions, the Kurds hurried their families away into caves, and harassed the Greeks with slings and arrows that pierced all their armour right through ; so that Xenophon's rearguard became more like a rout than an army. Progress was so slow and rations so scarce that, after a day or two, Xenophon and the other generals effected a second purge by clearing out the weakest of the pack-animals, the soldiers' belongings, and useless slaves, among whom, apparently, were some women whom the men had annexed *en route* ; for we read that here and there a soldier contrived to smuggle through a woman or even a handsome boy. But still Xenophon's detachment moved so slowly and suffered such heavy loss that he kept urging Cheirosophus not to press the van forward so fast. That general gave his reason for speed by pointing to a height in front over which the only visible road ran, and which was being rapidly occupied by the savage enemy. Xenophon replied that he had just taken two prisoners who might tell of some way round. One of the two refused, having a daughter married to a native of the mountain, and he was killed before the eyes of the other, who then revealed a fairly possible path round to the back of the main pass. Xenophon called for volunteers for clearing the pass by this *détour*, and many came forward. He himself remained at the foot of the pass, unable to advance owing to the huge masses of rock that the Kurds continued to roll down upon the road all night.

Next morning a trumpet from above told that the summit had been cleared, and the Greeks began to clamber up the height where they could, using their spears to help each other, as our mountaineers use ropes. Xenophon with his rearguard then went round by the *détour* because it was easier for the beasts, but he was obliged to ascend height after height, scaling the rocks himself with a few of his light-armed men, while his train suffered so severely that he was forced to negotiate with the Kurds through an interpreter for the restoration of his dead. This the Kurds allowed on condition that he did not burn their villages. So the Greek force was reunited on the top of the pass and, advancing, spent that night in a prosperous village with plenty of food and wine kept in large vats cemented as the custom still is in those wild mountains and in the Caucasus. Having returned the guide by agreement, the army proceeded by a somewhat easier route, but still continually harassed by the Kurds with bows so long that they rested one end against the left foot for purchase, and arrows so long that the Greeks used them as javelins to fling with thongs like slings. The passage of that Kurdish mountainous region took them a full week, and the loss was heavy. What became of the women left behind we are not told, but can easily imagine ; for women, like gold, have a universal value for possession or sale.

The Greeks had now before them the fairly level and fertile satrapy of the Armenians, the natural prey of highland Kurds, like the fatter sheep, in all centuries up to the present. But at the feet of the Greek army flowed the main stream of the Eastern Tigris. They must have been only about fifty or sixty miles south-west of Bitlis on Lake Van, a district of evil omen for the Armenians in a future age. But the river even there was too deep to ford, and on the opposite bank stood a swarm of cavalry under command of the Great King's Satrap. Meantime the Kurds were gathering in force upon their mountain slopes, ready to attack Xenophon's rear. The situation appeared desperate, but, as before, Xenophon was encouraged by a divine dream, and next morning two youths came to his tent (for access to him was freely open to anyone by day or night), and told him they had found a passable ford half a mile farther upstream where they had watched women and children bringing down washing, which the youths stole by crossing. By a clever stratagem Xenophon sent the main force to this upper ford while he made a feint at the lower, thus dividing the cavalry on the opposite bank. At the same time he turned his rear ranks about and charged the threatening Kurds, who fled back to the hills. He then followed the main body, and there was no more resistance on the Armenian side. In fact, when the Greeks had advanced to some large villages where the Satrap's palace stood, the Satrap himself offered a free passage on condition that the Greeks did not burn the houses. On these terms the army lay comfortably down, having plenty to eat and first-rate wine. But during the night snow fell heavily (it was mid-December), and before dawn Xenophon was to be seen without his cloak chopping logs for firewood, like a true high-hearted Athenian. By his example he aroused the men, who were comfortably covered with snow as with a blanket, and getting up, they kept out the cold by rubbing themselves with lard, turpentine, and sesame.

Hearing that the Satrap was gathering forces to close a mountain pass in their front, the Greeks attacked with good effect, hurried on till they had crossed the pass, and three days later they reached the upper course of the Euphrates, which rises in the same mountain mass as the Tigris, and forded it, though the water was up to their middles, and the cold painful. It became still more intense as they pushed forward through deep snow and in the face of a biting north wind over that high upland, probably where Erzeroum, notorious for its pitiless cold, now stands.

Here the men suffered from snow-blindness and extreme exhaustion, which Xenophon tried to check by giving out special rations with his own hands, but many died of cold and frostbite. They had to hold some black stuff before their eyes, and not to keep the thongs of the sandals tight at night, for the thongs froze into the flesh. Some were so wretched that, finding a patch of ground thawed by a hot spring, they settled down there and refused to move, asking Xenophon to cut their throats when he sternly ordered them to come on and pointed to the swarms of savages hanging on the rear in hope of plunder. Against these he was again obliged to turn his own rearguard about, which drove them down into snowy ravines. He promised to send back as soon as possible for the worn-out stragglers, and he found numbers more as he proceeded towards the van. So he spent all night without food in the snow, and next morning went back to collect all the men he could, and drive them on to a village where the van had made itself fairly comfortable. Somewhere in this freezing region the Greeks must have crossed a track which became the road from Erzeroum to Kars, and in a December many centuries later (1914) was to be strewn with Russian and Turkish corpses frozen side by side. The Greeks were now in the midst of villages rich but hardly visible ; for the houses were subterranean with entrances like wells, ladders down for the natives to descend, and sloping passages for the animals, which swarmed in the warm and roomy interiors to avoid the cold. The Greeks were there entertained with highland hospitality, pointing to any food they wanted —lamb, veal, pork, fowls, and so on—while they drank from great bowls of a heady but delicious wine, either through reeds or dipping their heads down and sucking it up like oxen. Having stayed a week with these amiable troglodytes, Xenophon gave the head-man of his particular dug-out an old horse to fatten up and sacrifice to the Sun, and they marched on through the snow, binding the feet of the horses with stuffed sacks lest they should sink up to the belly. The head-man acted as guide, but as he led to no villages, because, as he said, there were none, Cheirosophus struck him in a rage, and next night he ran home. Xenophon notices that he was angry at this outburst of temper, and this was the only occasion of ill-feeling between him and his brother general : a rare example of magnanimity on both sides.

A HAPPY WARRIOR

Marching forward, they then crossed a river which Xenophon calls the Phasis, but which was probably the early stream of the Araxes, flowing, not like the two great rivers of Mesopotamia into the Persian Gulf, but into the Caspian some distance south of Baku after its junction with the Koura of Georgia. Farther on they saw their way barred by a mixed host of tribesmen, and here a second quarrel almost ensued. For Cheirosophus proposed in rugged Spartan fashion to make a frontal attack, like Buller at Colenso, but Xenophon suggested sending a detachment round to the left over the long mountain range, so as to steal through unseen by night and take the enemy in the flank or rear. Unhappily, he added that he was not worthy to give this advice to the Spartan Cheirosophus, who, like all the noblest Spartans, had been trained to stealing from boyhood as an essential part of public-school education. Whereto Cheirosophus pointedly retorted that he had always heard the Athenians were particularly skilled in stealing public money, and the more they stole the higher was their reputation. Xenophon, of course, volunteered to lead the *détour*, but was requested by the other general to remain with his rearguard as usual. His ruse was entirely successful. The pass was cleared, and the way laid open to another fertile district.

None the less, the troops were very short of provisions when they came to a tribe of mountaineers which Xenophon calls Taocians. These had a habit, like the old Irish and our own ancestors on the Scottish border, of gathering in times of danger all their people, cattle, and possessions into strong and isolated fortresses. The fortress before the Greeks was nearly surrounded by a river, and the only approach was by a short but narrow defile, with high crags on both sides. Cheirosophus attacked three times in vain, for the natives rolled great rocks down from the cliffs, crushing and killing many. But when Xenophon came up from the rear, he suggested that the men should make their way singly through the large pines which covered the sides of the ravine, all but a short space of twenty yards at the farther end. The pines would protect them from sight and rocks, and the natives would soon exhaust their terrible ammunition. This manœuvre was also successful, the men vying with each other to be the first at the fortress.

Then occurred an event which Xenophon rightly describes as a terrible sight. For while the Greeks were passing through the defile, the women on the top of the crags flung their babies down and leapt after them, even the men following. One of the Greeks tried to stop a finely dressed native, but was caught in the other's arms and fell with him over the precipice to death. The scene reminds one of Byron's women of Suli in Epïrus, who, to escape the embraces of Turks, flung themselves over the cliff which you may see to this day.[1]

The army next had to pass through the savage race of the Chalybes, a name perhaps connected with the Greek word for steel. At all events they were a brave and fierce people, dressed in homespun tunics and kilts of cords, and armed with lances about fifteen feet long, and short daggers with which to slit the throat of an enemy when he was down and then cut off his head. They triumphed over each severed head with song and dance ; for they were head-hunters of the usual savage type, like the natives of New Guinea or Saráwak or the Senegalese serving with the French

[1] *Childe Harold's Pilgrimage*, II, lxvii, *The Isles of Greece*, Stanza xiii.

in the Dardanelles in 1915. At sight of the Greeks they shut themselves up in fortresses, refusing supplies, but hanging fiercely on the rear until the army crossed a broad river which Xenophon calls the Harpasus, perhaps the same to which the Turks give the name of Churuk Su, with their usual vagueness. A few days' march farther on they reached a largish town called Gymnias. Perhaps it was the modern Ispir, but the geography of all this part of the route is dubious. A guide there swore on his life that in five days he could lead them to a point from which they could see the Euxine. He led them by a devious track, first into the lands of a tribe hostile to himself, which he urged the Greeks to lay waste, and only then, but well within his time, to a high mountain which Xenophon calls Theches, the exact position of which has been much disputed. As Xenophon was climbing up the mountain, guarding the rear as usual, he heard such shouting in front that he supposed the van was attacked, and rode up with all speed to face the danger.

But on the way he at last distinguished the words, "The sea! The sea!" Then indeed all began running up the slopes. Even his rearguard ran. And gathering at the summit, they saw the dark horizon of the Euxine. All fell to embracing—common soldiers, generals, officers and all—and they shed tears of joy, as well they might. They piled up a great cairn of stones and broken weapons to mark the spot of their rejoicing, and, loading the guide with every kind of reward, they sent him away at nightfall, after he had pointed the path down.

There was some distance still to march, through craggy and difficult country, and one hard engagement to fight, decided by Xenophon's usual instinct for tactics, since he divided his line into eight battalions and stormed upon the enemy at so many points of a high but accessible ridge that they withdrew. Next, he was hampered by the discovery of large deposits of an intoxicating honey, which prostrated many of his men. At last, coming over the hill on which I stood and down the defile by which I had climbed, he reached Trapezus (Trebizond), and was safe in an Hellenic city again. There with merriment the army held athletic sports—flat racing, and hill running, boxing, wrestling, and the pankration, a match of boxing and wrestling, or " go-as-you-please-to-win ". In accordance with their early vow they also made thankofferings to Zeus the Saviour and to Heracles—both god and divine hero being then still living in full strength. For every god lives as long as he is worshipped.

While Xenophon watched these games and took part in the prayers, I can imagine no happier human being in all history. However we may fix his age, he was still in the prime of life. By that instinct for strategy and tactics which is a glorified common sense, by his tact in the management of men, his hopeful disposition, his refusal ever to acknowledge defeat, by his care for the army's provisions and his indomitable endurance of hardship and fatigue ; above all, perhaps, by his unerring sense of direction, with nothing to guide him but the sun, the stars, and his belief that if he kept steadily north he would somewhere reach the Euxine, he had conducted a large and diversified army through a mountainous and unknown country, mainly inhabited by unknown and savage tribes, and he had brought them at last to the sea and safety among races whose customs and language they knew. He himself had always acted with decisive courage in spite of that tormenting anxiety which enfeebles us all, and he had preserved throughout the perilous retreat a modesty, politeness, and moderation, partly implanted in his nature, and partly inculcated by the teaching of his master.

At the start near Sardis the force of all arms numbered about thirteen thousand (later increased to more than fourteen thousand) and at a review near Trapezus he reckoned about ten thousand, but some, including the women, had already sailed for Byzantium. The march to Cunaxa and on to Trapezus seems to have lasted about a year (from March, 401, to February, 400), and the distance has been estimated at about two-thousand-four-hundred miles, but exact estimate is impossible; for the Persian measure "parasangs" used by Xenophon varied from place to place and the average of three miles is probably too high by at least a third. However long in time or space, the adventurous task was accomplished, and as the accomplishment of an adventurous task is the highest happiness that can befall a man, we may account Xenophon supremely happy at the moment when he descended into the port of Trebizond.

On one other occasion I had the chance to consort with my great example's ghost. I was making my way on foot through Arcadia from the beautiful temple to Pan and Apollo at Bassæ, when in Elis night overtook me among the hills near Chrestĕna, only a few miles short of Olympia, and there I lay down to sleep among the sweet-smelling herbs and bushes abundant in Greece. I must have been close to the place which Xenophon calls Scillus and describes with affection towards the end of his *Anabasis*. For he lived there many years, an exile from Athens, and there one may suppose he wrote most of his books—the treatises on

Housekeeping, on Hunting, on Horsemanship, on the recent history of Greece, and on memories of his master, who had been poisoned by the democrats of Athens, very soon after Xenophon reached Trapezus. And there one may imagine that he wrote the story of his famous exploit, carefully following the notes he had made during the long march. Here, too, he built a shrine in gratitude to Artemis on the model of her temple in Ephesus, and here he liked to gather friends and visitors, entertaining them with the produce of his farm and the game he caught by hunting with his two sons, whom he had given to be educated in Sparta so as to train them to manliness. One of them was killed at the battle of Mantinea (362), where the Theban hero Epaminondas also fell. On hearing the news, Xenophon, in the midst of his grief, is said to have remarked, as a Stoic or Socrates himself might have done : " I never supposed I had begotten an immortal."

SCENE IV

"MY SERPENT OF OLD NILE"

How, being in Epĭrus during a Greek retreat, I beheld the battle of Actium

ON August the 28th, 1897, I was with the Greek army guarding the mountain pass that leads from the Greek town of Arta in Epĭrus to Janina, the chief town of Southern Albania, then still in Turkish possession. The Greeks wore their heavy blue overcoats, though the spring was hot, and small outposts had been set along the summit of a steep mountain ridge, which I helped them to fortify with loose rocks against the bullets that whined incessantly over our heads. Peering over the edge I could watch scattered bodies of Turks in their brown uniforms and Albanians in their little white caps approaching over a broad valley on the other side, and crowding into the shelter of dead ground at the foot of our rocky cliff. The Turks had two mountain guns which shelled the top of the ridge, and the Greeks brought up two similar guns, but the shells from either side seldom burst, and the rifles, firing black, smoky powder, were the only weapons that told. By their persistence and regularity of line the Albanians were evidently the best troops on the Turkish side. At intervals the firing was heavy, and a good many of our Evzone Greeks fell. But at sunset the sound of firing slowly died; for the Turks had a rule, probably a wise one, never to attack by night, and I went down to the empty, strongly fortified cottage into which I had forced an entrance in the mountain village of Karvarsaras, fairly well satisfied with the Greek advance. For it had penetrated some twenty miles into Turkish territory and Janĭna lay only about thirty miles ahead.

Next morning there was little firing, and the Turkish assault seemed to have failed. Instead of climbing the mountain barrier again, I walked up a low hill beside the road, from which the situation up to that point was clear. Northward I could see the snowy mountains of upper Albania from which I had lately looked down upon Metsovo, the entrance to the pass through which perhaps Pompey made his way over Pindus into Thessaly and so to his ruin at Pharsalia. Near at hand rose the great crag of riven stone which stands above Janĭna. Southward from my hill extended a wide plain, at the near end of which still smoked and flared the ruins of Philipiades, triumphantly burnt by the Greeks two or three days before. It had been a largish town, named, I suppose, after the Fifth Philip of Macedon. Farther on, beyond the plain, lay the great Ambracian Gulf, some thirty miles long by ten or more broad, shut in from the sea by two horns or promontories. At the end of the horn on this side the Turks had a strong fortress firing one big gun at intervals. It was called Prevĕza, and no one quite knew what the gun kept firing at, but, a little way nearer the mainland on the same promontory, Augustus once built the fine city of Nicopolis to celebrate his decisive victory over Antony and Cleopatra. And at the end of the opposite horn stood Actium, where was a temple of Apollo, beside which Antony's land forces were gathered. Farther beyond, out of the sea itself, rose the great mass of Leukas, and farther still the dome of Cephalonia, once Byron's home during his heroic effort to give Greece freedom. Hardly visible between them I could just make out rugged little Ithaca from which Ulysses longed to see the smoke ascending.

But associations with the past were suddenly interrupted by an intense increase of rifle firing on that very crest where I had been the day before. It grew into such a roar as portends the crisis of battle, and I saw the Greeks hurriedly dragging down their two mountain guns. Streams of blue figures came rushing and leaping over the rocky slopes. At once on the summit appeared equal swarms of black figures, waving their rifles and little red flags. A prolonged and high-pitched note sounded from among them. "That's the Turkish trumpet!" cried a peasant beside me. On her forehead a blue cross had been tattooed in girlhood, in defiance of Islam, and all her life she had known the fatal sound of that trumpet. Without a pause, she set off running back to the village, and as I followed her I met all the inhabitants of the neighbourhood hastening down from their scattered cottages to the narrow road. Down they came, carrying all they could carry, and dragging the rest behind them—children, cattle, ponies, pigs (one of the distinguishing marks of Christianity), clothing, bits of furniture, and the red peplomata or quilts which make the bedding.

Tying my small kit on the one little pony left me by my guide when he ran, I descended into the rout, and crawled along with the rest. All his life that pony had done nothing but crawl, and now we were jammed up with a jumble of soldiers, irregulars (*Andarti*), who hovered around the army, always ready for plunder or retreat, and women stooping double under their vast bundles. Some carried a wooden cradle on the top of the bundle, with a baby inside. One had lashed a baby to her back and a calf round her neck. Young girls also were doubled under bundles, and children scrambled barefoot along the rocky ground, each driving a goat or a sheep. And among the huddled mass whizzed and fell the bullets fired at random by the Turks on the summit. " Now we are in for a promiscuous massacre," I thought, " and Turks who enjoy killing can have it."

Sunset was at hand. Night would bring some cessation of the firing, and the Turks were worn-out with their long fast of Ramadan, as the Greeks were by Lent. But alarms continually renewed drove the indistinguishable rabble onward. We reached a long and narrow part of the road, shut in on our left by a steep mountain height, and on the right by black forest marshes stagnant and stinking, the overflow of the small river Louros, which runs into the Ambracian Gulf. The name set me thinking again of Cleopatra and her sudden flight, followed by Antony just at the crisis of battle. Mothers had put two weary children in front of me on the wooden saddle, and dreamily I thought of Cleopatra's line, " O happy horse, to bear the weight of Antony ! " The words awoke in me a vision of that irresistibly alluring queen.

Hour after hour we crept along under the malign light of a waning moon, though blocked at times by guns trying to join in the retreat, or by a struggling crowd at some little spring of water. For no one

"MY SERPENT OF OLD NILE"

drank the poisonous marsh, and the worst of all natural sufferings is thirst. As often happens when one is moving hour after hour on a crawling horse through the night, I went almost to sleep, filled with fantastic imaginings, and once when I was dimly aware that the mothers were taking the two children from my care, I perceived as in a dream tiny white or bluish lights dancing around me. I thought they were electric or telegraphic sparks in some way connected with the Turkish pursuit that might have rushed behind us at any moment and cut the whole mob of unresisting peasants and soldiers to pieces. But presently I realized that the sparks which rose and fell and circled round were only fireflies, and that it was likely I should sleepily fall off the wooden saddle myself. Coming to a point in the road where I felt sure the Greek army would make defence, I turned up the hillside, tied the horse by his halter to a large rock and lay down in a crevice to sleep.

That vast gulf, not many miles southward, was beginning to be just visible in the dawn of an early spring morning, and I seemed to see that its broad surface was again crowded with a large fleet. Most of the ships were of enormous size, larger even than the biggest in pictures of the Spanish Armada. They stood up from the water like castles, and were moved by ten banks of oars—the oars of the top bank so long and heavy that relays of slaves were kept ready to work them. The sides of the hulks were protected by thick baulks of rough timber, like the projections round our " blister ships ". On the upper deck rose high towers from which catapults flung huge rocks, so that the whole ship became a platform for projectiles, like the " Monitors " constructed for our fleet in 1915.

"MY SERPENT OF OLD NILE"

Behind these monster ships of Antony lay some sixty Egyptian vessels of lesser size, commanded by their Queen. The Antonian ships alone ran to five hundred, and his army on the southern entrance to the Gulf counted a hundred thousand, collected from various European and Oriental races, unused to solid war, depressed by the malaria which hangs about that wet and low-lying coast leading up to the sharp point of Actium, and the Roman levies had small enthusiasm for a Roman general who, it was rumoured, intended to fight on sea without their help. They even petitioned him to stick to the battle by land on which his fame as a gallant and energetic Roman general had been won. How could a general resist such an appeal? But Antony waved it aside.

On the opposite shore under shelter of the long promontory which would meet the point of Actium but for the half-mile or so of water that forms the mouth of the great Gulf, Octavian lay encamped with an army slightly less in numbers but made up of disciplined and fairly homogeneous Roman legionaries, some of whom might have fought under command of the great Cæsar, murdered only thirteen years before. The Octavian fleet was hanging outside on the open sea. Some of the ships were heavy monsters like Antony's, but most of them lighter and swifter, like the English ships under Drake. So there was Antony, suffering the fate of every commander who lays his fleet in a splendid harbour with a narrow entrance, like the Bocche di Cattaro, for instance, or the port in which the Spanish fleet at Cuba was "bottled up" in 1898.

Realizing the danger, Antony ordered his huge ships to break out through the narrow channel and form line upon the open sea. Cleopatra with her smaller Egyptian vessels followed them close behind, but as they emerged, all were confronted by the light Octavian craft, which dashed among them, rowing swiftly round and round, breaking the serried banks of oars, harrying the crews with spears and arrows, boarding with drawn swords, and flinging fire upon the decks. They were storming isolated castles upon the water. Big rocks fell crashing down upon them, slung by catapults on the towers. Arrows, spears, and swords met them from the bulwarks. Many ships were left in the Gulf, unable to emerge, but along the disorganized front upon the sea the clash of naval battle arose, and from the shores of the two enclosing promontories the rival armies looked on with terror or with exultation as the fortune of the conflict swayed, just as the Athenian army watched the naval battle in the Great Harbour of Syracuse nearly four centuries before. From both sides rose the roar of triumph or the groans of defeat, and from the embattled ships came the clash of brazen impact, the smashing of oars, the crackling of flames, and the screams of the dying.

Through the din and confusion Cleopatra commanded her own ship to wriggle out beyond the line. From her deck she saw Antony's great ship hard beset on every side, and almost incapable of movement. Some of his other vessels were in flames, some already occupied by the enemy. With her shrewd and rapid judgment, she felt the day was lost. Before the event she had agreed with Antony to sail together back in triumph to Egypt as King and Queen of the East. There they would meet their twins, called Sun and Moon, and their little baby Ptolemy, who was to carry on the immemorial dynasties of Egypt. Now, in defeat she would go.

"MY SERPENT OF OLD NILE"

All was not lost. Even without Antony she was Queen. A northerly wind arose. She signalled to the Egyptian ships still around her to follow. She hoisted her purple sails, and setting a south-east course for Egypt, she sailed down the Ionian sea.

From the deck of his vast flagship, dangerously beleaguered, Antony saw those purple sails puff out to the favouring breeze, as they bore away that " serpent of old Nile "—the snake-like little body of the woman he had loved for so many years. He signalled to a swift vessel with five banks of oars to come alongside. He climbed down from the bulwarks of his wooden castle, entered the swifter ship, and commanded the helmsman to follow the purple sails. His rowers soon overtook the Queen, and she invited him on board, but she hid herself in her cabin. Antony sat in the prow, and for three whole days he remained there, hiding his head between his hands, or gazing in despair towards the course before him. After futile delays and separations, they came together in Alexandria again. So to the lonely house, the last effort of war, the self-driven sword, the Mausoleum, and the asp—the pretty worm of Nilus that kills and pains not—the baby at her breast that sucked the nurse asleep.

That tragic figure of Antony, stationary at the prow as Cleopatra's ship bore him farther and farther away from Actium ! He was suffering the consciousness of a coward's crime, the worst torture that the mind of man can endure, or must die rather than endure. He had deserted the soldiers who admired and even loved him as a friend of the great Cæsar ; as a man of unflinching courage ; a general who had equally shared with them all the hardships and disasters of their recent campaign in the freezing uplands of the Armenian border, which Xenophon had known; and as a genial and friendly officer possessing that personal attraction which has sometimes doubled the power of great commanders. He seemed to hear the cries of rage and despair which arose from his army as they watched him sail away; the shrieks of his sailors whom he had abandoned in his great ships, which Octavian, cool, pitiless, and decisive as he always was, ordered to be burnt where they lay. One after another they flamed. They burnt to the water's edge. Hissing and steaming as water mingled with the intense heat, they disappeared beneath the surface, bearing with them the ruins of skilful construction, the masses of treasure hidden in their holds, and the souls of men, both slave and free. Soldiers and sailors, Antony had abandoned them all.

How noble would his reputation have been in Rome and in all history if only he had remained at the head of his legions or on the quarter-deck of his flagship, and cried: "Here I stand, your Admiral, your Imperator, your fellow-citizen in arms! Let the enemy do his worst upon me! Here I stand to the end." Thousands had died for him; thousands stood ready to die. He was a man over fifty, a man of unusual strength and of valour proved in many crises of fate. How could he abandon them, just to save his life, or to adventure upon a visionary Empire in barbaric lands? I thought of Napoleon at Moscow, and of the Kaiser at Spa.

Exquisite luxury had effeminated his body and impaired his power of decision. He had learnt to enjoy all the physical delights of a life that supplied them without his effort. Good things to eat and drink, silken clothes, cool or pleasantly heated rooms, comfortable beds with linen sheets—how pleasant they were to one who in war-time had never complained of hunger, heat, or cold! And, after the sweat and dust and filth of camps, in which the passion for woman is raised to almost unendurable longing, came Cleopatra, the small, lithe, and passionate embodiment of sensual womanhood, endowed with subtle genius and every art of various pleasing, and, as she pleaded in her defence, " No more, but e'en a woman."

He had seen her as a girl of fifteen, a lovely Greek girl just touched with the attraction of Oriental difference. Then in Rome as the great Cæsar's mistress, bringing with her their son, not long before Cæsar was murdered ; then as the goddess of beauty upon that barge at Tarsus ; and then in her chamber at Alexandria. No wonder that to Antony she was irresistible ; and he did not wish to resist. Even Socrates confessed himself to be easily overcome by beauty, and Antony was unlike Socrates in every other point. Her capacity for the gift and sharing of amorous delights long held him bound. Marriage with Octavia, sister of his present victor, was unavailing. A widow, a typical Roman matron with children, holy, cold, and silent, " a body rather than a life, a statue rather than a breather ", admired by the Roman populace as a worthy type of the mother of the Gracchi, almost as frigid as a consecrated Vestal. Beside such frigidity the memory of Egypt's snake-like body and amorous ways often recurred, and physical desire, so powerful a part of love, drew him back to the pleasures of sensual life, forgetful of Rome and Roman matrons. Disguised as Isis and Osiris, or, needing no disguise, as Venus and Bacchus, whom Antony impersonated with excessive

"MY SERPENT OF OLD NILE"

accuracy, they lived at ease, luxuriating in such pleasures as physical life can give without satiety; saved, perhaps, from satiety by the birth of three children, the cares of royalty, the designs of an Asiatic Empire surpassing the dreams of Alexander; or by a foreboding of the end which fell upon them at Actium.

So the tragic lovers sailed away to their doom, and in the twelve hours of that September day, thirty-one years before the birth of Christ, the course of the world was altered or confirmed. But for that day it is just credible that we might now be entangled among a host of unreasonable deities—the dog-headed, cat-headed, vulture-headed gods of Egypt, or even the elephant-headed, many-armed deities of India, melting into one another's forms and attributes like dissolving views. European history and religion have not much to boast of, but still one may trace in them some thin thread of reason, freedom, and definite forms of art—the thin thread which was not severed at Actium.

Dreams are quicker than thought, though thought is quick. But when I looked out from my crevice in the rocks, I found it was now broad daylight. A few straggling refugees were still stumbling along the road with their bundles and cattle, but not a soldier was in sight. The army had abandoned the strong position at Koumzádes, which I thought even Greeks might hold for a time, and there was nothing now between me and the Turks, whose habit it fortunately was to pursue slowly. As I rode along with the weary stream of refugees, I looked again over that wide lake-like Gulf, on the shining surface of which only a few pelicans were now floating. I looked to the promontories which almost closed the mouth, and I remembered that in the City of Victory—the Nicopolis which Octavian Augustus had built on the northern promontory to celebrate his conquest of Egypt and the East—a lame slave, exiled by Domitian from Rome, had once spent his thoughtful years instructing youth in the chilly principles of Stoical behaviour. Epictetus lived there to an enviable old age, and Arrian, the historian of Alexander the Great, thought it worth while to make notes of his lectures. Moral teaching has always been much the same—" Be good and you will be happy " (against which one might urge with exactly equal truth, " Be happy and you will be good ") ; " Practise self-restraint, especially from lust and cruelty " ; " Virtue can suffer no pain " ; " Nothing but goodness is good " ; " Even a slave can be virtuous ", anticipating the subtler saying of the Stoic Emperor, " One can be virtuous even in a palace ", and similar paradoxes or platitudes. But one saying had stuck in my memory : " When shall I see Athens again ? " some homesick student had asked. " Aren't you satisfied ", answered the lame slave, " with what you can see every day ? Is it better to see Athens than the sun, the moon, the stars, the earth, and the sea ? " Looking at the place where the City of Victory once stood and Epictetus once taught that stern morality, I rode on till the scent of orange blossom came to me from the orchards where families of refugees were wretchedly encamping in their dirt and smell. And so I crossed the Arachtos into the town of Arta by the ancient bridge into which the builder had been compelled to build up his beloved mistress to make it stand secure. The ancient ballad telling the story is still sung, showing of what love is capable.

"MY SERPENT OF OLD NILE"

On the way up the street to the telegraph office (which was closed lest the truth of defeat should be divulged), I passed the ancient Byzantine cathedral dedicated to St. Theodora, wife of the great Emperor Justinian, herself a striking instance of miraculous conversion. For in her beautiful youth she had in the public theatre of Constantinople displayed lascivious arts which Gibbon felt obliged to leave to notes in the original Greek. I found shelter for my horse in a half-ruined cottage, and at night, being seized with violent colic, I was attended by an old Greek woman, who performed various curative rites upon me, singing meantime magical charms such as the witches sang in Thessaly when Apuleius wrote the adventures of " The Golden Ass ". I felt that within twenty-four hours I had taken deep soundings into the abysm of time, and time was still continuing to form the abysm. For, at irregular intervals, the big Turkish gun at Preveza on the promontory of Nicopolis opposite Actium kept firing sullenly for some inconceivable purpose.

SCENE V

VIA DOLOROSA

How, being in Jerusalem, I saw the Roman soldiers and a rabble of Jews leading Christ to Cavalry

EVEN to an Englishman the first sight of Jerusalem is one of life's greatest events. That is still true, though few English children are now brought up on the Bible as we Evangelican children were in the middle of last century. To us the Bible was the Word of God, inspired or written by God Himself, and true for ever in every syllable, even of our translation. To question, to criticize, to expose errors or contradictions in it was blasphemy ; it was the sin against the Holy Ghost, which has no forgiveness. We were far better acquainted with the history of the Jews than with the history of the English. In the pious fervour of the time, we even transferred to ourselves the whole of Jewish history with its noble or evil examples, its warnings, denunciations, prophecies of doom and promises of deliverance, and when at Evening Prayer in our village churches we sang, " To be a light to lighten the Gentiles, and to be the glory of thy people Israel," we thought of the Gentiles as Jews, Turks, heretics, black or yellow masses of Indians, Africans, Chinese and other brands whom our missionaries strove to save from the burning ; but " thy people Israel" were ourselves, the English race; excepting only the Roman Catholics, who needed more light than even the Gentiles.

Imbued with childhood's knowledge that years never quite obliterate, I came to Palestine as to a home long familiar by report but never yet visited. The very names of places recalled an ancient history. Tyre and Sidon, the River Kishon, Nazareth, the Sea of Galilee, the Valley of Jezreel, the mountains of Gilboa, Beisan, the double mountains of Samaria, the hill country of Judæa—each name was filled with special memories, and at each place I could think to myself: "Here it happened. This is the very scene." Then I came to the high ground from which at last I could see a distant hill crowned with domes and towers and fortifying walls. It was Jerusalem, Mount Zion, the Holy City, the Centre of the Earth, the Emblem of Paradise.

If I, a foreigner, born and reared in a distant island, having no connection with Palestine either by race or history, could be so affected by the sight of that distant town upon a hill, how much more poignant must be the emotion of a Jew coming for the first time from any part of the world to behold the city which is his spiritual home! Here, long ago, his race had struggled for existence against the powers of enormous empires, had maintained a religious ritual divinely ordained for every detail of life, and had worshipped a spiritual and invisible deity, unlike the dog-headed symbols of Egypt on the south-west frontiers or, just across the desert to the east, the winged Assyrian bulls with human heads and curling beards. Here their poets had poured out impassioned odes of warning or encouragement, and love lyrics unsurpassed for the beauty of sensual passion.

VIA DOLOROSA

Here had been their temple, their sacred Ark, their house of the living God. What sense of holiness, what yearning of regret must fill the heart of every Jew as he stands where I was standing, and realizes his inseparable bond to the storied city! " And when he was come near, he beheld the city, and wept over it," we read of one who discerned the city's approaching doom, when the enemy should cast a trench about it and compass it round, and keep it in on every side, and lay it even with the ground, not leaving one stone upon another. And, with the yearning spirit of a Jew, we may read again the foreboding lamentation: " O Jerusalem, Jerusalem, thou that killest the prophets and stonest them which are sent unto thee, how often would I have gathered thy children together, even as a hen gathereth her chickens under her wings, and ye would not! Behold your house is left unto you desolate."

When those cries of passionate patriotism were first uttered, the city, rebuilt not long before, was still standing in mingled native and Greek or Roman form untouched by the Mohammedan and Christian temples and other buildings which even now leave it still the most beautiful of medieval towns. Though the site was left desolate for many generations, not one stone standing upon another but for the solid wall which had once supported the platform where Herod's temple stood, the consecrated hill remained. To Jews, who once had their capital there, everything that was then anticipated has happened. From age to age they have been despised, beaten, robbed, tortured and killed without mercy, even as a religious duty imposed upon Christians. In one point only was the speaker wrong in his anticipations. Thinking of the inevitable overthrow of Jerusalem by the

VIA DOLOROSA

Roman power which could not endure so rebellious and peculiar a people within the Empire, he said that there would be great tribulation, such as was not since the beginning of the world to that time, no, nor ever should be. It was then impossible to foresee how atrocious the persecution of the Jews would be for the next two thousand years. Roman persecutions were cruel, and when the Senate under Tiberius exiled to Sardinia four thousand freed men " infected with the Jewish superstition ", the comment was added that if they all died there owing to the unhealthy climate, it would be a cheap loss (*vile damnun*).[1] But for persistent cruelty, scorn, and exclusion from the comforts and pleasures of life, the Christians have far surpassed every torment that pagan Rome could devise, and up to the present year there has been no relaxation of Christian barbarity. The wonder is that, scattered in every nation, and powerless to resist every wrong, Jews survive as a separate people. In thinking that survival miraculous, Jews and Christians agree.

As I approached the city walls, I was met by a small party of Jews carrying in their midst two huge scrolls of the Law, which they were transferring from one synagogue to another, shouting, leaping, and dancing in front of the scrolls as they went. Certainly it seemed miraculous to me that they should be maintaining a form of religion so much older than any other form now existing, except perhaps among savages, and that they should still be rejoicing in the traditional worship of the five ancient Books of Moses, which are the Law. But there was nothing strange in their perpetual opposition to one of their own race who said he had come to fulfil the Law, and yet absolved them for disregarding many important points

[1] Tacitus, *Annals*, II, 85.

of the Law's ritual, such as the washing of pots and cups, tables, and even hands before meals, and the meticulous observance of the Sabbath as a day of complete inactivity ; one who repeatedly condemned in violent language the learned professors of the Law and those who boasted they lived with scrupulous exactness in accordance with ritual ; one who taught that the kingdom of God was within them, and insisted upon a worship with the heart and not with the lips only. From childhood I had seen how much easier the observance of ritual is than the worship in spirit and in truth, and now I could realize with what an uncomfortable shock the spiritual interpretation must have come to people accustomed to believe that the careful practice of traditional rites was all that religion required. There was nothing miraculous or even strange in that. I had often attended Catholic and Orthodox services and festivals in England, Ireland, Russia, and other Christian countries.

But when I passed the Anglican Cathedral about half a mile outside the walls, and later on the Roman Catholic Church and the Russian, Greek or Orthodox Churches, the behaviour of Christians did appear to me, not miraculous indeed, but inexplicable. All Christians must of necessity believe that Jesus was God, the Son of God, and that his teaching and commandments are of necessity the teaching and commandments of God. These ordinances must lay upon all Christians obligations at least equal to those laid upon Jews by the Law. From childhood Christians are made familiar with the words—" Blessed are the poor " ; " Take no thought for the morrow " ; " Consider the lilies how they grow, they toil not neither do they spin " ; " Sufficient unto the day is the evil thereof " ; " Judge not " ; " Resist not evil "; " Forgive unto seventy times seven "; " Blessed are the peacemakers "; " Blessed are the pure in heart "; " Let him who is without sin cast the first stone "; " Blessed are the persecuted ". We all know the words, and Christians must by their very name believe them to be divine. But they are utterly at variance with the habitual actions and beliefs of every Christian Government and nearly every Christian man and woman every day and night. Think of our savings-banks, our investments, our careful insurances for old age, our suits for debt, our tailors and drapers, our fashion plates, our delight in scandal and dirty stories, our advertisements, our brothels, our law-courts, and our successive wars! It is not miraculous, but it is remarkable that Christians who say they believe, and many who really believe, in the divine origin of these common-sense or paradoxical sayings and commands should produce the Christian world that we see extending over large parts of the two hemispheres. I can only think that so large a proportion of mankind has regarded Jesus as the Son of God because he was so unlike all the rest of us. Or perhaps we must compare Christian mankind of our present time to the man whose unclean spirit had gone from him, and who walked in dry places, seeking rest, and finding none returned to his house, which he found swept and garnished. The house was too clean and tidy, one must suppose, and so he took to him seven other spirits more wicked than himself, and they entered the house and dwelt there. It is a parable of the human soul, but it represents the history of Europe equally well.

None the less, as evidence of the continuous power of Christ's words, I remembered that once (in 1907) I was in Orissa, the southern neighbour of Bengal, as the guest of Madhu Sudan Das, a wealthy Hindu of Cuttack, who had written imploring me to come as witness to the desolation of his province. The floods of a great river rushing from the jungle hills had transformed the cultivated fields into a desert of sand, and, in spite of the well-intentioned efforts of the British officials, the villagers were creeping or lying about like skeletons barely covered with skin. Many came to Mr. Das entreating him to touch their putrefying sores, and in one case a man brought a bowl of water, praying him to dip his finger into it that his starving wife might be delivered in her dangerous labour. The child was safely born, and the reverence for Mr. Das continually increased. Indeed, his natural generosity would have given him power anywhere, but, though a highly educated Hindu, he told me he had become a Christian in early manhood, his faith being founded solely upon his admiration of Christ's prayer, "Father, forgive them, for they know not what they do." "The man who could utter that prayer while dying in torture was divine," he often said to me; "the moment I heard of the prayer, I recognized that truth, and I have never doubted it since." On the strength of a single saying Christ was accepted as divine because he was so unlike the ruck of mankind.

Thinking of all this, I passed through the walls by the Damascus Gate into the Holy City, and looked that evening from the window of a cell in the Austrian Hospice for pilgrims over the darkening lanes and closely packed roofs of Arab and Jewish homes. The scene of the immortal tragedy lay directly before me. No matter what destruction the Romans had wrought upon the city when they wiped it out as too dangerous for a frontier capital, here was the very place. Not in any of the old houses I could see, but in some house standing here before these existed was the upper chamber where Jesus gathered his few personal followers for a supper which he knew would be his last. His knowledge of his approaching execution was as certain as his knowledge of the city's approaching doom, and to him the bread and the wine upon the table became symbols of his own body and blood so soon to be killed and shed. He asked them to remember his death whenever they partook of that food and drink—the simple food and drink of all the pastoral and working people in that country.

As in the case of all sensitive and imaginative people, the foreknowledge of pain and death weighed upon him with increasing anguish. The suffering of fear came to its climax in that garden still lying there just across the steep valley of the brook Kedron behind the Hospice where I stood, and there he prayed with agonized earnestness that the coming anguish and the early end of a young and energetic life might be averted, if it were God's will.

But, as he had foreseen, anguish and death were close at hand. The expounders of the Law and the devotees of ritual held him encompassed, and would not let him go. This was the man who made light of divine and unreasonable laws, and who mocked at their pride in long robes and personal distinction. Here was a fine opportunity to mock in turn at his pretensions as a teacher and prophet. Taking him off amid a jeering crowd they blindfolded and mocked him in the Chief Priest's house, where in terror of the ruling class his most daring and impulsive friend denied any acquaintance with him at this moment of danger.

Night and morning, from one authority to another he was sent for judgment. The official representative of Rome was unwilling to act against the Roman idea of justice, but still more unwilling to offend against a subject and strangely superstitious people's idea of religion. Religious and civilian authorities of the turbulent city demanded the death sentence, and they were supported by the clamour of the mob, who always delight in a public execution more than in any other stimulus to their torpid sensations. Against his better judgment Pilate pronounced the death sentence, chiefly in order to get rid of a troublesome little affair such as confronts the Imperial Governor of a distant Oriental province almost every day.

From my window I looked down upon the rough road leading through the city from the Damascus Gate, and at a point a little way to my left I could see the entrance of a dark and narrow lane, rising at intervals by shallow steps up the slope of the opposite hill, on the summit of which I saw the flattish dome where tradition places Calvary. The lane has for generations been called the *Via Dolorosa*, and it is just possible that such Jews or even Christians as continued to subsist among the dust and rubbish of the old city when the Romans levelled it with the ground may have unwittingly preserved the tradition of the site. This tradition was supported by a discovery made in the middle of last century by a Jew who had become a Catholic priest (as uncommon an event as any authenticated miracle). Underneath the convent still called *Ecce Homo* by a similar tradition he excavated a Roman building and pavement where possibly Pilate's judgment seat once stood. It was called The Pavement, in the Hebrew Gabbatha, as we know from St. John's Gospel (xix. 13), and on the pavement thus lately disclosed are still to be seen shallow holes, perhaps scooped out by the Roman soldiers for some game like backgammon. For Pilate's guards gambled like all soldiers, and for Christ's undivided coat they cast lots.

It was not hard to imagine a pitiful little procession coming down the slope from the Prætorium or Judgment Seat. In the midst was Jesus, dressed as a Jew of the working class, for the soldiers who had tricked him out as King of the Jews, in a purple cloak and a crown of thorns, had taken the robe and probably the mock crown away, and given him his own clothes again, thus concealing the marks of the lash. As was usual in executions, he carried the cross to which he was to be nailed, but only for a time. He was enfeebled by the length of suffering through the night, by the examinations before one judge after another, and by the torture of scourging. So a casual passer-by was ordered to carry the cross, and Jesus went alone and unencumbered, in his usual clothes, very different from the flowing and majestic robes with which painters and sculptors have habitually and falsely sought to glorify him.

On guard around him marched a section of Roman soldiers, indifferent to the peculiar habits of excitable Orientals, and acting only under orders to preserve the life of the convict for his approaching death according to law. Close beside them came the priests and lawyers, equally anxious to save his life up to the appointed place of execution. Thick around the central group jeered and howled the crowding populace, such as always throngs to witness any scene of blood and horror, fearing only that in that narrow lane they might be thrust aside and come too late for the best part of the execution, which would be the stretching of the limbs and the nailing to the cross beams and the upright post.

VIA DOLOROSA

The hurried procession reached the Place of a Skull, to which the garden grave lay close. There they crucified him, as we read in four accounts agreeing with each other more exactly than most historical accounts of any episode agree. They crucified a man possessing a love of nature in flowers, birds, and beasts of all kinds, pitying mankind for having no shelter at night such as foxes and birds obtain without much effort—a man also who in his pity for mankind and in his deep perception into human nature uttered words of kindliness and guidance not only beyond his own time, but beyond any time since then. That life and that execution have been recognized as one of the decisive events of history even by modern critics of texts and tradition.

As in a vision, I saw again the fourth round of the Ninth Circle in Hell where traitors dwell, encrusted for ever in thick but pellucid ice, and the monstrous three-faced Emperor of the Inferno chews in the mouth of his vermilion face the head of one clutched deep within his moving jaws while the body lies outside, scarified with scratches to the bone, more painful than the champings of the head. So wrote the Italian poet, and it is hard for the modern apologists of Judas to modify such a judgment by providing for him the refuge of patriotism.

That evening I was present at a ceremony of the Abyssinian Church, held upon a platform constructed round a low dome, which forms the roof of the Empress Helena's subterranean chapel. For the chapel marks the spot where, during her visit to Jerusalem, some monks discovered for her the three crosses of the crucifixion—a fortunate discovery, no doubt fortifying her in the Christian belief which she handed on to her son Constantine, thus ensuring the position of

Christianity as the official religion of the civilized world. I do not know by what means the Abyssinians have claimed and established a right of worship on the roof of a chapel conspicuous for that providential discovery, but there I found a procession of them parading round the low dome above the Empress's altar. The Abbot or Chief Priest, a weary young man adorned with a mitre that glittered with diamonds, possibly genuine, walked in the centre of the group, preceded by a long lemon-shaped drum. Before and behind came priests or monks singing in the Oriental mode, and swaying to and fro with apparent ecstasy. They stopped, and the Abbot took his seat upon a throne richly embellished with gold or shining brass, and he held out a cross to be kissed by all who would. Two large umbrellas fringed with gold, and two smaller of green silk, illuminated with spangles, were carried before him and then gathered round the throne. Though the sun had set, the umbrellas were used to show that the pilgrims came from a country where it shines. The singing and rapidly gabbled prayers continued until an end came with unexpected suddenness, and the procession withdrew.

I believe the Abyssinian Church is still Monophysite, and the word raised in my mind dim memories of heated and bloodthirsty disputes in the early years of the Church and the early Middle Ages—disputes as to the meaning of the Holy Trinity and the nature of the Incarnation. Like a long series of wrathful skeletons or fanatical ghosts, the various sectaries of Christian belief passed before me—Arians and Athanasians, Gnostics, Ebionites, Docetans, Anthropomorphites, Armenians, Jacobites, Montanists, Nestorians, Chaldæans (if indeed they are not the same), Eusebians, Maronites (followers of a savage saint in Syria, whose church I saw in Tyre, and whose cemetery in Beyrout), Monothelites, and Monophysites, such as these Abyssinians and Copts were, or once had been in the thousand years during which Abyssinia and Upper Egypt seem to have withdrawn from active existence.

The distinctions between all these sects and heresies are hardly comprehensible except to the inspired subtlety of theological brains. Yet in the days of their origins the hardly perceptible differences and dogmas were matters of life and death, urged with a conviction so self-assured and a hostility so envenomed that hundreds of thousands of men, women, and children were slaughtered in their defence or denial, and controversies over the unity or double-nature of Christ's person or will caused as many violent deaths as the denial or assertion of his divinity. Even so we have not taken into account the more recent antagonisms among Christians—the Orthodox and the Catholics, the Uniates, the Old Believers (Rascolniks), the Molokans, the Lutherans and Calvinists, the Quakers, the Wesleyans, Methodists, Baptists, Congregationalists, Evangelicans, Anglicans, Christian Scientists and all ecstatic forms of American inspiration.

Similar spiritual and metaphysical distinctions and doctrines might well have existed in Europe apart from Christianity, as they have for ages existed in India, and with devastating results. Even before the birth of Christ we hear of philosophic feuds, though I do not remember records of slaughter between Platonists and Aristotelians, or between Stoics and Epicureans. But it appears strange that the most terrible religious or philosophic conflicts in history should have raged round that sensitive, infinitely charitable, and forgiving figure who was once marched to a peculiarly cruel execution up the very same lane upon which I was looking out from my Hospice cell. His foreknowledge of his death was natural, for all priests long to exterminate one who denounces their ritual as an empty form. No superhuman power of prophecy was needed to foretell the imminent destruction of Jerusalem, or the coming chaos of the world as the Roman Empire broke up. But how could so tolerant and open a mind as his foresee the incomprehensible divisions among his followers, the consequent brutish animosities, the cruel persecutions, and the bloody wars that would ensue upon his death and worship?

The horrible story is not a record of medieval ages alone. In England the animosity is comparatively mild at the present day, but go to an English village and still you will find a cruel social line drawn between those who attend the parish church with the gentry, and those who "sit under" the preachers in the Nonconformist chapels. When I asked the Anglican sexton of a village what was the proportion of Church people to Dissenters, he replied, " They beat us, curse them!" Even so Christ himself, foreseeing the future of his life and teaching, said, with deep insight into man's mental nature, "I came not to bring peace into the world but a sword." For though he said repeatedly that he revealed his truth to the simple-hearted people whom he called babes, the wise and prudent have never ceased to philosophize, meticulize, dogmatize, anathematize, and criticize over a teaching and a nature that to simple-hearted people seem so beautiful in their simplicity.

SCENE VI

THE GODS DEPART

How, on landing at Spalato, I heard the Emperor Diocletian discussing the world and saw him witnessing a martyrdom of Christians

IT was in July, 1913, an ominous date, for Europe was fermenting with wars and rumours of wars leading to the outbreak of one year later. The Balkans as usual were the danger-point, threatening explosion, and for some years I had known those beautiful and distracted homes of violent nationalism. In September, 1911, I had been in Albania with Edith Durham, whom the Albanians saluted with the well-deserved title of Kralitza or Queen. On behalf of a British Relief Society we were distributing what material for hut-building and medicine for malaria we could supply. For the Turks had stamped down an Albanian rising in the customary Turkish manner. As we were then riding along the coast near Alessio, we saw sudden disturbance among a large body of Turkish troops, and a German-speaking Turkish officer said to us : " The Italians have seized Tripoli. It's all owing to that cursed Abdul Hamid. We have no fleet. Only England can save us ! " Turning to me, Edith Durham said at once : " It is the beginning ", and her instinct, founded on knowledge, was right. For seven years Europe was to have no peace.

THE GODS DEPART

In the winter of 1912–13 I was with the Bulgarian army in its triumphant invasion of Turkey. For Bulgaria was part of the Balkan League, that miracle of temporary coalition arranged by Venizelos and James Bourchier, the famous correspondent of *The Times* at Sofia. In the summer of 1913 I was again sent to the Balkans, and journeyed to various points of Serbia and Albania, again, for the most part, with Edith Durham, a better protection than a cavalry escort. While we were in the Albanian town of Kortcha (Koritza), the Greek Commandant posted a telegram saying that Greece and Serbia had declared war on Bulgaria. That was on June 29th, another milestone upon the ominous road to death. The Balkan League was broken up. With characteristic treachery, Roumania struck Bulgaria in the back while her armies were occupied in defence against the attacks of Greeks and Serbs on her southern and western frontiers. I then foresaw the future alliance of Bulgars with Turks, which two years later led to the union of Bulgaria with the Central Powers against us, and so to the evacuation of our troops from the Dardanelles peninsula.

But those incomparable disasters were not yet realized as we wandered throughout southern Albania and visited the queer little Government of the newly independent country at Avlona (Valona). It was a rude Ministry of Moslems and Christians united for once by their bristling hatred of Greeks, Serbs and Montenegrins, and their suspicious dislike of all the Powers except England. They hoped that George V would send a prince to govern them, and I thought at the time how wise England would have been to give them Edith Durham as Kralitza, with two million pounds and me as her Grand Vizier. We should have ridden on white horses all through the country proclaiming the new Queen. We could not have made a stupider mess of it all than the Prince of Wied, who was soon after appointed Mpret. But the Albanians told us they insisted on " Blood Royal," which neither Edith Durham nor I could claim.

Long experience had taught me the murderous animosities of Balkan races and religions—Moslem against Christian, Patriarchist against Exarchist, Slav against Hellene, relics of the Turkish Empire against relics of the Roman, East against West, with hostile parties of the main European religions looking on, like vultures waiting for the future carrion. Irresistibly attractive as the Balkans always are by the nature of their lands and the childlike savagery of their peoples, it was a welcome escape to board a little boat carrying asphalte for a French company that was digging a hill near Avlona, and steam slowly once more up the Dalmatian coast, still fairly quiet as part of the great Austrian Empire, which claimed direct descent from the Roman Empire of the World.

Moving northwards point by point—past Durazzo, where Cæsar and Pompey the Great once waited to decide the future of Rome ; and Medua, the open roadstead for Albanian Scutari, then occupied by the Admirals of the allied fleets whose five flags were fluttering high on the castle, strung side by side like a Monday's wash ; and then past Cattaro, the splendid harbour of Montenegro, still held in those days by Austria ; and Ragusa, that beautiful town, once the port of exchange between eastern trade and Venice— so I came to the amazing city of Spalato. It was built by the Emperor Diocletian when, having saved the Empire once from the swarming barbarians of the north and east, he longed only to spend a quiet old age in that enormous palace, piously occupied with the worship of the Roman gods—the God of Heaven and the God of Health—and with the cultivation of the large vegetable gardens enclosed within the palace walls. To him it was a depressing sight to watch barbarians and Christians still persistently encroaching upon civilization. But he was growing old, he had accomplished his work, and he wanted to live in peace, warding off death as far as a mortal may. Knowing Europe as I did in 1913, and coming direct from the Balkans, I reflected that the anxious old Emperor need hardly have troubled himself so much with apprehensions about a religion that, with such futility, proclaimed peace on earth and goodwill among men. It seemed strange to me, besides, that a man of his genius and activity should ever have wished to retire into quietude and wake up every morning with no greater exploit before him than the maintenance of his piety and his health. But when the boat had tied up beside the quay where the colonnaded portico of the palace once stood, and I entered the city contained within the massive walls and towers, I saw a vision of the old hero himself as he lived—the last great Emperor of the Roman faith, a near predecessor of Constantine. The vision showed him about the year 306 of our era, some two years after his abdication and ten years before he failed at last in preserving his life.

"So the old man wants to return to power," he said, rolling up a letter and speaking rather to himself than to the officer who brought it.

It was a cool autumn morning in Spalato, and they were walking side by side along an arcade which ran the whole length of the front of the new palace, looking south-west across the sea. For more than two hundred yards the corridor ran, and at either end it was flanked with massive towers. Sixteen of them protected the fortress walls of the huge quadrangle within which the palace was constructed. In the centre of the colonnade stood a spacious entrance-gate, with steps leading down to the water, which lapped gently against them. For the bay was never rough, the storms of the Adriatic being warded off by low outlying islands.

Beside the entrance-gate a heavy barge lay at anchor. It had come at great speed from the Riviera, bringing the messenger of Maximian, ex-Emperor like Diocletian himself. Tied to their pivots, the banks of oars still rested on the surface ; the crews who had worked the ship were busy with breakfast, or lay sleeping in the newly risen sun.

" So the old man wants to return to power, and asks me to join with him," said Diocletian again ; and he stopped in his walk to look meditatively over the sea between the columns. " For twenty-one years I ruled the world—I, Diocletian, the slave boy from those Dalmatian hills down yonder. I saved the world—saved it from savages—Goths, Germans, Persians, Parthians, and the rest. Continually, like clouds in storm, they kept pressing down over the sunlit prospect of the Empire, and I drove them back to the dismal regions which they inhabit. All that is worth preserving in mankind I preserved. The mists and obscurities which threatened to envelop the clearest reason of the world I also swept away, as with a health-giving breeze. And now the old man wants me to return and begin all over again ! You must rest here, Julianus, for a few days, and I will give Maximian an answer."

" All your commands I obey," answered the officer ; " to me you are always Emperor."

"Please don't talk like a courtier," said Diocletian, though he bowed with a gratified smile; "I'm only a private citizen now—a self-made man enjoying well-earned repose, like any army contractor. And, like most retired speculators, I spend my declining years in planting trees I shall never see grow up, and in building a house I shall not long enjoy. At the best, I can feel the spring return only ten times more. For I suppose I am mortal, although I have long been declared divine."

He smiled again, and led his guest through a vaulted vestibule, on one side of which stood a great dining-hall, and on the other a library, guest-chambers, baths, and the ex-Emperor's bedroom and private apartments. The vestibule opened into a broad causeway or street, crossed at the centre by another street running at right angles to it, so that the two divided the quadrangle of the palace inside the surrounding walls into four interior quadrangles of about equal size.

Turning to the right, Diocletian led the way up some steps to a large octagonal building, like a tower with a pointed roof, and pushed open the lofty doors of decorated bronze. In the centre of an empty floor stood a large stone sarcophagus, carved in deep relief with historic scenes—legionaries hewing shaggy ill-armed barbarians in pieces, executioners beheading prisoners like poppies in a row, and on one side an emperor entering Rome in triumph, the standards and the lictor's rods and axes preceding his chariot, the spoils and long lines of captive kings and queens dragged behind, amid an applauding populace. It represented Diocletian's own triumph of A.D. 303—the last triumph ever to climb the Capitoline with the silent Virgin along the Sacred Way.

THE GODS DEPART

"As we were talking of mortality," Diocletian said, "I thought I would show you the tomb in which my carcass will lie for ever when, in the poet's words, my palsied head descends to heaven."

Again he smiled, and after contemplating the empty stone box for a while in silence, they turned to go.

"Observe the architect's skill," said Diocletian. "Outside, the mausoleum is octagonal; inside, it is circular. That is thought a clever piece of construction, and you can make what symbol you like of it—the circle of eternity at rest within the points of this angular life, or what you will. But these mysteries have no attraction for a rough old soldier like me. Look rather at the frieze running round the interior—a divine creature, you see, hunting boars and wild goats. That's more to my taste. I hold by the ancient gods as much as possible—partly, I suppose, because I am one."

He expected his companion to laugh, but Julianus only bowed, as if at a commonly acknowledged truth.

"I can't quite say why I had such a lot of stuff brought from Egypt," Diocletian continued. "All those granite and marble columns are Egyptian, and so are those sphinxes on each side of the doors, all covered with incomprehensible writing! They are said to be twice as old as Rome. A woman's face and breasts on a lion's body with eagle's wings! I suppose it all meant something to those old fellows. A queer country is Egypt! Like a huge coffin! And the priests worship queer gods with the heads of hawks, cats, dogs, calves, crocodiles, and heaven knows what! I'd like to ask them a question or two. But it's my belief that men and women will believe anything, provided it is ridiculous or impossible.

"You see those two statues in the pediment over

the door," he went on; "one is myself, the other is my wife Prisca, the ex-Empress. When I married her she was a beautiful woman, complacent and devout; born just to worship the genial goddess of fertility, the joy of gods and men. But now she is wrapped in fantastic superstitions—a kind of Jewess, they tell me—and has carried off our daughter Valeria with her. Heaven knows to what fate they are wandering through the world, now that I can no longer protect them. They are too distinguished to be fortunate."

"When last I heard of them, they were in the East," said Julianus.

"Howling over the crumbling ruins of Jerusalem, probably," Diocletian replied, with regretful bitterness. "Men are idiotic and swinish, but for real mania you must look to women. Notice that sarcophagus there, too. I had it brought here because of the beautiful workmanship: the story of Hippolytus and Phædra—another instance of feminine madness! The thing is over a century old. I've forgotten whose bones moulder inside; someone who was happy enough to live under the Antonines, I suppose, and saw the Empire complete and calm and uncorrupted. And there's a bust of Nero on that pedestal. What a fantastic man he was! And yet attractive, and capable of religious zeal. But now I should like to show you the temple of more genuine gods."

He led the way across a peristyle or roofless court surrounded by a colonnade of elegant arches, up the approach to an oblong temple, Corinthian in design, where they were met by a white-robed priest. He bowed profoundly to the ex-Emperor, extending his arms with hands turned down, and Diocletian answered the salutation with similar precision. The great doors were thrown open by acolytes who served the temple—sweeping the floor, shaking out the curtains, and keeping the altar-fires alight.

In the obscurity of the interior, into which a dubious light penetrated only through the open door, the visitor perceived a reduced imitation of the seated Zeus of Olympia, and the statue of a man in ancient Greek clothing, holding a scroll in one hand and a staff entwined with serpents in the other.

"As this is my only temple," Diocletian said, speaking low, "I chose to dedicate it to the gods of Heaven and Health combined—the greatest and the most useful of gods. My title of Jovius almost compelled me to select the one ; and indeed what greater god could one worship than him who rules the sky and directs the course of the firmament revolving round the earth and the Empire ? But my personal adoration is especially due to Æsculapius ; for though I am divine and immortal, where should I be now but for his aid when terrible sickness befell me a few years ago ? People who saw me even when I was recovering did not recognize the soldier and saviour of the world in the shrunken and enfeebled figure to which sickness had reduced me. I vowed at that time daily to worship the Healing God, and indeed I was engaged in his service as I walked the cool length of the esplanade when your ship put in. Other exercises I perform in his honour, as you shall presently see. For what is life—what is the life even of Divine Being—without the blessedness of health ?"

Taking a little incense from the priest, Diocletian raised both hands before the statues in turn and dropped it upon the smouldering fires of each altar. Tiny orange flames shot up from each, and a thin column of blue smoke arose. Julianus repeated the action before the statue of Jove alone, and as the ex-

Emperor waited for him to perform the other sacrifice, he said, " I have no need of health, being well already."

" Oh, youth, youth ! " laughed Diocletian as he turned to leave the temple ; and then he sighed and said little more as he conducted his guest around the rest of the palace buildings—the stables, the galleries of cells for slaves, the apartments of the stewards and cooks. Only when they reached the north-west quadrangle, which was built as barracks for the bodyguard, he said in his tone of sardonic irony :

" Yes, a thousand lusty men-at-arms are still required to preserve one life for a few years more. How many of the Cæsars have died except by violence ? Hardly half a dozen since Augustus, three centuries ago. Conquest has not saved a Cæsar ; public service has not saved ; still less has virtue. Good or evil, they have shared the same hideous fate. Slaughtered, murdered, stabbed, poisoned, torn in pieces, one after another they have gone—they have gone. Nor is abdication a defence. Fear lurks in ambush always ; and yet, though life is none too sweet, we cling to it."

Ashamed of an emotion thus revealed, he turned smilingly to Julianus and said, " Now you have seen the pleasant resting-place I have constructed for the peace of old age. The sun is glowing hot in spite of autumn. The midday meal will be served you, and you must rest for a few hours. This afternoon we will drive round the neighbourhood. There is a festival at Salŏna to-day. There will be the usual games and some necessary executions—no spectacle such as you young men-about-town are accustomed to in Rome, but just a simple entertainment good enough for us country folk."

Through the breathless hours of noon the palace lay

silent, basking in sunlight. Even the vast grey blocks of the outer walls glared in the heat, and the newly wrought marble of the colonnades and temple steps shone with dazzling whiteness. Except for the sentries at the main gates and on the corner towers, all the soldiers, household servants, and slaves slept or lay prostrate in the shade—all but two of Diocletian's secretaries, who, under his own direction, were cutting upon the marble wall of his inmost chamber a map of the Empire, the parts of which were variously coloured according to the dates of their acquisition or recent recovery. The regions which he had himself rescued from the barbarians were dyed with brilliant scarlet.

But toward four o'clock there was a stir throughout the palace. The guard was changed, servants moved to and fro on the streets, and presently a covered carriage drawn by six horses stood waiting before the ex-Emperor's portico. Diocletian entered it with his guest and drove slowly down the carefully paved causeway to the Golden Gate in the centre of the northern wall. Passing through the tunnel of its deep and vaulted entrance, the carriage emerged upon a broad road, lined with young cypress trees on either side; and directly the barriers of the fortress palace were left, an open country lay extended far in front, till rough lines of bare and rocky mountains closed the view.

Like one escaping into free air, Diocletian leaned back with a deep breath of relief, and fixing his eyes on the mountains he said, " I am getting on fairly well with my map, but have little satisfaction in it. We talk about the Empire of the world, but what do we know of the world? Look at those mountains! I was reared among them, only a few days' journey farther south. They are my native country, but what do I know of the lands behind them? They stretch away to the Danube and the Euxine; ridge after ridge of stony mountains, line after line of water-courses opening upon slips of plain, where outlandish people build little huts or pitch tents of skin; always on the move, always robbing and killing each other, speaking unintelligible and inhuman languages, and called by idle names which mean nothing at all. How shall I entitle that country on a map? One is tired of writing 'Land Unknown' all round the limits of our world."

" I once travelled along the great road which Rome built from Dyrrachium through such an unknown region," said Julianus. "We crossed terrible mountains and passed two big lakes. All was savage till we escaped through the ruined home of ancient Alexander to Thessalonica, and so to the city of the Bosphorus."

" And beyond that," Diocletian continued, " stood Nicomedia, where I once thought of erecting a new capital for the Empire. But the superstitious natives twice set fire to my palace after I destroyed their temple there, and I used that splendid site only to abdicate in despair. And beyond Asia lie Persia and Mesopotamia and the gates of India, which your ancient Alexander actually reached. But beyond those frontiers, what do we know? I have stood on mountain heights and looking eastward have seen again range after range of giant mountains, breadths of desert interminable, and unknown waters. You remember what some old Greek poet told about the wanderers of Asia, and people who pitch beside the lake at the edge of the world, and spearmen watching like eagles from peaks above the gulf of nothingness. But as I stood there, I saw the world's edge was not reached, and there was no gulf of nothingness before me, but always land, and land, and lands unknown."

"No doubt the surrounding world is larger than people used to think," said Julianus. "But, after all, our world gathered about this lovely sea, so full of glorious memories, is the only world that counts. We need not trouble ourselves with those dwellers in outer Cimmerian darkness."

"Yes, but we must trouble ourselves," Diocletian replied impatiently, "or they will trouble us. I've seen them out there upon the Eastern confines—tall brown men with faces like hawks; tall brown women too, large-eyed and athletic as Zenobia. And I've seen hordes of hideous creatures—dwarfish, having slits for eyes, and long arms like apes. And who knows what strange monsters Africa may beget— ludicrous, black, inhuman? No one has yet penetrated the farthest wilds of Britain or the islands west of it. But I have seen shaggy Germans beyond the Rhine, shaggy Scythians beyond the Danube. Innumerable they seemed. Mow them down by thousands, and next year there are thousands more, waiting for the sword. And beyond cold and misty seas dwell the Hyperboreans, from among whom the Goths descended upon us like a deluge of ice, devastating those bright cities of Asia, pillaging Thessalonica, Ephesus, and even Athens—Athens herself."

He paused, overwhelmed by the vision of those countless hordes.

"Little more than a century ago," he continued, "how secure and quiet the Empire lay! If peace was broken, it was usually broken by civil war. At the worst Rome then fought Rome. The victory was Roman, and it did not matter to the Empire who was Cæsar. Men went unconcernedly about their busi-

THE GODS DEPART

ness, hardly conscious of laws which stood firm and unquestioned behind them, the stronger because unnoticed. The inland sea was winged with merchant ships, always passing to and fro. Life slid by in beautiful cities, or among the isolated villas which gladdened the shores of the Province, and of Egypt, Asia, and Greece ; to say nothing of pleasant Italy with her bays and rivers sliding under ancient walls. ' Glory to thee, Saturnian land, great mother of fruits, great mother of men ! ' as our old poet sang. Then decent people could lay out their course of years as they pleased, beautifying their homes, pursuing the arts, and cultivating their minds or their gardens without thought or care. Under time-honoured forms, the established gods were reasonably worshipped. Newfangled notions were regarded with smiling incredulity or tolerant contempt, and from birth to acquiescent old age no sensible being suffered a disturbing thought, or aimed at greater happiness than the hope of a to-morrow repeating to-day.

"But, my dear Julianus, how appalling has been the change ! From every side an ignorant barbarism threatens to engulf that calm and placid world. Close beyond every frontier those huge clouds of savages are gathered, waiting to burst with inundation over all that Romans mean by the State, Civility, and Manners. For a few years I kept them back as Æolus once restrained the hurricanes of storm. For a few years I redeemed the world and renewed the Empire's life. But our peace cannot last. Close before us I see an age of tumult and unceasing war. Not an age, but ages following ages, during which Roman public life and civilized daily existence will disappear, perhaps, even from memory.

"Was it not time, then, that I turned from a ruining

world to build my palace, and for my final years to be still? You remember what the old Persian said: 'The worst torture man can suffer is to have many thoughts and no power.' I was unable to avert the evil I foresaw. We stand at the end of an age—the age of Rome. It has been a noble and beneficent age, blessing the heart and summit of the world. Egypt was not so great, nor was Assyria. Their ages passed; the age of Rome is passing now, and before mankind lies a whirlpool of savage obscurity."

"It is to save mankind," said Julianus, "that my master Maximian calls on you to return."

Diocletian made no answer. The carriage was entering the streets of a large and beautiful town, built beside a deep inlet of the Adriatic.

"Here we are in Salŏna," he said, rousing himself. "Isn't it a splendid situation? I intend to make it the capital of Dalmatia. You observe that I am strengthening the fortifications. Look at that mighty new wall! I am building that against the barbarians. Barbarians!—as if walls could keep out either barbarians or care or death!"

Diocletian descended at the gate of the large amphitheatre, from which the shouts of the spectators could be heard. As he and Julianus entered the imperial seats, the noise was hushed, and the spectators rose in silent reverence to the saviour of civilization. Even the gladiators paused in a mock engagement and saluted. Diocletian settled himself with deliberation upon a kind of throne, and placed on his head a diadem, retained for public occasions as a memorial of former greatness. He signalled with his hand, and the games proceeded.

There was nothing unusual in the programme. The amphitheatre was small—barely seventy yards long by fifty yards across. Within this narrow space trained athletes exhibited their strength and skill; gladiators contested with blunted swords, or with nets and tridents; wild bulls were incited to gore each other; strange animals imported from Africa at Diocletian's own expense—giraffes, hippopotami, zebras, and apes—were crowded together in a terrified herd, while the audience shouted to increase their panic, and were convulsed with laughter at their awkward movements, their bewildered faces, and wild efforts to escape. When negroes with long whips had driven them back to their stalls, there was an interval during which slaves cleaned the arena and covered it with fresh sand, while the spectators drank from wine-flasks and devoured the provisions they had brought with them in bags.

"The populace is awaiting the top of the climax," said Diocletian, looking round upon the crowded tiers with amused toleration. "After all, death gives the common mind its keenest emotion; you might almost say its one touch of poetry. To-day they celebrate a special sacrifice to Mars, and there are military executions in his honour. I take no pleasure in such things; I have seen too many deaths. No death can interest me now—except perhaps my own," he added, with his characteristic smile.

"Let us go then, Sire," said Julianus.

"Oh, no! I must see the end," Diocletian answered wearily. "The people would be hurt if we went. They are only carrying out one of my own decrees, and 'who wishes the end, wishes the means,' as the jurists say. Besides, you know old Martial's epigram—'Cato goes out from the theatre. Why, then, did he come? Was it that he might go out?' But here come the criminals. First there is a pack of deserters, murderers, brigands, and malefactors in general, caught in this neighbourhood or threatening the highways through the mountains."

From one end of the arena a squadron of ten criminals, armed as Roman legionaries, entered. They halted in single rank opposite the ex-Emperor, raised their short swords in salute, and clashed them upon their iron shields. The gate at the other end of the arena opened, and out swarmed a mob of thirty beings, leaping and shouting and brandishing stout spears and gleaming knives. They were decked like savages, with wigs of long fair hair, all matted and tangled, tunics and kilts of cowhide, bare legs, and oval shields of cowhide too. Without a pause, they rushed in a confused mass upon the supposed legionaries, who rapidly wheeled right and stood shoulder to shoulder in line to confront them. At the clash of the meeting forces the amphitheatre stood up and gasped with excitement.

At once the work of killing began. Swords struck with edge and point. Spears were thrust into the joints of armour. Daggers stabbed at throats. Within a few seconds, dead and wounded fell. Arms and hands were sliced off. The sinews of bare legs were severed. One head and then another and another rolled to the edge of the sanded oval. Screams of anguish mingled with the applause. The sand was stained with great patches of blood, bright red, crimson, and brown. The criminals who remained standing tripped over the bodies of the fallen.

Within twenty minutes only four of the legionaries and one burlesque barbarian survived. Slowly the four edged him back to one end of the arena, until they held him surrounded at the gate. Leaping upon him from right and left they clung to his arms while one quietly cut his throat, and the spectacle was over. The triumphant four saluted Diocletian, and received their pardon.

"This form of execution," the ex-Emperor observed to his guest, "is a device of my own. It gives the worst criminal some small chance of life. Besides, it encourages recruiting, for the legionaries always come off better than the barbarians, and some save their lives. The sight of blood and conflict is wholesome, too. It checks enervation and effeminacy. And, after all, it is pleasanter to fight for one's life than be slaughtered like a sheep.

"But now," he added, looking down on the arena again, "we shall be compelled to witness another execution. These are traitors who refuse to fight and actually prefer being slaughtered without resistance."

Two grown men, a youth of about eighteen, and a woman were pushed out from one of the doors, the keepers of the arena thrusting at them from behind with long poles tipped with iron points. They were dressed in the ordinary summer clothes of the respectable middle-class. The woman wore a girdle of yellow silk, and her black hair was tied with a fillet of the same colour. The youth held her by the hand, and all four walked slowly into the midst of the arena, with eyes uplifted to the open sky. Attendants followed, carrying a wooden statue of Mars, which they placed in the centre of the arena, and withdrew.

Straining their heads forward, the spectators watched what was about to happen. Taking one step toward the statue, the elder of the two men spat in its face, and in a loud voice uttered the words, "Get thee behind me, Satan!"

A yell of execration rose from the crowded amphitheatre. All sprang to their feet, gesticulating, and shouting for death.

"I feared the experiment would be useless," Diocletian said, regretfully. "The obstinacy of superstition surpasses reason. The offence is a crime against the Mars of Rome. Those two men are centurions who threw down their arms refusing to fight for the Empire's safety. The youth refused the military oath because his superstition commanded its followers not to bind themselves by swearing nor to resist evil. The woman has been added for propagating the same treason against the State."

Amid the storm of clamour, Julianus could hardly hear the words. His eyes were fixed on the heavy barrier of the opposite gate. It was raised. Two young lions and a leopard bounded upon the sand, and then stood still, bewildered by the light and noise. The two lions stooped to sniff the corpses still stretched in uncouth attitudes upon the scene of death. But the leopard, fixing his eyes upon the woman, cautiously advanced and crouched down for the spring. Instantly the youth snatched a bloody sword from the hand of a dead legionary and plunged it into the woman's body, low between her breasts. With a cry she fell. At the sight of the spouting blood the leopard sprang, tore open her garment with one scratch of his claws, fastened his teeth in her side and with half-closed eyes drank in ecstasy. Absorbed in the pleasure, he was an easy prey. With the dripping sword the youth struck once more, and the wild beast rolled over dead beside the naked form.

The spectators rocked with laughter. They yelled the obscenities common to mankind. They shouted admiration, too. Some called upon Diocletian to pardon the youth.

But it was too late for pardon. A lion sprang. The youth, still grasping the sword, made no resistance, and by one blow of a terrible paw his throat was torn out. One of the older men fell to the onslaught of the other lion, and the second centurion remained standing alone. " Depart in peace, most Christian souls ! " he cried, raising his hands. But while he spoke, a daring gladiator crept stealthily across the arena, seized him from behind, bowed his body down as if in mock obeisance to the gods, and struck off his head so that it fell at the statue's feet. Again the audience shouted with pleasure and applause.

" That is the end of our humble festivity," said Diocletian, rising. " Now we may go without offence."

The delighted crowd rose and cheered the ex-Emperor as he withdrew, saluting him with the title of Divus and Jovius. Looking back from the gateway, Julianus saw the bloodstained arena littered with dead bodies, and the two lions snarling with jealous satisfaction over their unwonted and delightful food.

The air was now pleasantly cool, and the sun was setting in lines of orange and crimson clouds over the Adriatic.

" Drive slowly round by the garden," Diocletian said to the coachman ; and as the heavy carriage began to move, he turned again to Julianus. " Such performances add variety to provincial life," he observed, " and prevent the agriculturists from flocking to Rome. The female prisoner was condemned also for persistently preaching the rites of an inhuman love likely to undermine our legitimate matrimony and hinder natural procreation. These heated and orgiastic mysteries are continually sprouting in the East, like poisonous growths on steaming dunghills. In olden times those Asiatics worshipped Astarte and

Cybele. Mithras came more recently to delude emotional minds, and now there is this.

"However, as I told you, it was merely for refusing to serve, or to continue service, in the army that the youth and the two deserters were executed. No more unpardonable treason to Rome could be imagined than a refusal to fight in her defence. These pitiful wretches enjoy the peace and splendour of Rome, but will not move a finger to protect or extend either. The City, the State, the Empire, are nothing to them. Such people brood only over their own condition and the preservation of their souls. They undertake no public duties. They refuse to act as judges or magistrates, and even their pleasures are private and selfishly concealed. They appear to live in a kind of ecstatic hysteria, scorning reason, avoiding social life, and looking forward with joyous expectation to the speedy destruction, not only of our Roman world, but of the whole human race. For the protection of humanity, I resolved some five or six years ago to extirpate their desperate superstition, and in that, at all events, I shall succeed."

"You are right," said Julianus; "if such treasonable opinions spread, no state—not even the smallest city—could survive in this world of perpetual conflict. And the best way of silencing pernicious opinions is to silence those who hold them."

"If those unhappy criminals had but shown a little reasonable compliance," Diocletian continued, "they need not have suffered. They might, for instance, have displayed a becoming reverence for myself," he added, smiling once more. "I make no pretensions to extraordinary virtue, but my private record compares well with my namesake Jove's.

"As you know," he went on, "I think it best to

maintain the ancient public gods. These new religions are too much occupied with personal states of mind, or else with oracles and soothsayers and the movements of stars and planets. What do the stars know about us, or what do they care? Solemn old philosophers used to say the stars twinkled in their pity for mankind, and the music of the spheres could actually be heard if we listened long enough. My friend, it is all childish folly. Not even Jews believe it.

"Then there was worthy old Marcus—divine, but still worthy; he always kept one eye turned inward upon what he called his soul. As though his soul mattered! He helped to build some decent towns, like this of Salŏna here; and he cleared the frontiers beyond the Danube. But all the time he kept grubbing into his own state of mind, his conduct and thoughts, calling them up daily for examination. That is not the way to greatness. He felt a kind of sympathy with all the world. He used to quote young Pliny's saying that, when one poor mortal assists another poor mortal, there is God. My dear Julianus, the gods are not pitiful and tender and effeminate. The gods are soldierly and civic powers. It was they who built the walls of Rome, and extended the empire of law and reason into the realms of barbarous and obscene night."

The carriage stopped at a large square enclosure surrounded by stone walls.

"Enough of these solemn abstractions," said Diocletian, with relief. "Here we are at my garden. Now I can show you something genuine—a real public service to the State."

Within the walls a vegetable and fruit garden was spread out in ordered rows and rectangular patches. Slaves were digging the rows and watering the roots by a system of channels arranged with sluices and locks.

"Isn't it magnificent?" Diocletian cried. "Look at those fennels, those onion-beds and cabbages, all in line! Just like cohorts drawn up for battle. And there are apple trees and plums, and a good big patch of vineyard for my special wine which I may drink without fear of gout. I come here to dig and prune nearly every day. It is healthy exercise, and much more delightful than ruling the Empire. You can tell your master Maximian that! And by the way, when I write my answer, remind me to put in a word of congratulation upon the marriage of Maximian's daughter to Constantine, son of my old friend and successor Constantius. He seems a promising youth. They tell me that he is one of the Cæsars already. But how many emperors exactly are there now? Do you suppose I care to become just one more among the number—I, who saved the Empire once?"

The carriage bore them to the Western or Iron Gate, and when they re-entered the palace the evening was almost dark, and the larger stars were already shining.

The town of Spalato is now built inside Diocletian's palace and extends beyond the walls. His mausoleum was converted into a cathedral dedicated to the Assumption of the Virgin about three hundred years after Diocletian's death. The High Altar marks the spot where his sarcophagus stood, and side altars sanctify the relics of Salŏna's first martyrs and of her first bishop. The temple of Jove and Æsculapius is now the baptistry, and the font, designed in the Lombardic style, has for six centuries served for the christening of the city's babies.

When I passed out through the Iron Gate and

climbed the steep and rocky height west of the town, I discovered a large stone cross upon the summit, and read an inscription cut on the base in fine Roman characters: "JESUS CHRISTUS DEUS HOMO VIVIT REGNAT IMPERAT."[1]

[1] Under the title "In Diocletian's Day" the main scene in this chapter is included in my book called *Original Sinners* (Christophers, 1920).

SCENE VII

ST. CRISPIN'S DAY

How, being with my colleagues at Rollancourt, I witnessed the Battle of Agincourt

IN July, 1918, I was quartered in the Château-Rollancourt, on the little stream called the Ternoise, about twenty miles south of St. Omer, and fifteen miles west of Montreuil, each in turn the Headquarters of the British Army. Hesdin was our nearest town, and St. Pol not much farther away to the south-east. The Château was one of the typical " Courts " of that district, designed, I suppose, for some nobleman of the early eighteenth century but escaping the Revolution, as most of these aristocratic mansions did escape. A green avenue led up to the front, which was " imposing ", having a broad classic centre and two wings of grey stone, an entrance portico, and windows opening upon the grass, as is the French fashion. But the front, though imposing, was an imposition, for there was little behind it. The mansion was one room thick, and had no more inside than a knife-blade. The creaking staircase and such interior walls as existed were hung with eighteenth-century engravings of aristocratic or dramatic scenes, such as might illustrate Molière, and with bookshelves of elegant volumes, all dating from the same exquisite century. The books apparently had never been opened, and certainly never will be read to all eternity. In the stream, which turned a mill in front of the gates, trout might be caught, and at the back of the house narrow paths led through shady groves, where once a bewigged and powdered Narcisse walked in attendance upon a bewigged and powdered Clarisse, who carried a shepherd's crook tied up with blue satin ribbon, and was perhaps followed by a lamb.

With me were four or five British correspondents —Perry Robinson, who had been with me at Christ Church, Beach-Thomas, who had followed me at Shrewsbury and Christ Church, Percival Phillips, scientific spectator of war, and Philip Gibbs, who earned the highest reputation in the war, but, much to his regret, was ordered home for a month just at this time. Both "Percival" and "Philip" had been out with me in the first Balkan War, and so, with Herbert Russell, the naval expert from Devon, we made a happy family. We were under the control of five censors, Major Neville Lytton, the artist, brother to Lord Lytton, being chief in command. All our censors had been seconded after severe wounds. Of the other four, the two most memorable to me were Captain Cadge, a Norfolk solicitor, an indefatigable worker on our behalf, and Captain C. E. Montague, a famous member of the *Manchester Guardian* Staff, a man of the highest literary power, and throughout his being of the finest and most gracious temper.

It was the custom that every night each of the correspondents should select some point on the advanced line which he thought best worth visiting, and should ask one of the censors to accompany

ST. CRISPIN'S DAY

him soon after daybreak. How different was our position from the correspondent's labour in the old days when we had to look out for shelter and food for ourselves, horses, and man (if we had one), and at the end of the day to go searching vaguely about for the censor and the telegraph office, never to be found where appointed ! Now, food, shelter, and a stationary board of censors were provided.

We might not choose our censor, but it was always a happy day when my turn for Montague came. One morning we drove together through Fruges, over the hill of Cassel and Mont des Cats, and on to the front's limit at Scherpenberg, looking across to Kemmel and the German outpost lines. We then walked back through the spot called " Hyde Park Corner " for its special danger, and having found the car again, we paused at Cassel to look over the extended view of the Flanders flats. In that interval of peace we fell to talking of *Henry V*.

I brought up John Masefield's attack upon a character so long accepted as one of England's noblest ideals. That true poet and discerning critic bids us regard Shakespeare's Henry V as " a callous young animal ", " a popular hero who is as common as those who love him ", " the one commonplace man in the eight plays ", " who woos his bride like a butcher, and jokes among his men like a groom ", " who cuts them (his former associates) from his life with as little feeling as he showed at Agincourt, when he ordered all the prisoners to be killed ". I admitted the play taken by itself was a poor drama, stuffed out with the Chorus, comic interludes, and common jokes about the difficulties of foreigners with the English language. Yet when the worst was said, I could not believe that the poet composed those four great speeches of Henry intentionally to make a mock of him. I knew that many lines in them have become hackneyed, but so have many lines of Hamlet and Macbeth. Montague reflected for a while as was his way, and then, instead of agreeing with me directly, he pleaded in Masefield's defence that when he wrote his excellent book on Shakespeare he lay much under the influence of Yeats, who certainly would never have taken Henry as his heroic ideal. So, looking over the coloured plain of Flanders in the golden sun while the big guns never ceased to throb, we let the question drop.

Whenever the King visited the front for a few days, it was part of the correspondents' duties to accompany him in turn, and my turn came next day. In long procession we drove across the Belgian frontier to Poperinghe and other familiar places, witnessing bayonet exercise in a field, a march-past of the K.O.S.B., and the movement of rations along a new light railway parallel with the front. At one point a shell plumped down a quarter of a mile away, and the whole cavalcade turned about, for the King might not be exposed to any risk. I wondered how far the death of a King or a Kaiser in action would affect the course of war. Would it be counted as victory for one side or the other? Or, after compliments, would the war be carried on in the name of the heir just as though nothing had happened?

Late that afternoon, having pooled my scrap of knowledge with the other correspondents, as we had agreed to do every day so that "scoops" were impossible, I borrowed the Major's horse, and rode out a few miles north on the road to Fruges. I passed an almost imperceptible hamlet—a farm or two built in Picardy fashion as a quadrangle round the great

ST. CRISPIN'S DAY

manure heap, that being the most precious possession, to be defended at all costs. Perhaps the little place was called Maisoncelle, if it had any name, and less than a mile beyond I came to a similar hamlet, where stood a little church of grey stone, with a little spire. It seemed to date from the early fifteenth century, and a farm-girl told me it was the church of " Azincourt ". That was its name, and she knew no more about it.

The ground rose slightly, very slightly, to a longish, narrow open space, partly ploughed, and flanked with woods on both sides. I stood with the grey church on my right, the hamlet of Maisoncelle close behind me, and in front the narrow plain of Agincourt. But instead of the August sunset, I felt the ceaseless drizzle and downpour of a late October morning. Just where I stood and along the open ground on both sides up to the woods I could see a small English force of less than five thousand archers and men-at-arms drawn up in a thin line, only four deep. There they stood, the men whose limbs were made in England, and they were speaking the language of Piers Plowman and Chaucer, not very different from the language that Shakespeare was to speak only a century and a half later. Henry, as Commander-in-Chief, might have wished to follow the tactics of his great-grandfather, Edward III, at Cressy (1346), which lay only about twenty miles south, beyond Hesdin. He might have wished to set the line of archers in front of the three bodies of the main army—the vanguard, the " battle ", and the rearguard—all three bodies consisting mainly of men-at-arms, covered from head to foot with plate- or chain-armour, and accustomed to ride on heavy stallions, though at Cressy Edward ordered all ranks to dismount. The Black Prince had then commanded the right of the vanguard, and ten years later he had adopted his father's method at Poitiers, except that he had mounted some of the archers, using them as " mounted infantry ", as we used the M.I. in the Boer War. But Henry's men were not nearly numerous enough for drawing up in the established order of battle. He ordered all to dismount, and placed the archers along the front or hid them in the woods on either flank. Otherwise the vanguard, the " battle " (under Henry himself), and the rear-guard were formed in one unbroken line four deep, the horses and baggage being bestowed under a small guard in the rear. The English numbers are recorded as 812 men-at-arms and 3,073 archers, besides 3 Royal Dukes, 8 Earls, and 18 or 19 Barons ; the French probably counted three to one but the figures given on both sides are vague and contradictory.[1]

The men were tired ; the archers ragged and bare-foot. In seventeen days they had marched three hundred miles from Harfleur, where for the first time British (or more properly German) gunners had beaten down a prolonged siege, during which Henry was said to have lost half his army by sickness. Why he had landed at Harfleur, or in France at all, remains one of the mysteries of the military mind. Perhaps he was ambitious to push the ridiculous claim of early English kings to the possession of the greater part or even the whole of France. Perhaps he sought, as rulers of discontented peoples still seek, to divert

---

[1] These figures are given as being " on record " by Mr. E. Burton in a letter to *The Times* (Oct. 26, 1933), supplementing Sir John Fortescue's account in his *History of the Army*. This record appears to me too small.

attention from troubles at home by the stress and glory of foreign war. Doctrinal Lollards and doctrinaire agitators had been a nuisance ever since the chaos of Richard II's time, and an open war with the French was never unpopular, even if success were uncertain.

Henry reduced Harfleur by aid of the German guns, and as his army was diminished to about half by death and sickness, he selected perhaps about five thousand of all arms, including the German gunners with their train, and set out for Calais provided with only eight days' rations. One can only suppose that the tradition of his great-grandfather's march nearly seventy years before worked in his mind. For Edward had accomplished a longer march with success. Starting at a point far beyond Harfleur on the Cherbourg peninsula, he had advanced through Normandy by Caen and Rouen along the Seine almost to the gates of Paris; had crossed the Seine, and then struck north through Beauvais, then a little west of Amiens and Abbeville, and so to a sandy ford near the mouth of the Somme, not far from the point where the single line to St. Valery now crosses. From there he had made his way north-east to the forest of Cressy, and so to the siege and reduction of Calais. If that prolonged march, the passage of two difficult rivers and a decisive battle had been possible for a great-grandfather, it was surely possible for a younger generation and a military instinct unsurpassed by Edward III, or even by the Black Prince.

A prudent king would have held Harfleur as Edward had held Calais, and withdrawn the relics of his wasting army to their own country. But Henry, then only twenty-seven, aimed at recovering the country's fame in arms, and with his little column of five

ST. CRISPIN'S DAY

thousand men—" we few, we happy few, we band of brothers "—set out to repeat the triumph of the earlier King. One can find no more definite object in the venture. Keeping along the coast near Dieppe, he came to the mouth of the Somme, where Edward had crossed ; but in war, as in everything else, " twice is impossible ", and the French now held the passage in strength. He was forced to move by rapid stages up the course of the Somme, searching everywhere for a practicable ford, and finding none. Past Abbeville the little army marched, and there they may have seen the builders just setting about the front of St. Wulfran's Church ; then past Amiens, where the cathedral was still new after its gradual building, and the completion not much more than a century before. So the column marched along that swampy left bank of the Somme which we were all to know five centuries later—the overflow of deep pools, the cultivated plain reaching away to Montdidier, Roye, and Chaulnes, with Corbie and Bray close beside the river. They came at last to the point just below the height of Péronne, where the course of the river running up from the south turns almost at right angles west. There by constructing two narrow causeways over the swamps it was possible to reach a ford still undefended, and there the column crossed. Henry himself worked among the men, taking charge of the dangerous end of one of the passages. The detail is in keeping with what I believe was the intention of Shakespeare's picture of the man.

The main French army, under an incapable Constable d'Albret, was already mustered at Péronne, and why they did not attack Henry in the confusion of his crossing is one of incapacity's mysteries. Instead of that, they turned north-west, and for a while the two armies advanced almost parallel to each other, the French passing through Bapaume, and the English crossing the Ancre somewhere near Miraumont or Thiepval or Albert, and proceeding just north of Doullens—names how familiar now to us all! On reaching Frévent, Henry heard that the French had succeeded in their object of placing themselves before him at St. Pol, cutting across his best road to Calais. Accordingly he inclined farther west, apparently trying for the road through Fruges and St. Omer. On this course he must have forded our little stream of the Ternoise, and marched right over the ground on which our Château-Rollancourt was afterwards to stand. So he reached Maisoncelle and the little grey church of Agincourt, if indeed it was then built, as seemed to me probable.

Here on that October morning, as the night's rain began to slacken, the English stood in their thin line—the archers holding their six-foot four-inch bows ready, the strings carefully kept dry through the rainy night, their quivers full of clothyard arrows, tipped with barbed iron points, flown with goose-wing feathers, and ranging up to two hundred yards. They also carried long stakes, sharpened at both ends, to plant into the ground as a palisade against cavalry, and in their belts were slung hatchets, hammers, and short swords, for the final push or defence. They deployed, and close behind them came the men-at-arms, ready to strike with lance, sword, or dagger, and carrying shields as well, but all dismounted, so that they were something like infantry in tanks. Henry himself rode along the front bareheaded. During their hard march the men would have learnt the look of that thin and resolute face, almost priestly or monastic in its asceticism, not in the least like "jolly Prince Hal". He made the men a short speech, reminding them of England's recent victories. All of the line would be well within hearing. All knelt and kissed the ground three times, one may suppose as symbol of the Trinity. Then the King dismounted like the rest, and took his place before the centre of the main body which he commanded. The German guns were kept in the rear, unable to move owing to the mud into which they sank.

Mud was the cruellest impediment to the French host. They had been formed up in the customary order of battle the night before—the vanguard, the centre or "battle" and the rearguard. The first two bodies were dismounted, the third was ordered to dismount but did not. Archers and some cavalry were posted on the flanks, and there were archers in the front, but all so crowded up with the men-at-arms that they could hardly draw bow. The crowding was the curse of the force. At least fifteen thousand men-at-arms, archers, and horse were jammed together upon that narrow slip of ground up which I was gazing. Some of the ground was plough, and all of it was sodden with continued rain. The men-at-arms in their heavy armour sank in mud till they could hardly move, and their ranks were so closely cramped together that they broke their lances short to use them with more freedom. They had spent the soaking night in confusion, shouting to each other in the hope of finding their comrades in the ranks. Now they stood there like a solid mass, almost incapable of movement even if they had been ordered to advance. They were thirty-one lines deep against the English four.

ST. CRISPIN'S DAY

As the French mass did not move, Henry, at the sign of an old knight who had gone in advance to reconnoitre, gave the command, " Forward banner ! " and the archers stepped out till within short range, the central line of the men-at-arms following slowly through the mud. The archers halted, planted their sharpened stakes in the soft ground, drew bow, and let fly their hail of deadly arrows. It was as when a machine-gun opens upon troops fully exposed in mass. The most terrible effect fell upon the cavalry, which attempted to charge the archers on both flanks. Though probably most of the horses were defended by armour, those barbed points either pierced through it or found bare spots in the soft and sensitive bodies. Maddened with anguish the poor creatures plunged, kicked, and fell writhing. Many turned in their pain and terror, forcing their way through the almost solid masses of the second and third lines of battle, breaking open gaps, and carrying panic among the mounted troops of the rear.

Wading knee-deep, the French vanguard, consisting mainly of the noblest families in France, who had contended for the honour of being in the front, began laboriously to advance. Some penetrated the archers' palisade, and attacked the King's own centre. One even cut a piece off the crown which he wore round his helmet. But seeing the confusion and gaps in the stationary crowd of living and dying human beings before them, the archers laid down their bows and rushed upon the helpless creatures exposed before them. They found the use of the axes, hammers and short swords tucked in their belts. With them they pounded and hacked upon the armour of the French, smiting and cracking it as one might crack the carapaces of large crabs. The French historian said it was like hammers beating on anvils. Too eager to wait for the trouble of killing, they dashed the helmets off the men-at-arms, and allowed them to clear away defenceless to the rear. The French vanguard was destroyed, the centre broke, the third line, having horses still alive beneath them, rode away in panic.

The rout and the slaughter were almost complete when a rumour ran that there was renewed fighting in the rear, and that Maisoncelle was in flames. Fearing that the crowds of unwounded prisoners in the rear among the baggage and horses might combine in another contest, Henry gave the terrible order that every man should kill his prisoners, disregarding the hope of ransom. The men refused, and Henry set aside two hundred archers to carry out the massacre. Many hundreds seem to have been killed in cold blood before the rumour was proved false. The murder of prisoners in cold blood was characteristic of a bloodthirsty age, yet it was but a forecast of that day in 1799, when two thousand to three thousand helpless prisoners were massacred by Napoleon's order upon the seashore of Jaffa.

That narrow plain of grassland and plough over which I looked had once been covered with many thousand French bodies and about one thousand English bodies closely intermingled. Some were stuck through with arrows, some battered with axes, others sliced with swords or pierced with lances. Such were then the best ways of killing men in the field. And intermingled with the corpses on the French side lay the agonized bodies of horses, who had not anticipated wounds and death, but had expected their usual food, water, and grooming from the men who rode them. As a result, Henry did reach Calais.

He did not survive to see the fruit and almost the memory of that bloody October day at Agincourt wiped out fifteen years later by Joan of Arc, a mere country maid, " the simplest shepherd girl you ever could see ".

That August afternoon in 1918 I left the peaceful scene, where not a single trace of battle remained, and rode back to Rollancourt, to hear at intervals in the night the hum of German aeroplanes seeking to drop bombs upon Abbeville, Etaples, or Montreuil, if they could find a fitting spot. Next day, as I shall recount in the last of these chapters, we were ordered to attend at the Headquarters of the Fourth Army (Rawlinson's) at Flixecourt, and hear the General's intentions for the great advance designed for the morrow (August 8)—the turning-point of the War.

SCENE VIII

THE ABBEY OF JOY

How, being at Chinon, I saw Joan of Arc, and dwelt in the Abbey of Thélème

EARLY in this century I was set the pleasing task of wandering through famous scenes of France. So passing south from Normandy, I crossed the drinkshed that separates cider from wine, and emerged into the wide and sunny valley of the Loire. All France is blessed with noble rivers, running with full stream, calm and silent but strong. They come from the Alps, the Auvergne, the Cevennes, and a few lower ranges of hill, and on their course they are the symbols of fertility, the quiet life of industrious villagers, and the patient fishermen who expect no reward for patience but fishing. The Somme, the Seine and Marne, the Moselle, the Rhône, the Dordogne, the Garonne—all strong and serviceable, but each with a separate beauty—what scenes of laborious but pleasant life the names call up; recent scenes of death and horror too. But of all the rivers the Loire and its southern tributaries, the Cher, the Indre, and the Vienne, are to me the most obvious evidence of the beneficent nature that pervades all France.

Their deep and eddying waters pass noiselessly through a land spread out to the sun for man's satisfaction and delight. Everything that is good to eat and drink swells and sprouts and spouts there at a touch, and one can hardly imagine hunger or thirst amid such abundance. Through banks of reeds and hayfields the rivers pass, or along the slopes of tufa hills well planted with vines, and sometimes they go sliding below the ancient walls of castles and pleasure houses, built there for kings and nobles and their ladies, because this was the best place they could choose for life.

So as I wandered down the Vienne and found myself in the old town of Chinon, only a few miles from the Loire, I knew at once that this was just the right place for the birth of Rabelais more than four hundred years ago. Here best he could create and rear his jolly giant. Here, as he tells us, in a region close beside the Loire, his young Gargantua, on waking, wallowed and stretched six or seven times in his bed, drank well, heard some thirty Masses, studied a paltry half-hour with his eyes fixed upon his book, but his mind on the kitchen, devoured an enormous breakfast, washed it down with a monstrous draught of white wine, and played three hundred games of cards and other parlour entertainments.

But later on in his education, under a learned tutor he listened to a three hours' lecture, when he was fully dressed, combed, curled, and perfumed. Then they sat down to table listening to some pleasant history of warlike actions long ago or discoursing merrily of the virtue, efficacy, propriety, and nature of all that was served at the table, as of bread, of wine, of water, of salt, of flesh, of fishes, fruits, herbs, roots, and of their dressing. They then made a thousand pretty instruments and geometrical figures, in some measure practising the astronomical canons ; then they learnt to play musical instruments, the lute, the virginals, the harp, the German flute with nine holes, the viol, and the sackbut. Next came another three hours' repetition of the morning's lecture, the boy learning to write handsomely in forming the antique and Roman letters, riding and jousting, mounting without stirrups, exercising with the battleaxe, the two-handed sword, the Spanish tuck, the dagger, the poniard, with buckler, cloak or target; next hunting the hart, the roebuck, the bear, the fallow deer, the wild boar, the hare, the pheasant, the partridge, and the bustard; playing at the bounding ball with foot or fist, wrestling, jumping, swimming in deep water on front, on back, with all the body, with the feet only, with one hand in the air holding a book like Cæsar; rowing and sailing, running up- and down-hill, climbing trees like a cat, running up the wall of a house, helped by two steel daggers and two bodkins, to the very top, throwing the dart and the bar, putting the stone, practising the javelin, the boar-spear, and the halbard; pulling the long bow and the steel crossbow, aiming by the eye with the hand-gun, reversing and planting the cannon, shooting to the front, to the flank, and behind; climbing with his hands by a cable to the top of a high tower, hanging by his hands to a pole slung between two trees, his feet touching nothing, and swinging to and fro upon the rope as fast as one could run; then shouting like all the devils in hell to exercise his lungs, besides lifting up two vast cows of lead and overcoming various champions at the clutch; after which he and his tutor sang to harmonious instruments, and engaged upon good discourse and pretty tricks until bedtime; but first at dead of night going out to see the face of the sky and look at the comets, if any were, as likewise the figures, situations, aspects, oppositions and conjunctions of the fixed stars and planets.

On rainy days after dinner they would recreate themselves by bottling hay, cleaving or sawing wood, and threshing corn in the barn; then they would practise painting and carving, watch the drawing of metals, or the casting of great ordnance, and the goldsmiths setting precious stones, and visit the alchymists, money-coiners, upholsterers, weavers, velvet-makers, watch-makers, looking-glass-framers, printers, organists, and other artificers, everywhere giving them something to drink. They went to hear public lectures on law, and the sermons of Evangelical preachers. They visited jugglers, tumblers, mountebanks and quacksalvers, besides the shops of druggists, herbalists, and apothecaries. After a thrifty supper, on wet or cloudy nights, the jolly giant went to bed, having profited by a strenuous day's education. But, to divert him from too vehement a strain on his spirits, his learned tutor allowed him once a month to go out of the city in the early morning to some neighbouring countryside ; there to spend all the day long in making the greatest cheer that could be devised, drinking healths, playing, singing, dancing, tumbling in some fair meadow, unnesting sparrows, taking quails, frogs, and crabs, all the time repeating pleasant verses from Virgil's pastorals, or Hesiod on Agriculture, or Politian on Husbandry.

As I went down the long and ancient street I saw in front of me a rollicking, laughing world revealed in which no one was modest and no one ashamed. Arm-in-arm, or with arms enlaced around alluring figures, men and women danced together in rows, singing, laughing, and making love as they went. Bouncing creatures they all were, and above the white edges of brilliant corsages the swelling breasts of women beckoned insidious, without attempt at veil, but as though panting for freedom. Fore and aft their trim shapes were displayed, like tidy craft sailing before a following wind. No shamefaced timidity held the men back, and the women thought no more of kissing than sparrows think of crumbs, or blackbirds of a cherry. Fearlessly they called things by their improper names, and nowhere could one hope to hear so many names for the same improper things; no, not even in the British Army.

So the gay-coloured lines of revellers danced along the merry old street, turning aside in couples now and then into a wine-shop, and bringing out goblets of wine for the others. Then I perceived that the variegated houses, seen in perspective, looked like a forest of wine-bushes. Over every threshold projected the symbols of mystic enthusiasm—pine branches, larch branches, stalks of fennel, twigs of willow, boughs of the beech with last year's leaves still hanging on them like burnished halfpence. A good wine needs no bush, but here every good wine had a hundred. Like the inscription upon the goblet that was dug out of the ancient monument as you go to Narsoy, each bush cried to the passer-by, " *Hic Bibitur*." Chinon with one voice has declared that within her municipality the thirsty soul shall never be driven next door for a drink. The door where he stands is nearer than the next, and at each door he is reminded of Rabelais's very words : " I drink for the thirst to come. I am stark dead without drink, and my soul ready to fly into some marsh among frogs : a soul never dwells in a dry place."

But as I climbed the hill to the castle, I heard a clear bell ring. It sounded three times, and I wondered whether it was the same bell that tolled when Henry II, one of our few wise kings, lay dying here. It was the same bell that Joan of Arc heard chiming the hours while she waited, bursting with inspiration, to be admitted in audience with the paltry King whom she had come to save, and who was so much less worth saving than herself as she traversed this stage on her way to the burning.

After this, I climbed to the very summit of the castle's tower, from which I could command a complete view of that famous Abbey of Thélème, founded and endowed by Gargantua himself as reward for the Monk after his victory over the Picrocholes. The Monk was permitted here to establish an Abbey after his own mind and fancy, his guiding principle being to make it as opposite as possible to all existing abbeys. In place of the vows of chastity, poverty, and obedience, any man or woman of the Order might be honourably married, rich, and free. No woman was admitted to the novitiate (at ten to fifteen) who was not fair, well-featured, and of a sweet disposition ; and no man (at twelve to eighteen) who was not comely, personable, and well-conditioned.

To ensure freedom and indifference to the time of day no walls or clocks were suffered in the Abbey. The building was hexagonal, having a great round tower at each of the six corners. It was six stories high, counting the underground cellars, and in it were 9,332 chambers, each chamber complete as a suite of rooms, like an American " apartment " except that each was supplied with an oratory besides the other chambers. From the centre of the hall sprang a winding staircase of porphyry and serpentine marbles, and from the northern tower led corridors sheltering

THE ABBEY OF JOY

great libraries of all books in civilized tongues, including Hebrew.

Into this transcendant Abbey bigots were not permitted to enter, nor hypocrites, puffed-up, wry-necked beasts, worse than the Huns or Ostrogoths, forerunners of baboons, nor hundreds of other ill-favoured beings, including lawyers, usurers, insatiable fiends and Pluto's bastards, makers of demur in love-adventures, peevish, jealous curs, sad, pensive dotards, firebrands of household broils, drunkards, liars, cowards, cheats, clowns, nor many more of similar evil quality. But gallant young men were there, jovial, handsome, brisk, gay, witty, frolic, spruce, jocund, courteous, blades of heroic breasts. And as to the women, we read :

> " Here enter you all Ladies of high birth,
> Delicious, stately, charming, full of mirth,
> Ingenious, lovely, miniard, proper, fair,
> Magnetic, graceful, splendid, pleasant, rare,"

and as many other sweet and comely qualifications as you may devise.

As to the dress, not indeed ordained (since there were no ordinances in Thélème), but customary, it followed the best fashion that the Founder had beheld or could imagine. And because every woman is at heart a Thélèmite and would be admitted into the Order if only her manner of life allowed, some details of the apparel may here be given. The ladies wore stockings of scarlet, crimson, or ingrained purple dye, which reached just three inches above the knee. Their garters were of the colour of their bracelets, and circled the knee both above and below. Their shoes, pumps, and slippers were either of red, violet, or a crimson velvet, pinked and jagged like a lobster's wattles :

THE ABBEY OF JOY

"Next to their smock they put on the pretty kirtle or vasquin of pure silk chamlet ; above that went the taffeta or tabie fardingale of white, red, tawney, grey, or any other colour ; above this taffeta petticoat they had another of cloth of tissue or brocade, embroidered with fine gold, and interlaced with needle work or as they thought good ; and according to the temperature or disposition of the weather they had their upper coats of satin, damask, or velvet, and those either orange, tawney, green, ash-coloured, blue, yellow, red, crimson, or white, and so forth ; or had them of cloth of gold, cloth of silver, or some other choice stuff, enriched with pearl, or embroidered according to the dignity of the festival days and times wherein they wore them."

Some days in summer, instead of gowns, they wore light, handsome mantles, made either of the same stuff as the attire or like Moroccan rugs of violet velvet, frizzled with a raised work of gold upon silver pearl, or with a knotted cord-work of gold embroidery, everywhere garnished with little Indian pearls. They always carried a fair panache or plume of feathers of the colour of their muffs, adorned and tricked out with glistening spangles of gold. In winter time they had their taffeta gowns of all colours, lined with rich furrings of wolves, or speckled lynxes, black-spotted weasels, martlet skins of Calabria, sables and other costly furs. Their beads, rings, bracelets, collars, carcanets and neck-chains were all of precious stones, such as carbuncles, rubies, baleus, diamonds, sapphires, turquoises, garnets, emeralds, beryls, and excellent margarets. Their head-dressing varied with the season of the year. In winter it was of the French fashion, in spring of the Spanish, in summer of the fashion of Tuscany, except on holy days and Sundays, when they were accoutred in the French mode, because they accounted it more honourable and better befitting the garb of a matronal pudicity.

There is no doubt that every woman would seek to be apparelled in such costumes, but for the inconveniences of poverty and of transport in modern vehicles. As for the dress of the men in the Order, it is of less importance, since men have abandoned emulation with women in beauty and magnificence. Enough to say that it was every bit as fine, and there was such a sympathy between the gallants and the ladies that every day they were apparelled in the same livery ; and that they might not miss, certain gentlemen were appointed to tell the youths every morning what vestments the ladies would wear on that day ; for all was done according to the pleasure of the ladies. In spite of all this splendour, no time was wasted in dressing, for the masters of the robes had all the raiments ready every morning, and the chambermaids were so skilled that in a trice the ladies would be dressed completely from head to foot. About the wood of Thélème was built a row of houses, very neat and cleanly, where lived the goldsmiths, jewellers, embroiderers, tailors, weavers, and other craftsmen, skilled each at his own trade and supplied with stuff by Lord Nausiclete, who every year brought seven ships from the Pearl and Cannibal Islands, laden with gold, raw silk, pearls and precious stones.

If one of the gallants wished to leave the Abbey, he carried along with him one of the ladies, namely her whom he had already chosen as his mistress, and they were married together, and if they had lived at Thélème in good devotion and amity they continued so to live to even greater height in their estate of matrimony, entertaining that mutual love till the very last day of their lives.

The pious Founder of the Order had observed with singular penetration that men who are free, well-

THE ABBEY OF JOY

born, well-bred, and conversant in honest company, have naturally an instinct or spur which prompts them to virtuous actions, and withdraws them from vice, and this is called honour. But the same men when brought under and kept down by base subjection and constraint turn aside from their noble disposition, and shake off and break that bond of servitude. For it is agreeable with the nature of man to long after things forbidden, and to desire what is denied. Therefore, as a final vision of the exquisite and enviable anarchy prevailing in the Order of Thélèmites, to which we all so fervently desire to belong, I quote the following clause :

> " All their life was spent not in laws, statutes or rules, but according to their own free will and pleasure. They rose out of their beds when they thought good ; they ate, drank, laboured, slept when they had a mind to it, and were so disposed. None did awake them, none did offer to constrain them to eat, drink, nor to do any other thing, for so had Gargantua established it. In all their rule and strictest tie of their Order, there was but this one clause to be observed :
> DO WHAT THOU WILT. *Fays ce que Vouldras*.[1]

As I started on the way from the valley of the Vienne over low hills and fertile fields to the valley of the Indre, I heard that ancient bell strike the four words, " Do what thou wilt " ; and again thinking of our wise king and of the little square-formed peasant girl, I wondered what was meant by " Wilt ", by " *Vouldras* ". Could I assume that Henry willed what he did ? Or the Maid—did she do what she willed ? Certainly neither enjoyed a life of exquisite delight as in the Abbey of Thélème.

[1] The full description of Thélème and its Order is in Rabelais's *Gargantua and Pantagrue*, Book I, 52–8 ; Urquhart's translation, 1653.

For most of us it is harder to decide what we will than to do it, and if Rabelais was right when he said we have naturally an instinct and spur which prompts us to virtuous action, it may be hard to do what we will even when we have decided, for we shall have set ourselves a rule more rigorous than the practice of all the Trappists, Flagellists, or the Fakirs of India. How, then, shall a man or woman keep the commandment " Do what thou wilt " when shut up tight in a subterranean cellar or a cage? What will, what power to do it had Cardinal Balue, Prince of the Holy Church, when for eleven years he was held confined in the castle of Loches beside the Indre? There we may see the vast wicker cage in which he was swung, as we are still told to believe, though historians doubt it; and no wonder! Could any mode of life be imagined so filthy, so indecent, as to be caged like an eagle or an albatross, without the bird's chance of splashing in a shallow bath or treading a freshly sanded floor? The Cardinal's only share in such happiness as a caged bird may enjoy was when the keeper came to thrust his piece of flesh between the bars. So there he perched year by year while eleven summers followed one by one, and only the chilling draught through the opened door told him that winter had come. He was released a few years before Rabelais was born, and with what a sense of timidity and exposure he must have emerged into the pitiless light of day, like a soft-skinned hermit-crab coming out to change into another shell! All who have been shut in hospital or prison for six months know that shrinking apprehension at release. I have known it after four months in a besieged town, and the great Cardinal, whether in a wicker cage or not, was besieged for eleven years, longer than Troy!

And Philip de Commines, the true historian, to whose portrait of his master, Louis XI, novelist and dramatist have owed so much—he too was shut up for many months here in the castle of Loches on the Indre, not swinging in a cage, to be sure, but fenced with a trellis of beams into a little window's embrasure, sunk in the thickness of the castle wall, as may be seen to this day. There he sat month after month, like a leopard clamped in a den far smaller than any Zoo would permit under the rules of the Society for the Protection of Animals, and there he had to meditate upon the incalculable course of history and the changes and chances of kings, a touch of irony being added that his particular form of den was the invention of his former master. Such royal treatment may add the strength of reality to an historian's style, but to myself that advantage would not compensate for the filth and monotony of life in a deep window-sill.

Climbing down still farther into the depths of the castle, one enters a square chamber cut in the solid rock upon which the castle stands, and there Lodovico, Duke of Milan, called Il Moro, spent the last eight years of his glorious life. In the noblest period of Italian art, poets and artists hailed him as the " Light and Splendour of the World ", but here he dwelt in a little grave, in darkness made visible by one narrow chink of window that cast a glimmer upon the opposite wall. Portraits of Il Moro are well known, and he had the good fortune to live at a time when a portrait was expected to have some resemblance to the original. At all events they all agree very well, but I see him after the first five or six years of his life in the dungeon—the smooth mass of darkish hair turned to a tangle of white, the keen eyes faded by atrophy like the eyes of subterranean fishes, the heavy jaw and throat shrunk into wrinkles like a lizard's. I see him night after night for eight years watching till the glimmer of dawn should appear upon the rocky wall, just giving light enough for his daily task of scratching sentences and figures upon the stone ; for he had always been an artist, and the greatest patron of the arts and sciences in all Europe.

The pleasures of memory never count for much, but perhaps, like Russian prisoners in their solitary cells, Il Moro kept a separate memory in his mind for each day or each week lest he should go mad with vacancy. Certainly he had enough memories to spread over eight years if he cared to dwell upon them one by one. As in a moving picture, he could pass before his mind the magnificent Court of Milan where his happy boyhood lay ; and the glory of his maturity when he was gathering at Pavia the ancient manuscripts that were to renew the face of the world like a second birth ; and when he was building the Certosa's façade, devising masques and revelries, decorating great churches, with Leonardo, the marvel of artists, at his side. And then he might think of Cecilia Gallerani, his wise and lovely mistress, whom Leonardo painted, and, next, of his child-wife, Beatrice d'Este, only fifteen, but already *la piu zentil* lady in all Italy, and such a huntress of wild boars as was never seen. All were gone now ; like a pageant they had swept down into the abysm of time —the stateliness and the gold, the gorgeous colours of city and clothes, the buildings elaborated with such art, the illuminated manuscripts that had taken a lifetime each to write, the exquisite mistress—all were gone, and the bones of the child-wife lay in the monastery where Leonardo painted the *Last Supper*.

The pleasures of memory never count for much,

and it was not to revel in them that Lodovico, Il Moro, Light and Splendour of the World, rose day by day in his chilly shirt from the rock in order to engrave upon the faintly glimmering wall the reminiscent words :

> "*Il n'y au monde plus grande destresse*
> *Du bons temps soi souvenir en la tristesse.*"

He scratched the lines so that some future prisoner in that Inferno might discover that a poet and an Italian had been there before him.

When Wordsworth was one afternoon sitting reclined in a grove, sunk in that sweet mood when pleasant thoughts bring sad thoughts to the mind, and feeling around him the joy of plants and birds and trees, he suddenly asked the profound and terrible question :

> "Have I not reason to lament
> What man has made of man ? "

With how much better reason might not the Cardinal, the historian, and the Duke of Milan have asked it ! It was man who had kept each of them shut up in a cage, or in a deep window-sill, or in a dark and rocky hole, and had converted a Prince of the Church, an intellectual writer, and the Light and Splendour of the World into warped and wrinkled rags of men, hardly able to confront the sun or the human face. Let a man travel for six months alone and without converse, he will begin to disintegrate. A scum mantles over his brain, and his courage is dulled. The soul brutalizes, and the heart will turn to the nearest wench for consolation.

Wandering alone in Central Africa, I have known that to be true. But I was in the sun and rain, not shut up in a cage, embrasure or pit for months or years.

THE ABBEY OF JOY

The Light and Splendour of the World died in his dungeon the year when Rabelais was a boy of thirteen, and our Henry VIII, who seemed another light and splendour of the world, was just about to wallow in his father's thrift. The fairy Abbey of Thélème was not yet erected, but even if they had belonged to the Order of Thélèmites themselves, how could those faded and worn prisoners have kept the Order's solemn commandment, "Fays ce que Vouldras"? Which among the Ten of Moses is so hard to keep?

SCENE IX

"NOT WITHOUT HONOUR"
St. Matthew xiii. 57

*How, walking in Aldersgate, I met Milton and
accompanied him to his home*

THE City is more haunted by living ghosts than is any churchyard in the kingdom. From Roman, Saxon, and Norman times they swarm—seamen, explorers, merchants, builders, dramatists, poets, and other masters of literature. The very names of the ancient and twisted streets, the churches, the Inns of Court, the river banks, the relics of fortifying walls bring them side with us as we pass, so close that at times we can hear their voices speaking as they used to speak when more definitely alive. So it was natural that ghostly forms and voices came to me very frequently in the 'eighties of last century when I was living in the East End, and had to traverse the City every day to my work in Bloomsbury.

Often on my return I would wander away from the straight route past the Post Office and along Cheapside to visit the outlying regions of Little Britain, Cripplegate, and Bunhill Fields. It was to be near the ghost of the supreme poet that I wandered there, and his presence threw over the whole region a solemnity of mind, an elevation of spirit, such as one may feel in approaching the Parthenon or the Cathedral of Chartres. At no time was it possible to escape that sense of awe as in communion with sacred perfection, but one day in especial I remember when most distinctly the glory of that revelation fell upon me as I was passing almost casually on my way to my home in Whitechapel.

Going down Aldersgate, I turned to the right into Jewin Street, which leads by a short passage into St. Giles's, Cripplegate, and its churchyard, where in a corner still stands an ancient bastion or watchtower or barbican of the great wall that once surrounded the City for limitation and defence. In Jewin Street itself the heavy offices and warehouses vanished, and in their place appeared a row of small Tudor houses just outside the City walls, through which one could pass either by a gate or perhaps by a tunnel running under the wall where the narrow passage into St. Giles's now leads. Behind the houses were largish gardens reaching out into the Moor or Moorfields, a desolate and unwholesome wilderness, much used as a place of settlement by the unfortunate families whose homes in the City were burnt by the Fire of 1666. The Tudor houses, though outside the walls, were too close to the City to be called suburban, but they had the advantage of access to open country to the north through the fen of Finsbury towards the village of Islington. In one of those houses John Milton was living in 1663, a year or so before his third marriage and removal to Artillery Row by Bunhill Fields.

It was June, and the noble figure, dressed in simple black but for a broad white collar, was being led along through St. Martin's-le-Grand and part of Aldersgate. His eyes, brilliant still though sightless, were turned up to the sky, and the setting sun shone upon him with genial warmth.

> "'Thus with the year,'" (he murmured),
> "'Seasons return; but not to me returns
> Day, or the sweet approach of even or morn,
> Or sight of vernal bloom, or summer's rose,
> Or flocks, or herds, or human face divine;
> But cloud instead, and ever-during dark
> Surrounds me, from the cheerful ways of men
> Cut off.'"

"Yes, sir, I remember the verses well. Indeed, I remember many fine passages in your vast poem, so far as you have gone with it yet."

It was Andrew Marvell who led the ageing poet by the hand, himself a poet of lesser range. Only five years before he had been Milton's colleague in the office of Latin Secretary under the great Protector, and at the Restoration he had used such influence as the moderate mind may sometimes use, though rarely, in averting imprisonment and perhaps execution from the supreme Republican, who had never hesitated to utter his indignant heart, and had earned the highest reward of courage by having two of his books burnt by the hangman.

"Keep my hand, Andrew," said the greater poet; "I feel here that we are approaching a purer air. I tried to give expression to the sense of it only this morning:

> 'As one who long in populous city pent,
> Where houses thick and sewers annoy the air,
> Forth issuing on a summer's morn to breathe
> Among the pleasant villages and farms
> Adjoined, from each thing met conceives delight;
> The smell of grain or tedded grass, or kine,
> Or dairy, each rural sight, each rural sound;
> If chance, with nymph-like step, fair virgin pass,
> What pleasing seemed, for her now pleases more;
> She most, and in her look sums all delight.'"

"NOT WITHOUT HONOUR"

"You did well, sir, to include the nymph-like maid," said Marvell.

"The passionate attraction of the male to the female illuminates or degrades," said Milton; "here it illuminates with an innocent radiance like the sunlight at dawn when the dark blue night slowly turns to brown and gold. I too have known that attraction in its utmost beneficence:

> 'And sweet, reluctant, amorous delay.'

Or again:

> 'Imparadised in one another's arms.' "

"I could give you passages of equal affection from your earlier poems," said Marvell, "before the civil troubles drove the Muses from our daily minds. But even better I remember those lines preceding what you spoke just now—the lines beginning:

> 'Yet not the more
> Cease I to wander, where the Muses haunt.'

And then you go on with the ennobling words:

> 'Nor sometimes forget
> Those other two equalled with me in fate,
> So were I equalled with them in renown,
> Blind Thamyris, and blind Mæonides,
> And Tiresias, and Phineus, prophets old:
> Then feed on thoughts, that voluntary move
> Harmonious numbers; as the wakeful bird
> Sings darkling, and in shadiest covert hid
> Tunes her nocturnal note.'

To complete such a poem as that, sir, you have a length of glorious toil before you."

"Yes, Andrew," said Milton, "but if you will quote me I will quote yourself against you. I remember that exquisitely wanton poem of yours containing the lines:

"NOT WITHOUT HONOUR"
> 'But at my back I always hear
> Time's wingèd chariot hurrying near.'"

"Nay, then, Master Milton," said Marvell, smiling with pleasure that the poet should have remembered his wanton poem and called it exquisite, "if we come to bandying verses between us, I am not one to forget the perfection of your own lines:

> 'Fame is the spur that the clear spirit doth raise
> (That last infirmity of noble mind)
> To scorn delights, and live laborious days;
> But the fair Guerdon when we hope to find,
> And think to burst out into sudden blaze,
> Comes the blind Fury with th' abhorrèd shears,
> And slits the thin spun life. But not the praise,
> Phœbus replied, and touch'd my trembling ears.'

It is full twenty-five years since Phœbus in those very lines gave you an immortality of fame. The wonders that you are now producing can but ensure it, or enhance."

"Alas!" cried the blind man in an outburst of despairing indignation, "what means fame, what can be called immortality in times like these? How brief and sufficient is that account I have written of myself in this newly elaborated poem:

> 'Though fall'n on evil days,
> On evil days though fall'n, and evil tongues!'"

And as I contemplated that lonely and passionate figure moving so close beside me when I turned into Jewin Street, I felt the depth of truth hidden in those poignant words. The high hopes for which he had striven with all his ardour for more than twenty years now lay shattered around him. The return of sumptuous courtiers, flaunting women, and fashionable wits had shattered them. More devastating still was the exuberant joy with which the crowd of ordinary people had welcomed the removal of restraint from their daily life, the return to their vulgar amusements, their childish games, drunkenness, and whoredom. He who had given up his life and his Muse for an ideal of grave living, and freedom of thought and speech under the guidance of conscience only, now beheld conscience imprisoned, freedom excluded from the country, and an uninspired and uniform church re-established with all its trumpery, inclining even to the foreign trumpery of Rome. He had seen the disinterred corpses of Cromwell, Ireton and Bradshaw exposed in Holborn to the mockery of the ribald crowd. The man who had intimately known the impassioned righteousness of Cromwell, whether at home or abroad, and the grave decency of Hampden's life, driven against his will to the sacrifice of his peace and very existence in the cause of England's freedom, now beheld the ruin of his country's reputation in Europe through the temptations of lascivious women, while men who had proved themselves staunch in the wars had forgotten the spirit of life and, like the dog, had returned to their own vomit again, or like the sow, to their wallowing in the mire. Like his own devils at the debate in Hell, Moloch and Belial, Mammon and Beelzebub were prevailing in his own beloved country, while Satan listened with malignant approval.

As the two poets passed along Jewin Street in the deepening twilight, sounds of shouting and wild songs of drunken pleasure were heard across the City wall, and Milton cried :

" Those are the cries of Belial come again—Belial, than whom a spirit more lewd fell not from heaven, or more gross to love vice for itself :

"NOT WITHOUT HONOUR"

> 'In courts and palaces he also reigns,
> And in luxurious cities, where the noise
> Of riot ascends above their loftiest towers,
> And injury, and outrage; and when night
> Darkens the streets, then wander forth the sons
> Of Belial, flown with insolence and wine.'

But leave me here, Andrew," he went sadly on, "I am near the house that I must call my home, and can now make my way there alone."

Alone he went on for a few steps till he could feel the gatepost of the little square of garden before his door. But there he stopped still as though struck dead.

From the inside of the house came sounds of music. Four voices were singing, or perhaps five. Two men's voices could be distinguished, and two women's voices, though one of those was dubious, and the part was sometimes taken by a younger, shriller voice. The music was composed in the Italian mode of the time—operatic, but entirely simple, like church music trying to be gay.

Listening intently, though he had no cause to listen, the poet heard the words:

> "Meanwhile, welcome joy and feast,
> Midnight shout and revelry,
> Tipsy dance and jollity,
> Braid your locks with rosy twine,
> Dropping odours, dropping wine.
> Rigour now is gone to bed;
> And advice with scrupulous head,
> Strict Age, and sour Severity,
> With their grave saws, in slumber lie."

Here a young man's voice interrupted: "Break off there, and let us go on at the more amorous part! Come, Anne, join in where you can. Put your arm round me, and never mind your small infirmity. Remember the learned Frenchman who said a man has never known full delight till he has made love to a lame woman. Let us begin at 'By dimpled brook'. Now, Mary, you lead off."

All the voices then took up the music:

> "By dimpled brook and fountain-brim,
> The wood-nymphs, decked with daisies trim,
> Their merry wakes and pastimes keep:
> What hath night to do with sleep?
> Night hath better sweets to prove;
> Venus now wakes, and wakens Love."

"That tune once again!" cried the young man's voice: "'What has night to do with sleep?'"

"Hist! he's coming!" whispered the youngest girl, and the singing stopped abruptly.

"Is it that hateful old tyrant?" whispered Mary, angrily. "I'm sorry, Charles, he's always dropping in to spoil our pleasure. Now both of you will have to steal out through the garden on to the Moor and work round into the City that way. Happily he can't see who you are. Here's a crown I've made for you by selling one of his tiresome old books. Kiss me, dear, and come again as often as you can. I'll signal to you when he's out."

"Nay, then, let go of me, Henry, and you do the same," whispered Anne's lisping voice. "Here's a bit of silver I've made for you by cutting down the house-keeping. You see he doesn't need much to eat or drink. He just sits dormant with his tobacco pipe all the evening. Kiss me gently, darling, and go out quietly through that garden door. Now, Deborah, you run out to meet him and say we're so glad he has come back safe."

Little Deborah, who was just entering her teens, ran out through the poet's sitting-room, but found him already at the door.

"I heard music—Italian music," he said, as though in sad reminiscence.

"Yes, father," said Deborah, "some of us children were just trying over a kind of a catch to some pretty lines. Very pretty lines, we thought, but I don't know who wrote them."

"*I* know," said the poet, as he felt his way to his accustomed armchair and sank down heavily into it.

SCENE X

"KING OF ALL HIELAND HAIRTS"

*How, being at my ancestral home in Westmorland,
I saw Prince Charlie and his Highlanders advance
and retreat.*

FROM Tebay Junction where the railway enters the Westmorland hills, the train pants up the steep gradient known as "Shap Level" for reasons unknown. On the summit stands the old village of Shap, with its Greyhound Inn. The place is still unspoilt because it offers no obvious attractions for visitors from the Lancashire towns. But I have stayed there at all seasons, for there I know that I have come to my native and spiritual home, and, like a prodigal son, I am welcomed by the mountains and moorland winds that run to meet me. Going down the fields on the west I come to the great tower and ruined aisles of Shap Abbey, where monks pursued in solitude the meditation of eternity, and from there I pass to Hawes Water, and climb to the Roman road that runs along the top of High Street, or find my way up Measand Beck and over the wild summit to Brothers Water and Kirkstone Pass. Twice on that devious track I lost the way in mountain mist, and once was baffled by driving snow and ice-coated rocks.

But more often I have followed the main Penrith

"KING OF ALL HIELAND HAIRTS"

road almost as far as the village of Clifton, and, turning off at a signpost labelled Little Strickland and Newby, have passed for a mile or two through the kind of country that strangers call dull or uninteresting—stone-walled fields of grass or oats, and lanes fringed in June with dog-roses and at every season, except the depths of winter, enlivened with stonechats and whinchats flitting along the walls, flights of plover in the fields, and a solitary or a mated curlew flying over from the moors with its lovely cry. As you approach Newby, you may look back due west to the Ulleswater hills with Saddleback and Skiddaw beyond, and then in front suddenly opens a wide prospect over the valley of the Eden, where Appleby and Kirkby Stephen lie hidden on the right, and on the left, north-east, rises the mass of Cross Fell, with Milburn Forest and the hills where the sources of the Tees and the Tyne both spring.

Just at the top of the low watershed, where the village street of Newby slopes gently down towards the Eden valley, some ancestor of mine in the middle of the seventeenth century chose a site for his family house—a suitable site for a modest squire who could farm sheep there, keep a few horses and a cart or two, drive to Penrith or Appleby for marketing, and attend the service of the Established Religion in the beautiful and ancient church of Morland, hardly more than a mile away for a Sunday's walk, and there be buried. The house was built of grey stone with a stone roof, in the simple and dignified Jacobean style often followed in Yorkshire and other parts of the north. Two short wings project from each end of the main building, making with it three sides of a quadrangle. A stone pavement leads down steps across a little grass court to the front door, over which stands a red-sandstone tablet with the Nevinson arms—spread eagles on the shield, and a spotted wolf for crest. The door opens directly into a large stone-flagged hall, with an enormous fireplace on one side, over which for generations swung a huge "kale pot", lately presented to me as a memorial by a recent tenant. From the hall staircases lead up to various small bedrooms, and at the top of one is a dark and secret chamber, from which legends of a mad wife and ghost have naturally grown up.

Outside lie spacious yards, cattle-sheds and a low-terraced expanse of grass, which may have been a garden or "pleasaunce" in ancient days. A stone gateway has led into it, with the initials I. E. N. carved on the arch, and the date, 1685. It follows that the garden archway was built only one year after John Nevinson, the famous and generous highwayman, was hanged in York, where in the Museum his iron fetters may be seen to this day. He was the man who, after plundering a coach on Shooter's Hill, crossed the Thames at Chatham, and actually rode one horse with hardly a pause to York, played bowls that evening with the Mayor, and established an alibi which saved him for that occasion only. I cannot doubt that his relations in Westmorland were proud of his exploits and lamented his untimely end. Across the village road from the house is a large paddock with low mounds as though meant for riding, and I like to imagine that my ancestral highwayman's indomitable horse was once a foal upon that grassy enclosure.

Horse and rider were still living memories when, sixty years after the execution, the Nevinson family were gathered round their wide hearth, over which

"KING OF ALL HIELAND HAIRTS"

the iron pot (now my waste-paper basket) was steaming, though parents and children were too excited for supper. It was a windy night in November, and strangers from villages along the road to Carlisle kept knocking at the door with astonishing and dreadful tales. An enormous host of wild Highlanders was pouring down the road from Scotland. They had crossed the Border where the Esk runs into the Solway. They had besieged William Rufus's great castle at Carlisle, and the garrison had surrendered. They were now marching along the road to Penrith, and would be there next day. Thousands were coming —seven or eight thousand, twenty thousand, a hundred thousand! They had cannons, lots of cannons, able to fling solid balls of iron three hundred yards. They had one gun of " innormowows length ", as a written message said. Those were English guns, taken at Prestonpans near Edinburgh, the capital town of Scotland. The battle had lasted only a quarter of an hour, and the savages from the mountains, charging with bare swords and daggers, had driven the English soldiers to run for their lives. Now here were the savages coming, wild as fiends turned out of hell, uttering squeals and growls like Hottentots, and hardly more decent in dress. They fed on oats like horses. They slaughtered all sheep and cattle on their way, and, failing those, they devoured children. Under their plaids they had nothing but butchering weapons and their own hairy skins.

What was to be done? Penrith was only ten miles off, and by this time of night they were there. One man rushed in to say he had actually seen two vast companies of mounted men entering Shap itself. They were billeting their horses in the barns and lying down beside them in the straw, while two Scottish Lords, who could speak a kind of English, put themselves up in the Greyhound. All of them, though cavalry, had behaved well, and had kept their hands off the women so far. But to-morrow the savages would be on them. It was like the old Border raids their fathers suffered centuries ago. All the villagers were herding up their sheep and cattle, and driving them far off the road down to Shap Abbey, or away down the valley of the Eden. If they were hidden, the savages could not devour them raw. It was well known that when oats were scarce in the mountain deserts, the men prodded their sheep and cows with their daggers, and the women caught the blood and mixed it into cakes. What else could be expected from people who lived among unknown mountains in filthy huts, with a fire in the middle and a hole at the top for the smoke to go out, and where the women did all the work while the men fought the other savages, stole their cattle, drank a home-brewed fiery spirit, and sang unintelligible rigmaroles? Knowing what his fate would be at the hands of Papists, the parson of Morland had left his comfortable home and fled to Kirkby Stephen. The savages were bringing back the grandson of Popish James, and the horrors of Bloody Mary and Smithfield would be renewed.

So rumours were whispered in the hall, and hour by hour the apprehensions increased. Every knock at the door might mean a band of unintelligible murderers come to plunder the food, cut the throats of Roger, John, and Henry, and ravish pretty young Eliza and Jane in their own bedroom. They barricaded the doors, front and back, and all night long they sat together listening to the roaring wind, whis-

"KING OF ALL HIELAND HAIRTS"

pering to each other, and drowsing with sleep upon the table and benches. But nothing terrible happened, and when a grey light first showed through the windows, Mrs. Nevinson and the maidservant began to set out such breakfast as had not been hidden for safety in the dark and secret chamber upstairs.

It was the morning of November the 22nd—a wild autumn day, the earth smelling of rain, and the trees around the paddock shedding their last leaves before the gale that was sweeping over them from Skiddaw. Hearing no unusual sounds, the father unbarred the doors and said he would walk to Morland to see whether anything had happened there, but all the family were to stay at home on peril of their lives. So Roger and Eliza, being the two eldest, eluded their mother by escaping into the backyard and into the fields, where they stole from wall to wall down the slope towards the Penrith road. As they went, carefully watching over the top of each wall and then running across the field to the next, they suddenly heard a strange sound borne upon the wind. It was like a continuous shriek, but rather of a wild beast in agony than of a man or woman. "That's the savages coming!" whispered Roger, and they ran together over the next field till they reached a point from which they could see a length of the main road. Hiding behind a rock and peering over the top of it, they waited.

The screeching sound steadily increased, and all at once the children saw two lines of men coming along the road and blowing bagpipes fit to outroar the wind. No kind of tune could be perceived but a succession of shakes, twists, turns, and shrill screams, while without ceasing a deeper note buzzed and groaned. A single drummer beat the marching step in front. But close behind the pipers marched another solitary figure—a tall young man of about twenty-five, his long yellow hair partly hidden by a powdered wig, and on the top of it a little blue cap or " bonnet ". The face was singularly attractive, smooth and browned with health and weather, the nose and mouth finely formed, the eyes dark brown and extraordinarily brilliant. He was wearing a short tartan coat without plaid, and a large silver star shone on his left breast. His breeches were tartan too, riding boots reached to his knees and were bespattered with mud after the few miles' march from Penrith. His horse was there, but the leader was sharing the march on foot with the men. He marched with resolute step, as an heir full of high spirits at coming into his rightful heritage. But as he turned his face left towards their side of the road, the boy and girl dodged down behind the rock, and when they peeped out again he had passed.

Now the road as far as they could see was crammed with marching men—the fighting Highlanders of thirteen clans—wild-looking men with long hair and unshaven faces, some bareheaded, some wearing blue bonnets, all with various tartan plaids fastened round the left shoulder, little tartan jackets and skirts, in front of which swung a long hairy purse or bag, and when the wind blew the skirts the children could see the men's bare thighs still gleaming with water from a deep rivulet they had lately forded. On the back of each man was slung a firearm, and in the right hand, or lashed round his waist, each carried a big sword, often without sheath, in the left hand a piercing dirk, and on the left arm the foremost ranks held a round leather shield, with a long spike

"KING OF ALL HIELAND HAIRTS"

of steel projecting from the centre. The crowd marched rapidly, taking little count of step or rank, falling out when they pleased, but always rejoining the body of their own tartans, which the chief of each clan was leading. Like the Prince they marched in high spirits, every now and again shouting barbaric cries, and sometimes falling out in little groups to turn round and round in peculiar patterns by the roadside, lifting up their skirts to let the wind dry their naked bodies. As they danced they renewed their savage outcries with extraordinary enthusiasm.

Absorbed in the amazing sight, the Nevinson children watched the disordered army go past—thousands of them, nearly eight thousand in fact. And in the rear came those terrible cannons, with carts carrying the big iron balls that could kill men at three hundred yards. With inspiring pipes and joyous shouts the last invasion of England was passing before their eyes, and they saw it disappear into the grey village of Shap. Then the shrieking of the pipes died away, and a deeper silence fell upon the hills and moorlands.

But the invaders pressed tumultuously on. They joined the bodies of horse under Lord Elcho and Lord Balmerino at Kendal, and hastened forward through Lancaster, Preston, and Wigan to Manchester. Prince Charles's cause depended absolutely on speed. Though inexperienced and untrained, the man had an instinctive judgment in war. After his occupation of Edinburgh and the rout of sleepy John Cope at Prestonpans, he rightly proposed to strike old Marshal Wade's army in Northumberland, and fight his way down the east side of England, trusting to enthusiasm and the terror of the Highland charge. Few regular troops could stand the onset of wild mountaineers who, regardless of death, charged till within musket's length, fired their " pieces " right in the face, flung them down, to be gathered up at leisure, and dashed through the smoke, smiting the English or Hessian soldiers down with heavy claymores, and finishing them off with the dirks, or piercing them with the spikes sticking out of their targets. Their charge was like a Zulu onset with assegais. But the Prince was over-persuaded by Lord George Murray and other senior soldiers, and so the western route by way of Carlisle was tried. Hitherto old Marshal Wade had remained fixed about Newcastle, putting out his head like a tortoise now and then, and always drawing it back. But there he was, still threatening the Prince's advance from across the Pennines. And what was worse, the King's ruthless and experienced son, the Duke of Cumberland, was waiting with an army in Staffordshire, uncertain whether the Prince was coming down through the Midlands or through the puzzling mountains of Wales. The latter seemed likely when the Highlanders reached Manchester, but they turned aside through the Peak district and appeared at Derby. With great skill the Prince had eluded the armies to left and right, numbering together some thirty thousand trained soldiers. His one chance now was to slip between them and strike at London itself. Nothing stood in the way but a ramshackle camp at Finchley, of which Hogarth has left us a picture.

Here again the Prince's instinct to attack was right. London lay terror-stricken before him. Wealth and religion were united by common fear. The Bank hoarded its gold and made payments only in silver. The Lord Mayor and merchants presented loyal

"KING OF ALL HIELAND HAIRTS"

addresses to King George, who had just returned from the complicated wars in Germany. Young gentlemen of fortune interspersed and spiced their pleasures with military exercises. A regiment of lawyers was formed under command of the Lord Chief Justice, with the King as Colonel. The City Companies subscribed to an emergency fund, and contracts were concluded for the supply of twelve thousand pairs of breeches, twelve thousand shirts, ten thousand woollen caps and stockings, one thousand blankets, twelve thousand pair of woollen gloves, and nine thousand spatterdashes. With such luxurious clothing the Royal Army would be suitably equipped to encounter the nakedness of Highland savagery. Even the Quakers were moved to compromise with their pacifism by supplying woollen waistcoats for troops engaged upon the Devil's work of war. All Jesuits and Popish priests were driven from London to a circumference ten miles outside the City's boundary.

But the panic subsided like a bubble. On December the 6th, the Prince held a Council of War at Derby, and a Council of War is always a sign of weakness. His passionate and wise desire to rush forward on London at all risks was overruled by Lord George Murray and other advisers of cautious apprehensions, and at last the high-spirited design was abandoned. On that day the melancholy retreat was ordered, and in deep despondency the Highlanders turned upon their tracks. No mistake could have been greater. Half London Society would have opened both arms to welcome the handsome young Prince who came to them endowed with all the charm and pathos of the Stuart blood. Even wealth and religion might have made terms. Throughout

"KING OF ALL HIELAND HAIRTS"

the country people admitted they were uncertain which was the Pretender—George or Charles. In England there was no such enthusiasm for the Stuart tartan as the Scots had felt for a leader of the Clans, but the Hanoverian Court did not inspire enthusiasm either, and no one sang " Georgie is my darling, my darling, my darling " ! If the worst had befallen, it could not have been worse than what befell. The young Prince and his Scottish Lords might have been executed with noble display on Tower Hill, as some of the Lords were executed. The Highlanders might have been slaughtered as most of them were slaughtered or hung withering on Carlisle yetts. But the White Rose of the Stuart name would still have been adored as a symbol of Royal greatness. Royalty that seeks safety in flight can never be recovered. We know that well.

In sullen silence the Highlanders turned about and began the retreat. Within a fortnight of leaving Manchester on the gallant advance they passed through it again, and one may suppose it was then that some unknown poet and musician conceived the song, " Farewell, Manchester, noble town, farewell ", a eulogy sounding strange to us who have known that industrious city. At Lancaster the Prince wanted to stop and fight the leading detachments of Cumberland's army, now following with the silent pursuit of a cat watching her prey. But again he was overruled, and the miserable retreat was continued through Kendal and up the Penrith road to Shap, which was reached on December the 16th. The guns and ammunition carts had been checked by some mishap at Kendal, but the main body of the Highlanders pressed on towards Penrith through " a night of dreadful wind and rain ". In the depression and disappointment of defeat, the Highlanders were no longer content with their simple ration of bread and cheese and beer, and even that was running short. For pay the men got sixpence a day, the two front ranks (who were called " gentlemen " and seem to have had a special privilege in carrying targets) got a shilling, and the captains half-a-crown. But there was nothing left to buy in Shap, and the hungry men went ravaging for meal, poultry, or sheep in the farms and moorlands around.

Rumours of the retreat and the dangers to which isolated farms and villages were exposed reached Newby from Tebay, Kendal, or Windermere, and the Nevinsons again barricaded their solid stone house and drove their livestock into hiding. But, as before, Roger and his sister slipped away just after the December sunset and waited in their former hiding-place while the west wind blew the rain against them in soaking gusts. They watched the road till the night was almost black, and then they heard the scream of the pipes again. But now the sound came from the south, and suddenly it stopped as though conquered by the storm. They crept down till they were close upon the road, which gleamed with rain under the moon's fitful light. Then they saw a crowd of men coming slowly towards them and going past. First came the lines of pipers, silent now. Then followed a drenched and miserable crowd, a disordered and uncontrolled jumble of men marching in silence. Last, but still at the point of greatest danger in retreat, came a solitary figure, walking with head hanging down, hair dripping over his face, and a plaid wrapped carelessly round his body. He carried no arms, but tramped desperately along through water and mud. He walked like one whose life is over. So the boy and girl, standing in the gorse and bracken by the roadside, saw the Stuart Prince with his despairing crowds of clansmen depart. The retreating army reached Penrith early on the 17th.

Next day the sound of firing was heard at Newby. Lord George Murray, having secured his guns, had marched with the rearguard from Kendal, pausing for a few hours at Shap, and had pushed along the road to a hill called Thrimby, only a mile from the village of Clifton. There he was overtaken by Cumberland's dragoons, each of whom was said to carry a foot soldier on the horse behind him—making four thousand men in all. The foot soldiers, we must suppose, slid off the hindquarters of the horses, and ran out into the hedges and ditches of the fields on both sides of the road, while right down the narrow road itself, a small number of dragoons charged the rear of the retreating Highlanders. With enviable decision Lord George Murray turned his men about, and, glad to be actually fighting, they dashed against the horsemen with their broad claymores, many of which broke upon the skull-caps of the dragoons, and strove to finish them off man by man with the dirk. As had happened before, the maddened horses and their riders could not withstand the impetuous onset, repeated again and again. Parties of the clansmen leapt into the fields and moors to rout out the English foot who were trying to work their way round and cut off the retreat. The scattered Highlanders succeeded in checking this manœuvre, though, as a contemporary witness tells us, " the loose-tailed lads " suffered from the thorns and prickly gorse. The fighting continued far into the moonlit night, but before morning Murray had brought his men

"KING OF ALL HIELAND HAIRTS"

off to Penrith, and thence he pushed straight on to overtake the Prince at Carlisle. From Kendal the rearguard had marched forty miles without sleep and on short provisions. They had done all that a rearguard should, and had brought off the guns in safety. It happened nearly two hundred years ago, and that evening and night the Nevinsons, in their grey stone house which now stands so quiet, were listening to the firing, the outcries and the trampling of horses in the last battle hitherto fought on English ground.

Still formidable the Highlanders passed back into Scotland, and moved to and fro with various fortune, till in April of the next year the Duke of Cumberland met them again at Drumossie Moor or Culloden, seven miles from Inverness. They were then eight thousand strong, but it was the end. Burns, born only thirteen years later, and well acquainted with the story, sang the lament of the lovely lass of Inverness:

> " Drumossie moor, Drumossie day,
>   A waefu' day it was to me!
> For there I lost my father dear,
>   My father dear and brethren three.
>
> " Their winding-sheet the bluidy clay,
>   Their graves are growing green to see;
> And by them lies the dearest lad
>   That ever blest a woman's e'e!"

There follows her curse on butcher Cumberland, the Royal Duke. So to the music of the most beautiful Scottish songs the Highland host passed out of history into the abysm of time, with all their pipes and clashing swords and barbaric yells.

Bonnie Prince Charlie alone is living still. Mankind's yearning for romance has kept him alive for many generations now. All of us eagerly long for something to shake us clear of the chains that bind us in the commonplace—something to raise us into a sphere where, in the old Greek phrase, we may become greater than ourselves. We know his subsequent story. He suffered the cruellest fate that can befall any human being. He outlived himself. Against his better nature, he had yielded his mind a victim to the reasonable caution of older and more experienced advisers. After escaping from Scotland, he went on living, a man forbid even to himself. The curse of his failure in that one great exploit dragged him down into the slough of despond, and he sought in vain the natural ways of escape—those natural refuges that afford a brief oblivion to despair. He took to women, and he took to drink. After a few years had passed, no one would have recognized the bonnie Prince in the sullen, intemperate wreck. His one redeeming virtue remained—his insistent entreaty to be allowed to return from France and " perish with the people I have undone ". How many of those people had he undone ? On the field of Culloden alone, within twenty-five minutes three thousand of his Highlanders are said to have died. And after Culloden the butchery followed.

But still the young and radiant hero lives as he appeared in his early triumphs—handsome, vital, filled with courteous generosity, amazingly chaste, being, we are told, cool and indifferent even among the welcoming ladies of Edinburgh ; full of wisdom's hope, and inspired by the daring that sets prudence aside as a tedious couch or a physician's bottle. That was the attractive youth whom no Highlander would betray though a reward of thirty thousand pounds was set on his head, and it was he who still lives in the songs which spontaneously sprang from the soul of a gallant and imaginative race.

SCENE XI

REVENANT

How, being at a performance of " Samson " in Wales, I heard the composer conduct

FROM my boyhood Cader Idris has been to me the ideal of a stern and beautiful mountain. Before I was in my teens I scrambled up a steep and rocky path to the summit, alone. For me in those days it was something of an adventure, and between me and the mountain there grew up a friendly and understanding relationship, far more intimate than with my relations by blood. I have felt it whenever I returned, either walking across from the Schools at Shrewsbury through Welshpool, Can Office, and Dinas Mowddwy to Dolgelly, the dark peaks of Cader seen in perspective always nearer as I walked; or when the sudden vision of the front, crimson in sunset, rose before me as I emerged from the wooded foot-hills, and there it stood—the wide central precipice above the volcanic llyn, flanked on either side by the supporting buttresses, so different in shape and so balanced in power. To me Cader has always remained a magic mountain, and though I have seen the Himalayas and crossed the Rockies and wandered in the Alps and the Caucasus, no mountain has been for me so filled with mysterious influences such as haunt the Celtic world.

I was especially aware of those magic influences one New Year when I was staying on business in the little grey town at the mountain's foot. The cliffs and crags of the precipitous range towered high above the town, and the summits were hidden in clouds and mists, now and again just blown away by the screaming tempest to reveal some crest unexpectedly high and covered with thin and drifting plumes and gullies of snow. Cataracts of brownish water streamed down every cleft in the mountain-sides, and the main river, flowing through the town under an ancient bridge, had flooded the neighbouring streets and houses. To myself such a scene appeared as beautiful as stern, but beauty has little effect upon the native mind, and the inhabitants of the town were to all appearance grim, silent, and unlovely. Gloomy-hearted men and hard-featured women they seemed, battling through long generations for very existence against the hardships of the country they inhabited. Their lives depended chiefly on sheep, and the sheep depended on the mountains. The houses were built with thick walls of grey and partially hewn rock, in the hope of shutting out the deluges of rain and the blasts of the wind. What little time the people could spare from the struggle for food and warmth was given to the contemplation of eternity or the more soothing visions of drink. Not that they were a drunken race. Drink was their temptation, as being the readiest way of escape from this vale of tears; but, conscious of their impious longing for that premature escape, large numbers of them had from childhood been pledged to resistance, and had succeeded in keeping themselves inwardly dry. Perhaps all the more on that account their thoughts were turned to the prospect of the doom awaiting the great majority of mankind after death, and to the remote chance of escaping it offered only to elect human souls.

Various ideas about the surest means of escape had prevailed among them from age to age. At some dim period it was the Druid way, and many rites and customs of that primeval religion still survived. At a much later time it had been the way of the Roman Church, but hardly a trace of Rome remained. The Anglican way never penetrated far into the mountains, for it was the way of a hostile and conquering race, and the Anglican priests had regarded the natives as barbarians hardly worth the laborious task of saving. Cultivating the leisured ease of their own country, they had shrunk from the toil of mastering the unknown language dominant among the mountains—a rude language hardly changed since the invaders from the Continent savagely drove the British from their fertile plains. But, with the coming of Wesleyans and Methodists and Baptists among a generation fast reverting to paganism, the people had recognized a new way appealing to their souls. It was stern, but it gave a possible vent to their passionate longing for emotion and excitement. Under the crust of that dour and uncommunicative exterior, a fire of unexpected passion lay smouldering—a passion sometimes revealed in an outpouring of stormy eloquence, and sometimes in crimes of unusual horror, as when pieces of an unfortunate girl were found distributed in the river, or when a man left the body of his murdered wife up among the crags to be eaten by the ravens. The enthusiastic converts stood combined against the external foes from Rome or England, but among themselves they hated each other like members of one family.

Religion was good, and so was the sin of drink if one yielded to it, but it was in music that the people found their greatest consolation for the miseries of this world and the apprehensions of the next. Some played the harp, some the fiddle, many the harmonium, and all, without exception, sang. They sang as naturally as we English people swear. And in my little grey town New Year's Day had long been the festival of music and song. The winter that I was living there it was to be celebrated as usual, or even with higher religious solemnity. As a local paper truly observed, " It was a red-letter day for the Eisteddfodwyr, for all roads led to the metropolis of the county on that day." So all the Joneses and Thomases and Williamses and Hugheses and Morgans and Evanses and Pughs and Lloyds and Edwardses and Wynnes and Griffithses and Merediths and Ellises and Owenses and Davieses and Prices came flocking down from the hillsides and neighbouring villages into the narrow grey streets of the metropolis, crowding the tiny station and over-running the little square where stood the hall for the performance. There, too, stood the inn for the teas that cheer and the cups that do more.

All morning, amid a deluge of rain, the competitions proceeded without a hitch—competitions in solo singing, in harp playing, in memorial poems, in the carving of walking-sticks, in brass bands, and native dramas. In the afternoon came the event of electing the Bard for the year. There were sixteen competitors, and the appointed subject was " Y Tanguefeddwr ". The Druidical judges declared all the poems too long as poems so often are, but ultimately the prize of four guineas was bestowed upon the well-known Bard Brifdir, and he was then installed in a carved oaken chair in accordance with the rites traditional among "Bards of the Isle of Britain" from the age of the Druids downwards. In fact, four of the Christian clergy present, in their enthusiasm for the background of time, seemed to relapse into that older form of religion, and, belonging to the Ancient Order of Druidical Bards themselves, they proudly escorted their newly elected Brother in the chair, which thereupon became his private property. As this was by no means the first triumph of his Celtic inspiration, he may have possessed a complete set of that poetic furniture.

But in the evening unexpected trouble came. The market hall was crammed with an eager audience waiting for the concert promised by the Choral Society of the county. It was an unusual and long-anticipated occasion. Splendidly daring, the Society had ventured to announce a performance of the Oratorio called "Samson", and both chorus and orchestra had been practising for many weeks, sometimes separately, sometimes together. One of the soloists was a native of the metropolis, the other three had specially come down from London, also a metropolis. It was fifty years since the Society had attempted such an enterprise, and in the profoundly musical assembly all were glowing with expectation of delight. The inn was empty, the city square around the new war memorial was almost deserted, though a few shepherds still hung about it, fully exposed to the drenching rain, which was not their second nature, but their first.

All was ready. The lady at the piano gave the note —the A—for the orchestra. She gave it several times.

REVENANT

She struck the appropriate chords. The stringed instruments tuned, and tuned again. The chorus of divided men and women sat nervously attentive. The audience began to whisper. A few stamped with impatience. Nothing happened. No conductor appeared. A boy was sent to the inn on the chance that the conductor had been delayed there, warming himself. No oratorio could be decently performed without a conductor, and still the audience and the performers were waiting.

A telegraph boy ran in and handed a brown envelope to the Society's President. With deep emotion the President announced that the veteran conductor's motor stood helpless in the middle of a flooded ford, and as it was twenty miles to walk across the hills he feared he would be too late for the evening's performance. Eloquent sighs and groans and lamentations arose on every side.

But from the front seats there rose a strange and unexpected figure. He was dressed in old-fashioned clothes—a long brown coat and knee-breeches. From the wig which surrounded his large and deeply wrinkled face one might have mistaken him for a judge. Quietly mounting the platform, he told the President that he was himself fairly well acquainted with the music, and would do his best to fill the conductor's place, with the kind permission of the singers, the orchestra, and the audience. A gasp of astonishment went round, but, without waiting, the old gentleman borrowed the President's walking-stick, and took his stand at the conductor's desk. The first violin offered him a book of the score, but he said it was unnecessary, though he thanked him all the same. Then he gently raised the walking-stick, his left arm also uplifted to call the performers together. As the right hand moved decisively down, the orchestra struck the full, loud chord, and the overture—*andante pomposo*—began.

Such a performance as it was! Orchestra, chorus, and soloists were like men and women inspired. They played and they sang as though their souls were transfigured into tremulous or blazing flames. " Total eclipse! no sun, no moon! "—what an appalling depth of darkness! " Why does the God of Israel sleep? " " Return, O God of Hosts! Behold Thy servant in distress "—what pathos of despairing supplication! What a hopeless wandering in the orchestral part, as of sheep lost upon the mountain without shepherd or dog! " But hear me, hear the voice of love "—it was the voice of Dalila the traitress, but no matter. What affectionate entreaty! How feminine! How irresistible to any man!

And when the chorus came, " To song and dance we give the day ", performers and audience alike went wild with sudden joy. True, it was the Philistines who sang, but what did that matter? The verse ended, " And sweep this race from out the land ", and who should the race be but the hated invaders who themselves had swept across the eastern frontier? The whole hall rose to dance and sing. But the crowd was too thick. There was no space for dancing, and out they all trooped through every exit, the old gentleman at the head of the singers, and all the orchestra following in their train. Round the little square, singing and dancing, they went. In front of the war memorial the old gentleman stood still and mounted the few steps, while all the performers gathered close round him. There, with passionate fervour, the chorus of Israelites shouted, " With thunder armed, great God arise! " Then the Samson, who had begun to feel " some secret impulse ", launched into the joyous air :

> " Thus when the sun in's watery bed,
>   All curtained with a cloudy red,
>   Pillows his chin upon an orient wave !
> The wandering shadows, ghastly pale,
>   All troop to their infernal jail,
>   Each fettered ghost slips to his several grave."

At those words the bewigged conductor was observed to smile, but, waving the unusual baton, as though he were conducting the heavenly choir of cherubim and seraphim, he moved on towards a steep and narrow road leading into the very heart of the mountains. All the performers, all the audience, all the population of the metropolis followed at his heels, singing and playing as though all had practised that glorious music for years and years.

So they came to the open summit of a hill where upright rocks, ranged in a circle, marked the scene of ancient Druidical rites. In the middle of that rocky circle the aged conductor took his stand with the performers, while the thick crowd pressed around the outside of the ring.

The rain had stopped. Far up the estuary the glimmer of the rising moon revealed long wisps of storm-tossed cloud, which clung to distant mountain summits. With upturned faces barely visible, the transformed assembly stood in silent adoration. After Manoah's recitative, " Come, come ; no time for lamentation now—— To his foes Ruin is left ; to him eternal fame ", the conductor stood illumined by some internal radiance, gazing around upon all with grateful benevolence, as though recognizing the passion of a musical race. Then once more he raised the transfiguring wand. The orchestra played two andante but joyous lines, and the Israelitish woman, the native singer of that rugged metropolis, raised high and loud the immortal strain :

> " Let the bright Seraphim in burning row
> Their loud, uplifted Angel-trumpets blow ;
> Let the Cherubic host, in tuneful choirs,
> Touch their immortal harps with golden wires."

The trumpets blared. The precipices re-echoed. " Angel-trumpets blow ! " Again and again the glorious sound was repeated. Then all the Israelites —all that wild, stern people, suckled on music and excelling in music alone—joined in the chorus :

> " Let their celestial concerts all unite,
> Ever to sound his praise in endless morn of light."

The celestial noise rose to the drifting clouds, and through a gap among them a few stars were seen. Exultation and joy filled every heart. Wesleyans and Baptists beamed on each other. The Methodist minister embraced the Anglican priest. Strange shapes of ancient, bearded men, dressed in transparent grey robes and wearing wreaths of mistletoe, hovered high above the circle of upright stones. When the superb chorus ended with the final chord of united voices, all the performers and population pushed into the Druid circle to embrace the conductor. But he was no longer there.

SCENE XII

"L'HOMME"

How, leading a running party of students at Jena, I witnessed the battle, and the intrusion into Goethe's house at Weimar

THERE is a peculiar beauty about a German forest in autumn. The damp ground strewn with the rich brown leaves of birch and beech sends out an autumnal smell, and so do the dark forests of pine and fir. In early morning one may feel the sharp touch of frost, and almost certainly a white mist will hang over the valleys, lakes, and rivers. But about ten o'clock a pale sun is visible through the mist, and by noon its light will be golden, and the sky bright blue. If you go far into the hills, you may hear the pattering of potatoes that a green-coated forester throws down for the wild boars and roebucks. In a few minutes the forest creatures come stealing out of their coverts, and cluster around you as in a fairy-story or a mediæval picture of the Creation or Christ's cradle in the hay. Twilight comes slowly, and as the still air darkens into blue, orange lights of fires and lamps suddenly appear in the cottages on the hills and in the ancient houses surrounding the open square of a little town.

Such an autumn I spent as a student in the old University of Jena in 1886, while Bismarck still reigned

"L'HOMME"

supreme in Germany, and one may almost say in Europe, serving his master, the sturdy old William I. Only a few years had then passed since the two between them, with Moltke as a third, having overwhelmed the armed forces of Denmark, Austria, and France, established the German Empire on foundations of permanent might, as it then seemed. Since I was not rich enough or skilful enough to join a fighting Corps and expose my face heroically to be slashed and gashed by pliant foils without buttons on the points, I enrolled an athletic club for football, to be played under "soccer" rules and with a real English ball in place of a leather case stuffed with straw and kicked about regardless of rules! But what pleased me better than the football were the "Runs" in which with difficulty I induced about a dozen or twenty fellow-students to join. I didn't bother about hares. As in my old school at Shrewsbury, we ran for the sake of running, just as we learnt Greek for the sake of learning it. And so on fine Saturday afternoons or other holidays I led out my little pack to run far through the beautiful forests and villages of Thuringia, up and down the swift-flowing Saale, up and down the Fuchsthurm and Forst, hills overlooking the town, or to Ziegenhain, where the best white beer ran, or along the winding, uphill road called the Schnecke or Snail, which was the way to Weimar.

The students, though excellent gymnasts, were unaccustomed to run long distances for fun, and their exertion was an amazing sight to the townspeople and villagers. But in time they came to enjoy it almost as much as I did. One day's Run I especially remember. It was October the 14th, and when we started from the Jena market-place, the mist still hung so thick that we could hardly see the tall church tower with its clock.

"L'HOMME"

Up the twisting Schnecke, lined on both sides with solemn pines, I led the way till I saw a chance of turning sharply to the right and following a track which brought us out upon the wide plateau on the top of the hill or cliff called the Landgrafenberg, which looks steeply down upon the town of Jena to the south and on the valley of the Saale to the east.

Here I halted for the whole pack to come up, and watched the mist rising till all the high-pitched roofs below us were clear. Then I led the panting "hounds" gently along a country road north-west, passing through two tiny villages, and so to a larger one, with the distinctive name of Vierzehn Heiligen. There in a little beerhouse I halted again, as the pack showed signs of a German thirst. Wondering who were the Fourteen Saints who gave their name to such an outlandish village, I sat with a splendid *Seidel* of "*helles*" in my hand, but just as I began to drink, my keenest "hound" purposely jogged my elbow for a joke, and I poured the cooling beer right over his head instead of down my throat—a disappointing loss.

So we sat long into the sunny afternoon, drinking *Seidel* after *Seidel* and devouring chunks of the yard-long sour loaves with chips of powerful Limberger cheese. But realizing the date of that charming day I could not but recall the scene that was there enacted just eighty years before. Only eighty years! It would be quite possible for aged men around us in the village to have been living babies then; and then, as to-day, it was a morning of thick white mist through which the sun was breaking by ten o'clock.

Early that morning Napoleon stood on the summit of the Landgrafenberg peering vainly into the fog. He knew that a great Prussian force lay just in front of him, but he was strangely ignorant as to its size and importance. On the previous day he had ridden from Gera, more than twenty miles away to the east, and had found Jena already occupied by Lannes, who had only just cleared the town of the Prussian rearguard of Hohenlohe's army, which had been there the day before. He had then climbed the Landgrafenberg with Lannes at his side, and stayed there all night. He spent many hours encouraging the men to climb after him to the summit of the commanding position, and he even assisted their efforts to bring the guns up two steep ravines where the wheels stuck in the marl. The men were wearied by their long marches since the army had left the Main. But the sight of the Emperor actually among them filled them with renewed ardour, and by 3 a.m. troops and guns were in position. So true was Napoleon's own saying: " In war men are nothing, the one man is everything." When all was arranged he himself bivouacked on the summit with his five tents, as usual.

That night the greatest military genius of history stood at the height of his genius and his genuine power. At Austerlitz he had extinguished Austria eleven months before. On the Continent only Prussia now remained unsubdued, and the Prussian army lay before him. It was trained and supported on the traditions of Frederick the Great, but Frederick had been dead just twenty years, and Frederick-William III was no successor to genius. Nor was his Commander-in-Chief, the wavering old Duke of Brunswick, a successor. His idea of generalship was to hold Councils of War, definite in nothing but evidence of weakness as I have said in a previous scene. Blücher, Scharnhorst, and Gneisenau, great names in coming history, were among his generals, but his counsels swung this way and that, till at last, like

"L'HOMME"

a wavering compass, they appeared to settle into a direction pointing north. He would retire up the Saale valley to the Elbe and stand there ready to check any possible advance upon Berlin. The retirement was to be slow and well protected, for he left forty-seven thousand men as rearguard under Hohenlohe, while Rüchel had a large force ready in front of Erfurt to defend the left flank of the retirement. What was called his main army had thirty-five thousand chosen troops of the old Frederick model under his own command. In all his scattered forces he could dispose of only one-hundred-and-twenty-eight thousand men, while Napoleon had mustered two hundred thousand. The great mass of these were in Jena or around the city, commanded at various points by marshals of splendid fame—Lannes, Ney, Soult, and Augereau, under Napoleon himself, with Bertier as Chief-of-Staff. More significant still of Napoleon's strategy was the presence of Davout and Bernadotte nearly thirty miles farther northward up the Saale at Naumburg and Kösen, standing ready to threaten the right flank of Brunswick's retiring army, or even to cut off its communications with Berlin. It is in the communications that the secret of warfare lies. That has been the maxim of all great strategists before Napoleon and since.

On the night of that 13th of October, while the tired horses and gunners were dragging the guns up the ravines, and the troops swarmed up the face of the cliff, Napoleon was justified in telling them that victory was a mathematical certainty. He was almost justified in the overweening pride of his saying: "It is truly a proof of the weakness of the human mind that people think themselves able to resist me." As usual he waited till after midnight to issue his final orders for

"L'HOMME"

next day's battle. His design was simple. Lannes with the main force, supported by the reserve of the Guards, was to advance in the centre towards Vierzehn Heiligen, starting from the summit of the Landgrafenberg, and moving over the plateau behind a screen of skirmishers. Soult and Ney were to hold the right wing, protecting Lannes from being outflanked. Augereau on the Schnecke and the road to Weimar was to hold the left, checking any similar threat in that direction. Murat with a force of twenty thousand flashing cavalry was ready for the terrific glory of the pursuit. But he chiefly watched the left, for it was there that Hohenlohe had massed his greatest strength, believing that Napoleon's attack must come along the Schnecke and the Weimar road. He had neglected the Landgrafenberg in consequence, and that was why Napoleon and Lannes were able to climb it and establish troops and guns there on the late evening of the 13th.

So it was that at first sign of light on the morning of the 14th, Napoleon stood there peering in vain into the thick white mist. He believed that the main Prussian army under Brunswick lay only a few hundred yards in front of him. That was his great mistake throughout the day. It was not the main army, but Hohenlohe's powerful rearguard that was hidden there. For Napoleon it was indeed a fortunate mist that veiled the position on both sides, for some sixty thousand of his central force were thickly crowded upon the summit, a mark through which Hohenlohe's guns could have ploughed long and bloody furrows, as the round shot flew and bounced among their congested and helpless ranks. But by ten o'clock, when the white sun began to glimmer through the mist, the troops had deployed upon open ground, and the advance began.

"L'HOMME"

The Prussian line also advanced, marching in close formation as on parade in a barrack yard. That was the Great Frederick's method of warfare, as it had been his eccentric father's. But before they had come many paces they found themselves checked by a buzzing swarm of scattered skirmishers. Their cavalry, which should then have charged in irresistible mass, were trained to charge only in driblets of small bodies together. Lannes's mass of infantry, supported by Ney on his right, pushed forward with crushing weight, and before midday had driven the Prussian line back upon Vierzehn Heiligen, and after two assaults had overcome resistance there—just where, only eighty years later, I was sitting at ease with my *Seidel* of "*helles*". It was in vain that Rüchel then appeared, his men advancing also in regular Prussian order. He was an hour too late, and on the field an hour means life or death. Soult from the right and Augereau from the left brought up their forces to surround the confused and unhappy Prussians on both flanks. At noon Napoleon called upon his Guards and all reserves to crash into the centre of the conflict, and by two o'clock the whole of Hohenlohe's fine and courageous army was drifting away northward in helpless retreat, with Murat's inexorable cavalry slashing at them from behind.

That was bad enough, but the height of the tragedy was to come almost at once. As we have seen, Napoleon had made the mistake of supposing he was faced by Brunswick's main army, whereas he had only Hohenlohe's powerful rearguard before him. But conjecturing by the insight of military genius that Brunswick would endeavour to retire north-east, so as to cover the approach to Berlin, he had set Davout and Bernadotte at Naumburg far down the Saale to outflank or check the retirement. As soon as they perceived that the main conflict must take place near Jena, Bernadotte moved rather slowly up the Saale to the heights of Dornburg, where the Dukes of Weimar had an old residence or castle, but he got no farther, and could claim no part in the battle. Davout, on the other hand, having acquired a certain genius for war as though by infection from the master to whom his whole being was devoted, crossed the Saale at Kösen, about six miles south of Naumburg, and advanced west and slightly south, over the open plains dotted with small villages to Auerstädt, about six miles north-east from the weaving town of Apolda. Whether he expected it or not, there he came upon Brunswick's main army with King Frederick-William leisurely carrying out the retirement towards the Elbe, of which the Saale is a tributary.

The fog was still thick when Brunswick perceived a great mass of French troops drawn up across the main road in front. Blücher charged and charged again, but his cavalry could not be brought to act in mass, and as the main army tried to advance along a deep gully in the road the French had them at their mercy from the higher ground on both sides. The losses were heavy. The wavering old Duke himself fell mortally wounded—he who had suffered defeat at the small but decisive engagement of Valmy, which Goethe, who was present, proclaimed as marking a new epoch in the history of the world (September 20th, 1792). Scharnhorst, who now succeeded to the command, was in a distant part of the scene, and the unhappy King, who had no spark of the Great Frederick's intelligence, was at a loss what to do. Like most people at a loss, he could think only of retreat. He gave the fatal order for the main army to fall back upon the support of Hohenlohe's powerful rearguard.

"L'HOMME"

A fine support! Swinging round past Auerstädt in the direction of Apolda the unhappy main army of Prussia had to seek support in the confused and panic-stricken mobs of the rearguard scurrying away as fast as they could, pursued by Murat's slashing sabres, and already struggling far from the field of Jena. Main army and vanguard became inextricably mixed. The confusion was barely imaginable. By evening all was over but the running. The pitiless pursuit continued far into the night, and indeed for the next few days. The Great Frederick's army, the model of discipline, the terror of Europe, had ceased to be. Another Power had fallen. Berlin lay open to Napoleon, and again he seemed justified in that overweening claim that any thought of resisting him was a proof of the weakness of the human mind.

Military genius he displayed at every point, but his highest genius was shown in placing Davout and Bernadotte far away forward on his right to check the Prussian retirement, the direction of which he divined by a kind of spiritual instinct. At the same time, sitting there in the inn at Vierzehn Heiligen, where the storm of the battle had passed northward soon after four o'clock eighty years ago, I did not forget that, owing to Davout's genius in striking with a far inferior force right across the direction of the main Prussian army's retirement, he had given his master a great and devastating victory instead of a local success which must have been followed up with speed by tired troops, and probably with heavy loss at the passages of the Saale and the Elbe. We read that in private letters to Davout Napoleon acknowledged this vast debt, though in public, in accordance with his nature, he took the whole glory of the day on himself. Davout's blow was decisive, and historians still speak

"L'HOMME"

of Jena-Auerstädt as one and the same overwhelming victory.

As I dreamily sat there in the inn at Vierzehn Heiligen on the eightieth anniversary of the battle, I recalled the scene as in a vision—" the little Corporal " of genius standing there in his cocked hat and long grey coat, his famous Marshals moving the French columns to the field on this side and that as his midnight orders had directed, the invincible body of his Guards massing on the summit of the cliff and moving forward like a deluge of destruction straight upon the little village where I was ; and then the faithful Davout, infected by genius, sweeping across the path of Brunswick's doomed army from the north-east and driving them back to join the confused crowds of the defeated rearguard, only to add to the piteous confusion. Gathering my pack of student hounds together, for many of them were fast asleep, I led them jogging back across the open plain, well cultivated in strips without hedge or fence, as is the thrifty German way of agriculture, and so we reached the height of the Landgrafenberg, and saw below us in the twilight the lamps of Jena, and the square with its ancient Town Hall, in the vaulted cellars of which we would that evening enjoy a students' supper of soup, sausages, and beer, at sixpence a head. But as we went along the earthy tracks and over the strips of plough, I heard from every clod the cries of many thousand voices lamenting their early deaths, and in tongues once hostile, uttering the words " Oublié " and " Vergessen".

As we crossed the entrance of the Schnecke and the Weimar road, I heard again the shouts of Murat's cavalry with drawn swords thundering past me to join in the pitiless pursuit. I could picture them galloping

"L'HOMME"

hard along that ten-mile road which I had so often walked on visits to my Weimar friends. Weimar must be reached, for it had been Brunswick's headquarters, and Carl August, Duke of Weimar, had thrown in his lot with the Prussian cause. So in the early evening Murat's squadron of Hussars arrived in the little Ducal town upon the Ilm, and saw the park laid out along the river banks, and the Duke's palace newly built in German-classic style. But as they rode through the streets crowded with refugees, soldiers in flight, and soldiers bleeding from wounds, they came to a simple but substantial dwelling-house which seemed the right sort of place for comfortable billets. Accordingly sixteen Alsatian Hussars quartered themselves there. It was Goethe's house.

The poet was then fifty-seven. After his return from Italy in 1788, he had lost something of his zest for life and poetry. His passionate friendship with Charlotte von Stein had cooled, owing partly to misunderstanding, partly to the presence in his house of the beautiful young girl, Christiane Vulpius, as his mistress and the mother of his son. He had devoted himself mainly to the study of Optics and Botany, and it was only after some years that Schiller's friendship aroused him, as he said, from " the charnel house of science ". But Schiller had died the year before the French invasion. Herder too was dead, and the dreariness of late middle-age fell heavily upon a poet seldom now stirred by passion or poetic fervour. To the world he was still known only as the author of *Werther*, and at nearly sixty to live upon fame won at twenty-five may well be bitter. It is true he had published *Faust, a Fragment*, in 1790, and had been adding bits to it from time to time, as his unfortunate manner was. He had written *Wilhelm Meister's Apprenticeship*, many exquisite lyrics, and a few dramas that were praised and left to grow even colder than they were. An edition of his *Collected Works* had fallen moribund, and the splendour of the *First Part of Faust* was still unknown except to a few.

But there in his simple but substantial house upon the Frauenplatz the poet was, when the French Hussars came trotting into the town. Even then his own fine saying was true of him : " For myself I am happy enough. Joy comes streaming in upon me from every side. Only, for others I am not happy." When all began fleeing from the town, he remained quietly at home with Christiane and their boy. He gave what he could in the way of clothing and food to the unhappy refugees from the villages. The aged sons and daughters of those very refugees have themselves told me what their fathers told them of the horrors of that day : how the French slaughtered all their cattle and fowls, took the bread from the ovens, drank all the beer and the milk, ripped up the bedding and coverlets, such as all Germans love, and scattered the feathers to the October winds. But Goethe refused to move.

The sixteen Alsatian Hussars quartered in his house may have been surprised and pleased to hear the dignified old gentleman speak the French language, though indeed as Alsatians of those days they themselves probably spoke the kind of German dialect which Goethe remembered from his distant youth when he was making love to Friederike Brion at Sesenheim, within a ride of Strasbourg. We may imagine the sixteen cavalrymen after such a day settling themselves fairly comfortably for the night with food and drink, sofas and carpets, not knowing or caring for a moment that close beside them was one of the great poets of the world. After midnight two drunken sharpshooters forced their way into the house, demanded to see the master, compelled Goethe to drink with them, and afterwards crashed into his bedroom—a small chamber looking out upon a garden at the back—and threatened to kill him. At the moment of extreme danger Christiane sprang upon them and with the help of some neighbours, also hidden for shelter in the house, flung them out upon the street. When we read the rich and varied works accomplished by Goethe in the next twenty-six years, we might remember that, but for the courage of that still beautiful woman, they would not have existed.

That night Napoleon himself remained in Jena, conscious of a triumph which he had from the first announced as mathematically certain. But next morning Marshal Ney arrived in Weimar fresh from the corpse-strewn plain, and he remained for some hours in conversation with Goethe. He set a special guard upon the house, and the order of protection was renewed by the Marshals Lannes and Augereau, who came a little later in the day. Thus a poet's house was preserved in honour of his poetry, as Pindar's house was once preserved, and as Milton appealed for similar protection in his well-known sonnet. Often while I lived in Weimar I have gazed at that house in passing to the famous theatre, and have mentally beheld the strange events which have happened there, and tried to estimate the wisdom and beauty once uttered and created by a living man behind those simple windows.

Two years later when Napoleon and Goethe met at Erfurt, Napoleon, as is well known, exclaimed to him, " *Vous êtes un homme !* " (or " *Voilà un homme !* ") It was rare praise for a poet. Napoleon called Goethe a man, and, since Nietzsche invented the word, Napoleon himself has been acclaimed as the very type of the Superman. But after all, which is which? There is something more of a Superman in the poet, so elevated above the national prejudices and animosities which we all feed upon like a delicious poison, that when in later years German Nationalists condemned him for not having written war-songs, and taken a leading part in the popular uprising against Napoleon and the French, he calmly replied:

"In all my poetry I have never shammed (*habe nie affectiert*). What I have not lived through, what has not touched me to the quick, I have never uttered in verse or prose. I made love-songs only when I was in love. How could I have written songs of hate without hatred? And between ourselves, I didn't hate the French, though I thanked God when we got rid of them. How could I, to whom civilization and barbarism are the only two differences of importance, hate a nation which is one of the most civilized on earth, and to which I owe so great a part of my own mental development?

"In general," he continued, says Eckermann, to whom he was speaking in March, 1830, "national animosity is a peculiar thing. In the lowest degrees of civilization it is always strongest and most violent. But there is a point where it vanishes—where we can stand, as it were, above the nations, and we feel the happiness or misery of a neighbouring people as though it were our own. That degree of civilization was suited to my nature, and I had become firmly established in it long before I reached my sixtieth year."

To stand as it were above the nations and feel the happiness or misery of a neighbouring people as though it were our own—that is a position more worthy of the Superman than spreading plains and valleys with a top-dressing of dead bodies, for which a victorious nation will erect exultant columns and other memorials of glory.

SCENE XIII

"THE PILGRIM OF ETERNITY"

How, being at Newstead Abbey, I felt the presence of Byron, whose heroic end I witnessed on my way through Ætolia

ON July the 16th, 1931, among the crowd at Newstead Abbey, I met Venizelos for the third or fourth time in his career. There he stood in a gay little pavilion, over which the Greek flag waved in the sunshine and breeze. As Prime Minister of the Greek Republic, he had generously come over to read a speech in recently acquired English to a variegated audience of Greeks and English people gathered in that most beautiful of English parks. He was the guest of the City of Nottingham, to which the Abbey and park had been presented by the owner and a wealthy citizen in combination. He had lunched with the Lord Mayor in the new Council House; tea in silver teapots awaited him in the long dining-hall of the historic Abbey; and he was dressed in the most rigorous fashion of the English gentleman—shining top-hat, long black coat, grey trousers with black stripes, everything irreproachable. With his fine pale face, short white hair, short white beard, spectacles, and benevolent expression, he looked the very model of a highly educated, elderly statesman, as indeed he was. One of the most influential personalities in this century's European history, he would have passed for an associate of Wellington, Melbourne, Sir John Russell, or Gladstone in youth.

I had met him before in crises of the Balkan League, which he and James Bourchier contrived to create as by miracle; and again during his contest with King Constantine of Greece when we first landed at Salonika in 1915; but my mind went back to a very different scene when I was probably with him eighteen years before that. After the disastrous war of 1897, when the Turks had driven the undisciplined Greek armies out of Thessaly and Epīrus, and might easily have occupied Athens herself if the Powers had not intervened, I was ordered to Crete by Massingham, the famous editor of the *Daily Chronicle*, who stood passionately on the Greek side. The rising of Cretans against their prolonged oppression by the Turks had given occasion for the recent war on the mainland, because a Greek battalion under Colonel Vassos had come to assist the rebels. The rebellion was still simmering. All the Powers except Germany had sent out mixed naval and military detachments, nominally to support Turkish sovereignty, really to watch lest one of them should grab the fine harbour of Suda Bay, where some British warships among others were lying to protect two or three little Turkish ships, which looked as though they were built about the time when our grandfathers first heard with bewilderment that iron ships could float.

Steaming leisurely along the northern side of the island, we touched at Candia, and I walked over the hill of Gnossos, without knowing what wealth of early history lay hidden under the mounds, only waiting for Arthur Evans to discover it. At Canéa, just on the highest point of the old fortifications, the flags of the Powers fluttered round the Sultan's flag like ornaments on a birthday cake for a good child. They looked over a chaos of burnt and ruined streets, houses, and shops which had been the Christian quarter of the town. The cathedral stood intact, and as a place of refuge was crammed with furniture, bedding, pots, pans and babies saved from the Turks and the fire. At the farther end of the quay, French and Armenian enterprise had erected a flimsy little café, called with some justice "*Au Concert Européen*". For there the French and Russians sat at the tables drinking international healths till the world went round, and concluding commercial arrangements with feminine apparitions who sat in the corners and were wonderful linguists. They had undergone strange and varied fortunes. Originally the apparitions had counted but three, until the economic law of supply and demand stepped in to curtail monopoly, and one afternoon a steamer hailing from Smyrna brought fifteen or twenty more similar imports. They tried to land at Candia and at Retimo, but the Turkish Custom-house authorities refused them as contraband, and, with shame and defiant tears, they steamed on to Canéa, only to be encountered with a like refusal by Turkish austerity. But it so happened that an Italian officer stood watching, and calling upon two Italian sections, he brought his men at the double along the quay to the rescue of womanhood in distress. With fixed bayonets in two lines they stood drawn up on each side of the gangway, and between the lines the dainty shoes and chiffons and wayworn faces were escorted into the town in grateful security, to the eternal glory of the Powers and the European Concert.

"THE PILGRIM OF ETERNITY"

One afternoon I left the city gate which was guarded by a grimy Turk and a Seaforth Highlander in queer combination, and climbed cautiously among rocks to elude the French who were watching the " neutral zone ", in which one may be shot at by both sides indifferently. I arrived by happy instinct at the very headquarters of the rebels, over which the Greek flag flew. By shouting the Greek words for *Daily Chronicle*, I secured a rapturous welcome, and, crowding round me, the rebels conducted me to a mouldering cottage where they set me on a table, while three of their captains sat on a bed, and the house was soon crowded with Cretans—fine-featured men, all wearing the black Cretan handkerchief twisted round their heads, and black cotton trousers like undivided bags with the feet thrust through separately at one end. All were armed with rifles, revolvers, and sheathed Cretan knives, eighteen inches long. With the help of an interpreter, I accomplished my mission of finding out what the rebels demanded—namely, the withdrawal of the Turkish troops from the island, and union with Greece. Both these demands were ultimately won, chiefly, one is proud to remember, by British action. But the point that I recalled that day at Newstead was that almost certainly one of those captains seated on the cottage bed was Venizelos, then an unknown Cretan patriot, in rags and going in daily danger of execution. Now as a model European statesman, famous throughout the world, and Prime Minister of Greece, he was reading a speech in English to the Lord Mayor and Corporation of Nottingham.

From my seat in front of the pavilion where the rebel turned statesman was speaking, I could look up sideways to a window high upon the sham-Gothic front of the building attached to the old but poorly constructed Augustinian Abbey. It was the window of Byron's bedroom, where his canopied bed still stands, surrounded by the furniture he actually used, including a looking-glass, now a little grey with age, that had once so often reflected the proud but irresistible young face, and the head fit for the sculpture of Pheidias, as Venizelos had just told us. From that window, in boyhood and youth, Byron had looked over the garden lawns to a lake drained by an artificial cascade into the monastic fish-ponds below, and beyond the lake and ponds to part of the vast domain which was all his own. With its gardens, wastes, and relics of old Sherwood Forest, his domain was one of the loveliest estates in all England. In the midst of its beauty, haunted by memories of medieval monks and the merry Robin Hood of our ballads, the boy grew up into that wayward, passionate, high-hearted, imaginative being whom all the civilized world was soon to know, vituperate, and adore.

Looking into that mirror and over the expanse of garden or forest which he owned was one whose youth was very different from the youth of Venizelos, the Cretan bandit. Byron enjoyed all such advantages as a wealthy Englishman may purchase at a public school and a famous University. He was never short of food and drink. His reckless high spirits, physical energy, and the vital passion of sex attracted the youths and women who rejoiced in youthful excess and immoderate pleasures. His rush of wit and power of phrase made him famous even before he won his fame. At times in debt, and then again endowed with riches beyond the dreams of any poet; a courted and luxurious traveller, visit-

"THE PILGRIM OF ETERNITY"

ing Europe, even in its wildest and least known regions; and a member of the House of Lords by family inheritance, he had become conspicuous for his genius and his fascinating errors even before *Childe Harold* made him famous at twenty-three. It is significant of the depth of his nature and the gallant defiance of his spirit that, just before *Childe Harold* was published, he made his great speech in the House of Lords in defence of the frame-breakers of Nottingham. It was a speech that, for its eloquence and passionate sympathy with the working people, even the Labour Lords in the present House might envy and imitate, appearing as they do like shipwrecked sailors scattered upon a vasty deep.

The speech was made in February, 1812, and, though it is easily accessible in Moore's *Life of Byron*, its temper may here be shown in a few extracted sentences, all the more that they apply with singular exactness to our present discontents:

> "When we are told", he said, speaking of the Nottingham machine-breakers, "that these men are leagued together, not only for the destruction of their own comfort, but of their very means of subsistence, can we forget that it is the bitter policy, the destructive warfare, of the last eighteen years which has destroyed their comfort, your comfort, all men's comfort;—that policy which, originating with 'great statesmen now no more', has survived the dead to become a curse on the living, unto the third and fourth generation!
>
> "Can you wonder that, in times like these, when bankruptcy, convicted fraud and imputed felony are found in a station not far beneath that of your Lordships, the lowest, though once most useful, portion of the people, should forget their duty in their distresses, and become only less guilty than one of their representatives? But while the exalted offender can find means to baffle the law, new capital punishments must be devised, new snares

of death must be spread for the wretched mechanic who is famished into guilt.

"I have traversed the seat of war in the Peninsula; I have been in some of the most oppressed provinces of Turkey; but never, under the most despotic of infidel governments, did I behold such squalid wretchedness as I have seen since my return, in the very heart of a Christian country.

"And what are your remedies? After months of inaction, and months of action worse than inactivity, at length comes forth the grand specific, the never-failing nostrum of all state physicians from the days of Draco to the present time. After feeling the pulse and shaking the head over the patient, prescribing the usual course of warm water and bleeding—the warm water of your mawkish police, and the lancets of your military—these convulsions must terminate in death, the sure consummation of the prescriptions of all political Sangrados."

In this as in his other few speeches (for instance in his plea for the Irish Catholics) Byron was years before his time. All great men are before their time, for they have to create the time in which their influence will come to fruit. One can easily see that if Byron had remained in politics, he would have anticipated the Radicals of last century and the Socialists of our own. It might well have been so if he had not turned from the rhetoric of eloquence to the rhetoric of verse. And, after all, it was by verse that he won his immense influence in all civilized countries. England has produced many great poets —more, I suppose, than any country but Athens— and yet the majority of English people dislike verse, and regard poets with amused or contemptuous indifference. But Byron's early works were passionately absorbed by thousands who had despised verse before. What was a still rarer achievement, he created a new and infectious mood—the Byronic mood—and the young, who alone are open to moods, adopted it with the eagerness of poetic despair. To them that proud, self-conscious melancholy was fresh and irresistibly alluring. Its strangeness harmonized with the dawning romanticism of the time, and the sadness of its disenchantment was the natural result of a prolonged and terrible war. Goethe, who followed Byron's career with increasing admiration, on the appearance of *Manfred* wrote, " In this tragedy we find the quintessence of the most astonishing genius —born to be its own tormentor." Coming from Goethe, who himself had created a similar mood by his *Sorrows of Young Werther* and his early scheme of *Faust*, that judgment is remarkable for its tribute and its insight. All the youths of the world, if not born to be their own tormentors, became so.

If *The Giaour, The Corsair, Lara, The Siege of Corinth, Parisina, The Bride of Abydos*, and *Manfred* were to appear in our own days, they would be laughed at as easy-going and immature rhetoric ; and yet how alluring to youth even of our own day is the thought of solitude among mountains and torrents, the scorn of mankind, the reproach of a cruel God, and the gloomy contemplation of an unappreciated self !

The descriptions of foreign parts have secured for *Childe Harold* an immortality in guide-books, but apart from guide-books how many of the lines have passed into the common language of mankind !

" Hereditary bondsmen ! know ye not
Who would be free themselves must strike the blow ? "

" Can tyrants but by tyrants conquer'd be,
And Freedom find no champion and no child ? "

" Yet, Freedom ! yet thy banner, torn, but flying,
Streams like the thunder-storm *against* the wind."

"THE PILGRIM OF ETERNITY"

"The Niobe of nations ! there she stands,
Childless and crownless, in her voiceless woe."

"Butchered to make a Roman holiday."

Childe Harold was finished just before Byron was thirty, and not till it was finished did he enter upon the true sphere of his genius. He became the greatest satiric poet in our language, with the possible exception of Pope, whom he admired deservedly for the perfection of his satiric art. *Beppo* is exquisite because, though it says nothing in particular, it says it so very well. But *Don Juan* is supreme. It has more laughter, more good humour than Pope, and the métre is more charming, more capable of variety and of that " sudden glory " which the surprise of laughter sheds. Like *Childe Harold*, the stanzas of *Don Juan* abound with lines that have become commonplaces of quotation, invaluable to politicians :

"It opened half the turnpike-gates to heaven."

"Man, being reasonable, must get drunk ;
The best of life is but intoxication."

"And Haidée being devout as well as fair,
Had doubtless heard about the Stygian river,
And hell and purgatory—but forgot
Just in the very crisis she should not."

"You're wrong.—He was the mildest manner'd man
That ever scuttled ship or cut a throat."

There are many others in that exquisite scene of Juan and Haidée alone upon the seashore. Or take the still more familiar quotation from the scene with Julia in Canto I :

"A little still she strove, and much repented,
And whispering ' I will ne'er consent '—consented."

Or from the same beautiful scene, as an instance of consummate ease and " sudden glory " (in the fifth line), take the stanza cxiii :

> " The sun set, and up rose the yellow moon ;
> The devil's in the moon for mischief ; they
> Who call'd her chaste, methinks, began too soon
> Their nomenclature ; there is not a day,
> The longest, not the twenty-first of June,
> Sees half the business in a wicked way
> On which three single hours of moonshine smile—
> And then she looks so modest all the while."

And, for satire upon the mutability of things and the absurdity of war, read Canto XI, stanza lxxxii :

> " I have seen Napoleon, who seem'd quite a Jupiter,
> Shrink to a Saturn. I have seen a Duke
> (No matter which) turn politician stupider,
> If that can well be, than his wooden look.
> But it is time that I should hoist my " blue Peter ",
> And sail for a new theme :—I have seen and shook
> To see it—the king hiss'd, and then carest ;
> But don't pretend to settle which was best."

And Canto VIII, stanza xiii :

> " There the still varying pangs, which multiply
> Until their very number makes men hard
> By the infinities of agony,
> Which meet the gaze, whate'er it may regard—
> The groan, the roll in dust, the all-white eye
> Turn'd back within its socket—these reward
> Your rank and file by thousands, while the rest
> May win perhaps a riband at the breast ! "

After reading Canto I, Shelley wrote, " Every word has the stamp of immortality. It is something wholly new and relative to the age, yet surpassingly beautiful." Goethe welcomed *Don Juan* as a new form of comic art such as no German could ever hope to rival. And Walter Scott, in his generous lament over " that mighty genius which walked amongst men as something superior to mortality ", added that the poet "appears to have thrown off the verses of *Don Juan* with an effort as spontaneous as that of a tree resigning its leaves to the wind".

One would think so, to judge from the consummate ease with which the stanzas run, line following line, rapid, definite, inevitable as the minutes of the clock. Indeed, Shelley and other friends who were with him at Pisa and elsewhere evidently believed that Byron wrote with great rapidity and assurance. One cannot doubt that they were right, though he made plentiful corrections. Shelley speaks of him as "cheerful, frank, and witty. His most serious conversation", he said, "is a sort of intoxication." That extraordinary facility of wit and expression, the rush of inborn vitality, is seen equally in his letters. That ardent and spontaneous vitality was the secret of his genius and fame.

And yet, in spite of all appearances, Byron found writing a hard matter. When Moore wrote of his own trouble in writing that "he felt about his art as the French husband did when he found a man making love to his (the Frenchman's) wife: 'Comment, Monsieur—sans y être obligé!'" Byron replied:

> "I feel exactly as you do about our 'art', but it comes over me in a kind of rage every now and then, like . . ., and then if I don't write to empty my mind, I go mad.—I feel it as a torture which I must get rid of, but never as a pleasure. On the contrary, I think composition a great pain." (From Ravenna, 1821.)

Those may seem strange words, coming from one whose work at its best appears the triumph of ease, and at its worst a slovenly exuberance! But, though he could not escape the torment of that conscience which acts as a gadfly upon writers, he was never the literary man complete, and most writers only bored him. With the exception, indeed, of Shelley, of whom he wrote, " Of all men Shelley thought highest of my talents—and, perhaps, of my disposition " (1823).

From the first he always felt the longing for action. In his Diary of 1813 we find the note : " I think the preference of writers to agents—the mighty stir about scribbling and scribes—a sign of effeminacy, degeneracy and weakness." Writing to Moore in the following year, he says, " Half of these Scotch and Lake troubadours are spoilt by living in little circles and petty societies." And, again to Moore, in 1817 : " I do not think literature was my profession." The Contessa Guiccioli, who, by attaching him so rigidly to herself, may be said to have rescued him from his brief period of promiscuous abandonment, tells us that he frequently said to her, " A man ought to do something more for society than write verses." In *Beppo* we read, " One hates an author that's all author." And from Venice, writing to Moore in 1816, and telling of his endeavour to learn the Armenian language, he said :

> " I found that my mind wanted something craggy to break upon ; and this—as the most difficult thing I could discover here for an amusement—I have chosen to torture me into attention."

It was in his nature to want something craggy for his mind to break upon, and it was only in action that he could find it. As though to anticipate Garibaldi, he had tried to organize rebellion among the Italian Carbonari. The news of the increasing and partly successful movement in the Morea and other parts of Greece to shake off the intolerable oppression of the Turkish conquerors recalled to him the happy days of his early visit to the beautiful and historic land. His poems had then created that ardent sympathy with the Greek people which was now expressed in a body of English Philhellenes, anxious to give help even by arms. But apart from his genuine devotion to the cause of freedom and his memories of the incalculable service of ancient Greece to mankind, he recognized an opportunity for his own personal deliverance.

He was only thirty-five, but he saw himself ageing. His misuse of women, wine, and spirits had been for his health excessive, though probably it was not above the average of his time. But even more injurious to health had been his pernicious diet adopted in the hope of keeping his figure slim. The stoutest constitutions must quail under courses of vinegar, cucumbers, and magnesia. He became alternately too pale and too red, too fat and too flabby. He was now subject to " seizures " and fits of uncontrollable rage, stamping, grinding his teeth, and pouring out streams of violent abuse. His dress had become ridiculous, and visitors stared at him as at a relic of fame outlived. The blaze of glory is all very well, but it is a bonfire that needs repeated feeding.

And how depressing his surroundings had become! There was Shelley's widow, certainly no good friend; Claire Clairmont, who had pursued him passionately till she became mother of his daughter; there was Lady Blessington, a disappointed lion-hunter; Count d'Orsay, the fop; Trelawny, the model *poseur*; Leigh Hunt, the casual sponge; Mrs. Leigh Hunt, the slatternly spendthrift, and her six slovenly children, with another coming; there were the dogs, the monkeys, the parrot. Worse than all, there was the Contessa Guiccioli, rather dull, rather plain by now, whom he had taken on as a temporary amusement and was forced to retain, much as a ship's captain must retain a barnacle that has eaten into the hull and been broken short, fixed there for life. What a set for the poetic hero of Europe, once so adored!

From the entanglements of drooping age, withering fame, and such a lot of men, women, and animals, nothing but action could save him, perhaps nothing but war. To lead in war alone would clear the mouldering scene and restore his repute from the abyss of dingy failure. Like another poet, whose short-lived youth was almost equally attractive, Byron might cry, " Now, God be thanked Who has matched us with His hour." He might be glad to leave:

> " Glad from a world grown old and cold and weary,
> Leave the sick hearts that honour could not move,
> And half-men, and their dirty songs and dreary,
> And all the little emptiness of love."

One can well imagine Byron repeating with sympathy—" and all the little emptiness of love ". Of whom would he think—of Mary, or Augusta, or Caroline, or Annabella, or Claire, or the Contessa, or how many besides? Chiefly the Contessa, one would suppose, for she was of the present, and the others were transfigured by time.

I have often entered or left or crossed the Gulf of Corinth at its mouth between Patras and Missolonghi, and never without the thought of Byron. Sixty or seventy years ago Matthew Arnold said the English were beginning to forget him, but I suppose every Englishman still thinks of him as the ship passes the lagoon and fatal marshes of Missolonghi. To myself the vision of his end came most clearly when, as I was riding down from Arta during the Greco-Turkish War of 1897 to reach the telegraph station at Patras, I came nearest to the wretched village but could not turn aside since it lay out of my course to the ferry-boat. As it was, the ride on a crawling horse through the little-known district of Ætolia had taken me three days. On his first happy journey in Greece, Byron himself had passed along this route. It is a strange and haunted land, for the ancient gods came there early and left it late, as though reserving it as a retreat for their discredited old age. Nourished by long lakes and brimming water-courses, which flow through forests of ilex and the dark Valona oak, it is different in character from the rest of Greece, and in old times the Greek inhabitants there spoke dialects almost as rude as barbaric tongues. On the track I passed the solid ruins of Stratos, where a detachment of Athenians who had heard Pericles and watched the Parthenon building were surrounded by the semi-barbarians and destroyed. And I passed the white torrent of the Achelous (Aspropotamo), and Agrinion, the market town of Missolonghi, and Kalydon to which Atalanta, the swift runner, came from Arcadia northward, " a blast of the envy of God ". But, haunted as was the road by visions of ancient heroes and death, Missolonghi lay amid the marshes on my right, and from it arose a grander and more terrible vision.

Among the muddy flats, the natural homes of the malarial fly, and a shallow lagoon which no tide ever cleanses, I could see the squalid village which the western Greeks had chosen as a kind of headquarters for their rebellion, in the vain hope that it might command the entrance of the Gulf, and that the marshes would make it inaccessible. There, as in a vision of the past, I saw a ramshackle cottage, which a few men in the cellar could shake in sport like an earthquake; so frail that it has since been cleared away, and the space put to the filthy use that all open spaces are put to in the Balkans. I saw rain falling incessantly, and the village lanes knee-deep in slush, but at intervals low-lying, rocky Ithaca was just visible across thirty miles of open sea, and next to Ithaca the great dome of Cephallonia, where Byron had spent his last few happy weeks before Mavrocordato urged him to come over to the pestilent lagoon, with the vague hope of attacking Lepanto on the opposite coast of the Gulf.

In an upper room of that ramshackle house the splendid and adored hero of Newstead, of London, and all Europe was lying in the extreme misery of malarial fever, acting upon a corrupted and weakened frame. He lay almost alone. Trelawny, the self-centred imposter, and Colonel Leicester Spencer, doctrinaire Benthamite and helpless literary man, had both left him; no great loss certainly, but still, in danger and solitude, one may regret the departure even of fools. A few personal attendants remained —William Fletcher, Tita Falciere, and one or two besides his two main doctors, Julius Millingen, a young Scottish student, and Francesco Bruno, whose only remedy was to bleed the patient and bleed again, no matter how strongly Byron objected. And there was Count Pietro Gamba, young, enthusiastic, devoted, and incapable, and William Parry, who had been sent out by the London Philhellenes as an expert in gunnery, of which he knew nothing. Though given to drink, and rough in manner, Parry was devoted in service and a comfortable contrast to the fools. Among this little assembly of friends, ill-assorted but for their honourable affection for an heroic nature, the great satirist, so favoured by fortune, genius, and fame, lay dying in a dirty house —dying at thirty-six, and in a hopeless cause.

He had long known the cause was hopeless. He had no belief in the Greeks, for they had been too long enslaved to be capable of heroic and combined effort. Like all Greeks, even in ancient times, they were better in word than in deed, and their patriotism was fissiparous as a jellyfish. Soon after he first began to know them, Byron wrote, " I like the Greeks, who are plausible rascals, with all the Turkish vices without their courage." " They are such barbarians ", he had written lately from Cephallonia, " that if I had the government of them, I would pave these very roads with them." He found himself surrounded with mutinous and murderous irregulars, never to be trusted, and always clamouring for money and food. His chosen bodyguard of five hundred Suliotes mutinied and deserted him. The various clans and parties hated each other more than they hated the Turks. On Easter Sunday, April the 18th, the day before he died, he said to Dr. Millingen : " Your efforts to preserve my life will be in vain. Die I must ; I feel it. Its loss I do not lament ; for to terminate my wearisome existence I came to Greece. My wealth, my abilities, I devoted to her cause. Well, there is my life to her." He could not know that by heroic action in a cause which he knew to be hopeless, he was establishing that very cause for which he died.

On the Thursday before that Easter Sunday, William Parry, in a full and apparently true account of what Byron then said, tells us he spoke of strange feelings and gloomy thoughts, mentioning even an idea of going to America. Then he added a strange confession :

"THE PILGRIM OF ETERNITY"

"When I left Italy I had time on board the brig to give full scope to memory and reflexion. It was then I came to that resolution I have already informed you of. I am convinced of the happiness of domestic life. No man on earth respects a virtuous woman more than I do, and the prospect of retirement in England with my wife and Ada gives me an idea of happiness I have never experienced before. Retirement will be everything for me, for heretofore my life has been like the ocean in a storm."

Still later, on Easter Sunday evening, he called again on the child he had never seen, on his sister Augusta, and even on his wife :

"Oh, my poor dear child ! My dear Ada ! My God ! could I but have seen her ! Give her my blessing, and my dear sister Augusta and her children—and you will go to Lady Byron, and say—tell her everything—you are friends with her."

That was the report of his faithful servant Fletcher, who adds : "His Lordship appeared to be greatly affected at this moment", and, after some indistinct muttering, Byron said, "Fletcher, now if you do not execute every order which I have given you, I will torment you hereafter, if possible." But Fletcher protested he had not understood, and Byron could only reply, "Oh, my God ! Then all is lost, for it is now too late "; and then again, "My wife ! my child ! my sister !—you know all—you must say all—you know my wishes ! " He also said, "I am more fit to die than people think ", but of his few last words, spoken in delirium, when often the real self awakes and reveals itself, I like best to remember his cry, shouted, as Parry says, in English and Italian on the last evening of his life : " Forward ! Forward ! Courage—follow my example—don't be afraid."

"THE PILGRIM OF ETERNITY"

So on Monday evening, April the 19th, 1824, at six-fifteen that noble spirit vanished from the world. A terrific storm raged over the mouth of the Gulf, and hearing the roar of thunder, the armed men and the shepherds, cowering in the filthy streets, said to each other, "The great man is dead."

As my Greek pony plodded along the road between Agrinion and the coast, and I looked across the marshes to Missolonghi on my right hand, I witnessed again the departure of that courageous and exuberant soul. I heard again the words, "Forward! Forward! Follow my example! Don't be afraid!" And I was glad to think that, within my narrow limits, I had followed his example, and shared in his conflict for freedom against the same oppressor of the same people he had sacrificed himself to save. And when I reflected that, but for him, though at the time he failed, the Turk would still have remained for many years supreme over the land of Greece, I was content to honour the man who had done this, and besides had shaken the self-complacent presumption of Church and Society in our own country. As to his weakness, his evil behaviour, I would leave, with meekness, his sins to the literary scavengers, who, no doubt, have grubbed a lot of lucrative leavings out of the refuse.

SCENE XIV

"DAILY SELF-SURPAST"

How, while exposing the slave-trade in Angola, I witnessed Livingstone's noblest sacrifice

ON the 10th of June, 1905, I put in for a day at the ancient port of Loanda, the capital city of Portuguese Angola. It stands about two-hundred-and-fifty miles south of the Congo's mouth, and is the only place worth calling a city upon the west coast of Africa between Tangiers and Capetown. I was in one of the Portuguese ships that ran about twice a month carrying mails, passengers, general cargo, and slaves. Our vessel having picked up consignments of slaves at the more southern ports of Benguella and Novo Rodondo, was now waiting at Loanda for a final consignment of forty-two, making up the full cargo of two-hundred-and-seventy-two head.. Of these, however, two died on the eight days' voyage, so that at San Thomé we landed two-hundred-and-seventy men and women in prime condition, not counting the babies, who went free as possible investments for future interest. Or perhaps only babies were taken, still pinkish and crinkled from the womb, to maintain the health of the milch mothers ; for I noticed that no young children, boys or girls, were brought away with their parents. One man tried to escape by swimming ashore off Ambriz, but was soon overtaken by a boat, beaten on the head by the oars, and brought back to be " tamed ".

If the word " slaves " sounds harsh, by all means let us use the polite and legal terms " serviçaes " or " contrahidos " ; let us call them " contract labourers " or " workers under bond ". It made not the smallest difference what word was used. These African men and women had been bought and sold for money ; they had been forced away from their homes in the interior ; had been marched down to the coast in gangs, shackled up at night ; had been assigned at Benguella, Novo Rodondo, and Loanda to one purchasing plantation or another, and were now on the voyage to one of the islands, San Thomé or Principe, in the Gulf of Guinea, to work the cocoa plantations till they died. They had not the smallest hope of return, and they never did return. If that is not the very definition of slavery, what more fiendish title can we invent ? But if it soothes humanitarian feelings to call slaves " contract labourers ", let it be so. One would always like to avoid hurting the sensibilities of tender-hearted manufacturers and the Diplomatic Services. So I use the word " slaves " only for brevity and truth.

Since I was first in Loanda, during the previous winter of 1904, I had penetrated some five hundred miles into the interior of the Angola province, covering about one thousand miles or rather more during about seven months of wandering on both sides of my route. Starting from Benguella in an ox-wagon I had crossed the barren and mountainous region that fringes the coast as far south as Mossamedes, and so reached the high forest plateau that pours down the tributaries of the Congo on the north side, and of the Zambesi on the south. Not that the water

"DAILY SELF-SURPAST"

on either side necessarily joins one or other of those great rivers. The Cuanza, for instance, though flowing north, emerges into the ocean south of Loanda ; and the Okavango, whose fairy-like source I found on the southern side of the main watershed, after wriggling like a snake for hundreds of miles, loses itself at last in Livingstone's Lake N'gami, discovered by him in August, 1849.

As I passed along that broad watershed of Central Africa, continuing my way on foot with a few carriers, I found myself in the heart of the Portuguese slave-preserve. It is inhabited by various Bantu tribes in villages stockaded against lions and leopards. There are the Bihéans, or Ovimbundu, for the most part traders and carriers, speaking Umbundu, which is useful as far as the centre of the continent, where it meets Swaheli, used by the Arab traders. There are the Luimbi, the Luvale, the Luchazi, and the Chibokwe, who are the cleverest and most artistic of the tribes, though they are reputed the most savage. They file their teeth into points and, though no longer cannibal, are believed to eat human beings who have met violent death. Each kraal among the various tribes had its chief or headman, privileged to live in a finer hut, to decide disputes, and to afford a larger number of wives, according to wealth, as is customary in all countries. While I was in the country there were no railroads and no open roads, but here and there an ox-track through the forest, and always paths leading from kraal to kraal, by which communication could be maintained from one side of the continent to the other. But the paths were so narrow and hollowed out by rains that I found walking along them difficult, unless I adopted the native manner of bringing one foot round in front of the other at each step, like a chimpanzee or gorilla.

All the plantations in Angola, whether of coffee or sugar-cane (for rum), were worked by slaves, and I was told of an enterprising speculator at Mossamedes who kept a stock-raising establishment for the production of slaves to meet the market. But domestic and plantation slavery was so universal in most parts of Africa that my attention was chiefly given to export slavery from the mainland province to the two islands close to the Equator on the Gulf of Guinea. This traffic was very profitable for everyone concerned, except the slaves. They were obtained very cheap in the interior by organized raids or tribal wars, for breaches of ancestral custom or Portuguese laws, or on charges of witchcraft, to pay family debts, by purchase from uncles (who have control over a sister's offspring), or by mere exchange, as of an old brass-studded flintlock for a healthy woman.

At various points of the route into the interior I met an owner leading along a slave in chains for sale. But as a rule the slaves were collected till a gang of about thirty or forty was assembled, and then the lot were marched off in single file by stages to the coast. The gangs were easily distinguished from trading carriers because they were guarded by three or four half-bred Portuguese armed with guns, and they carried no loads on their heads beyond a few little rags of their own and the wooden shackles with which their hands or feet or both were pinned together at night. Some of the shackles that I found hanging on the trees for future use were long enough to pin the feet of two men or women together side by side. But the majority of the shackles were just conveniently sized for the hands or feet of a single slave, and they were used every night, at all events till the long stretch of deserted forest called the Hungry Country was passed. I found by far the largest number of shackles hanging on the trees or lying on the path upon the last stages of the Hungry Country coming west before the Cuanza was reached. For after that point the drivers knew the slaves would have no hope of escape and return, as the uninhabited desert extends for five or six days' march, and there is nothing to eat on the way. For the same reason that part of the route was most thickly strewn with the skeletons of slaves who had fallen on the march or been murdered there because they could not keep up with the gang. A worn-out slave was killed by a blow from an axe at the base of the skull, and owing to a queer conception of property, slaves were not buried, though carriers were.

After descending the paths down the last hill to the coast, worn white by the passage of slaves for generations, the gang sometimes shed a few of its members in the little town of Katumbella. I stayed there for some days, and as I passed among the scattered houses in the evening I would hear the blows of the palmatoria (a wooden slat specially designed to give as much pain as possible to the open palm) and the still more cruel blows of the *chicotte*, a riding whip of hide or rubber. With the blows came the screams of tortured slaves being " tamed " or reduced to civilization. But a Dutch trader in the town told me that he never wasted much time over the taming process. He gave the slave a good flogging, and, if that did not avail, he sent him straight on to Benguella, where he could depend on getting the fair price of sixteen pounds for him.

Benguella was at that time the chief slave-market for the cocoa islands, and the gangs, having been marched along the flat piece of coast from Katumbella, were herded into large yards till the day before the fortnightly ship arrived. They were then ranged up before the Governmental Curador, who asked them whether they were willing to go as labourers to San Thomé. As a rule no answer was given, and in no case was the slightest notice taken of an answer. Each was given a disc with a number and the name of the agent who had secured him, and a tin cylinder containing his name and the date and place of origin. By diplomatic hypocrisy this process was called " redeeming " the slave and converting him into a " contracted labourer ". All the slaves were then decked out with brilliant coloured cloths, blankets and caps, and herded aboard the vessel which in eight days was to land them in San Thomé, there to be allotted to the plantations which had requisitioned for them. In one or other of the two islands they were doomed to live as slaves for the rest of their lives. When I was there no one had ever returned. For which reason the natives called the voyage Okalunga, or the Abyss.

As to profit, the licensed agents at Benguella would give from sixteen pounds to eighteen pounds at the port, and a planter on the islands would give from twenty-six pounds to thirty pounds for any man or woman delivered in good condition. But the apparent profit was not net. What with licence, stamp duty, and landing charges, the Government took about thirty shillings, and the steamboat company charged two pounds per head for the voyage. The Curador had to get something, the ship's captain got four shillings per head for every slave safely landed, and

"DAILY SELF-SURPAST"

the ship's doctor got two shillings for maintaining the health of the slaves on the voyage, during which an average of only two per cent died. Still, when all deductions were made the agents' profit on the two-hundred-and-seventy men and women slaves safely landed from my ship, for instance, secured them a considerable income, even as slave-trading went. Dutch traders told me the agents cleared about four pounds a head of the livestock when the whole transaction was completed.

For nearly three weeks I stayed in Benguella, being offered lodging with one of the Dutch traders, and watched the stages in the whole process of " redemption " and embarkation. Bunyan's precept " To live each day as 'twere your last " may be good in theology, but it brings no reassuring comfort in daily life, and warnings of my danger at the hands of the Portuguese slave-traders came to me from café gossip, the British engineers working upon the beginnings of the first railway, the officials of the telegraph office, and the Dutch traders. Two or three of the British, including a man named Rawstorne, who had known me in Ladysmith, made themselves into a kind of bodyguard, accompanying me everywhere I went at night, without telling me of their purpose. But nothing unusual happened till the night before the Portuguese ship was starting. Then I was seized with the common symptoms of violent poisoning, and in the morning Rawstorne carried me down to the pier bluish, cold, and repeatedly fainting. Doctors have told me the poison was probably aconite, but its nature was unimportant. No one was surprised at my condition, for all the Portuguese and the British were quite aware that the object of my journey was to expose the suspected abomination of the slave-

"DAILY SELF-SURPAST"

trade in the Portuguese provinces. Large wealth for the Government and the traders was involved, and what was the life of one unknown traveller in comparison? Skin for skin, yea all that a man hath will be given for a comfortable income. There were recent instances of honourable Portuguese who had set out for Portugal to expose the infamy, but had never arrived.

When we came to anchor in Loanda on the 10th of June, 1905, I knew that I must still spend about three weeks in visiting the cocoa plantations on the islands of San Thomé and Principe. Then only sixteen days to Lisbon. Then a British ship, and only four or five days to Liverpool and home! From Loanda I could fairly expect to be home by July the 20th. Home, friends, decent meals, a real bed, and security! It was one of the radiant moments of life.

I looked down upon the fo'c'sle of the steamer and saw the two-hundred-and-seventy slaves now collected to their full number. They were lying about the deck in stupefied indifference or despair. No going home for them; no security, no decent meals or beds, no expectant friends, nothing but ceaseless toil in a steamy atmosphere like a hothouse—ceaseless toil day after day till death ended it and their bodies were flung away into the forest. It was a different fate from mine, and as I turned I found standing close beside me the shrivelled and worn figure of a man with something striking about his face and bearing, though he was obviously in the extreme stage of fever and tropical disease.

There was no mistaking that famous and noble ghost. I knew that fifty-one years before he himself had emerged at Loanda from the interior. And after

"DAILY SELF-SURPAST"

what a journey! I suppose the greatest journey of exploration ever accomplished in the history of man, unless Marco Polo's journey equalled it. He had left Capetown in June, 1852, and he reached Loanda in May, 1854, having in two years traversed about three thousand miles of almost unknown country in the south and centre of Africa. Upon that uncharted course he had been confronted by all the perils of savages, wild beasts, and disease. He had passed among tribes whose method with enemies was to hew them in pieces and fling the limbs to the crocodiles in the rivers. He had travelled by ox-wagon, by riding-ox, and on foot, and those who have known what long marching is in Central Africa know the anguish of feet festering with jiggers or inflamed by the bites of other poisonous insects. He had made his way among drenching rains and had waded through flooded swamps, soaked to the skin by day and night, with never a chance to dry. Various fevers had held him torpid for many days together, and dysentery had drained the blood of his body till he could hardly stand upright or sit the riding-ox. Most of his outfit was stolen early on the journey, and before he reached Loanda he had little but rags remaining. Yet he had mapped his route by the stars as he went along, and had traced the course of many unnamed rivers. His observations of wild beasts, birds, insects, and plants were so accurate that they hold to this day, and his knowledge of the native customs and laws laid the foundation of a modern science.

Travelling slowly northwards from the Cape, as he had travelled two or three years earlier, he had passed through Griqualand, Bechuanaland, and, skirting the Kalahari Desert, had entered the wide dis-

"DAILY SELF-SURPAST"

trict then called by the general name of Barotseland. It was partly inhabited by the tribe of Makololo, whose young chief, Sekelétu, became very friendly and accompanied Livingstone on a long journey about the unknown land, proceeding with him even as far as Naliele, which was nominally the chief village or town. But the main centre of Livingstone's life among the Makololo was again Linyanti, a largish place on the River Chobe, a tributary of the Zambesi. It enters that great river a few days' journey above the Victoria Falls, which Livingstone did not see or name on this occasion, though he heard much talk about it. He reached Linyanti in May, 1853, and he returned there in November in order to make it the starting-place for the final stage of his great journey.

His desire throughout had been to reach the sea at the centre of the west coast, and from Linyanti the nearest point was certainly Benguella. But to reach Benguella he would have to pass along the main route of the slave-traders, then, as it still was the main route when I passed along it fifty years later. When he was still at Linyanti, Livingstone had not realized the full horror of Portuguese slavery. But he knew already that a slave route was likely to be difficult and dangerous, the natives being aroused to suspicion and hostility towards any white or whitish man. In August, while still at Linyanti, he made a significant note in his Journal : " The slave-trade seems pushed into the very centre of the continent from both sides. It must be profitable." From the east coast it was always being pushed by the Arab traders, but from the west coast I can only suppose that it was being pushed back into the centre because British cruisers had been sent to Loanda to watch any possible export. The main export of slaves had originally run from Angola to Brazil or the Southern States of America. Their chief product was then coffee. I am not sure when the export to the Portuguese islands actually began, but almost certainly the export increased with the growing popularity of cocoa and chocolate in all civilized countries during the second half of the nineteenth century. At all events, upon his first great journey, Livingstone avoided the main slave route, and at Linyanti resolved to make for Loanda, though Benguella was the nearest point on the coast—about two-hundred-and-fifty miles nearer.

On my own journey along the great watershed of Angola it was always a matter of intense pleasure, as of a reflected glory, to remember that at some point of the way my own route must have crossed Livingstone's. I think the point was probably somewhere close to the Portuguese " Fort " still called Mashíko (or Maxico), just beyond which I camped for a time. Mashíko was a powerful and quarrelsome chief of a Barotse tribe, always at variance with Livingstone's Makololo, but at intervals amenable to Livingstone's personal power of persuasion and good sense. It was not impossible that the name of so conspicuous a man should become attached to a district and remain so for at least fifty years. It is true that the names of places in Central Africa are repeatedly shifting, owing to the cleanly habit of the natives to burn their huts and villages every few years, just as civilized nations ought to burn their slums. I have walked over the site of a town or village invariably marked large on every ancient and modern map, but have been unable to see or hear of any vestige to recall the memory of such a place. In Mashíko's

"DAILY SELF-SURPAST"

case, the building of a fort in the midst of the former chief's wide territory may have preserved his name.

The Makololo themselves were equally anxious with Livingstone to explore a possible trading route from Barotse to the coast. Accordingly twenty-seven chosen men were appointed to accompany him all the way. He calls the men Zambesians, and says only two of them were real Makololo, the rest coming from various neighbouring tribes. Being naturally afraid that, if Livingstone died on this new and most dangerous part of his journey, they would have trouble in returning through hostile tribes beyond the dominion of their chief Sekelétu, or in persuading the white people of South Africa that they had not purposely brought the great Doctor into peril, various pledges were arranged for the future, and a great volume of Livingstone's Journal was left, to be forwarded to his father-in-law Moffat in the south to prove that all was above suspicion. So at last, in November, 1853, the small party started in canoes down the winding and branching River Chobe, and Livingstone gives a full list of his stores. For defence and shooting for food he took three muskets, a rifle, and a double-barrelled smooth-bore, besides ammunition distributed for safety among the baggage. For food, to avoid heavy loads, he took only a few biscuits, a few pounds of tea and sugar, and twenty pounds of coffee, which, without milk or sugar, he found the most refreshing drink after fatigue and exposure to the sun. For clothing he took one small tin canister filled with shirting, trousers, and shoes for civilized life, if he should ever reach it, a bag for spare change, a box for medicines, another for books (a Nautical Almanack, Thomson's Logarithms, and a Bible). Another box contained a magic lantern, which he

"DAILY SELF-SURPAST"

found of great service in impressing the natives. The sextant, artificial horizon, thermometer and compasses were carried apart. He also had twenty pounds of beads for bargaining, a small gypsy tent to sleep in, a sheepskin mantle as a blanket, and a horse-rug as a bed. As he remarks himself, the outfit might seem spare, but he always found the art of travel consisted in taking as little baggage as possible; for failure chiefly lay in want of pluck or in carrying such a lot of things as to excite the cupidity of the tribes.

At the junction of the Chobe with the Zambesi (here called the Leeambye) he turned north up the main river till he passed Libonta, and reached the territory of the Chief Shinte. Here he left the canoes and set out upon a march inclining westward in the direction of Loanda. This was the most difficult part of all his journey. He entered the tropical forest where there was no track except the narrow paths leading from kraal to kraal blocked by dense growth on either side. Rain fell incessantly. His clothes went mouldy, and his tiny tent rotted. The wet was his chief enemy. As he wrote at the time, he did not care much for fatigue. Marching did not hurt him, but when stopped dead by pouring rain, fever laid hold on him and he had to lie dormant, soaked through in his worn-out tent.

Every other disaster that can befall the traveller in tropical Africa followed. The chiefs were rapacious and hostile. At one place the appointed guides refused to show the way unless paid extra in cloth on the spot. On reaching the wide territory of the Chibokwe, he had serious trouble with some of the tribes, and saved his little party from destruction only by arranging his Makololo so as to surround the excited and violent enemy, and showing himself in a stronger position even with only five guns. Then he told them he was quite ready to fight but they must strike the first blow. Once when the fever was at its height and his men thought him dying, they broke into open mutiny, jeering at him and refusing to obey his orders. Whereupon he rushed out at them with his double-barrelled pistol, and proved to them that their lives as much as his own depended upon discipline in the camp. Mutiny never recurred.

But the most critical moment for any African traveller is when his men fling down their loads and refuse to go any farther. Livingstone's men were indeed worn out. Continually harassed and dogged by hostile, thieving, and murderous tribes, they despaired of their leader's power to bring them to the sea. They urged him to turn back and seek the safety of Linyanti again. He replied that he would go on alone, and when he withdrew to his tent, they presently came to him saying they would die for him and never leave him. He was at that time so reduced by fever that he could neither ride the ox nor march, and his men had to lead him along, one on each side, to prevent him from falling. Happily they had now almost reached the border of Portuguese territory, and after crossing the Quango, Livingstone was hospitably received by the Commandant of the fort, and given a negro guide down to the coast. This kindliness to a man who had appeared like a shrunken and powerless corpse among them without warning or credentials lasted all down the forest paths till the sea was visible and the descent of the hill into Loanda began. In his Journal he naturally speaks with gratitude of the Portuguese

"DAILY SELF-SURPAST"

traders, many of whom, as he then believed, disapproved of the slave-trade. But we read that to several of these passages he afterwards added " an expressive series of marks of interrogation ".

His Zambesian men, having more knowledge of Portuguese slave-trading than in those days he had himself, were terrified lest when they came to the sea they would be kidnapped and sold into slavery. Understanding their fears he made them his final pledge : " I am as ignorant of Loanda as you are," he said ; " but nothing will happen to you but what happens to myself. We have stood by each other hitherto, and will do so to the end." None the less, at the end of Chapter XIX in his great book, he adds the paragraph :

" They were now somewhat apprehensive of suffering want, and I was unable to allay their fears with any promise of supply, for my own mind was depressed by disease and care. The fever had induced a state of chronic dysentery, so troublesome that I could not remain on the ox more than ten minutes at a time ; and as we came down the declivity above the city of Loanda on the 31st of May (1854), I was labouring under great depression of spirits, as I understood that, in a population of twelve thousand souls, there was but one genuine English gentleman. I naturally felt anxious to know whether he was possessed of good nature, or was one of those crusty mortals one would rather not meet at all."

He need not have feared. In Mr. Gabriel, the British Commissioner for the suppression of the slave-trade, he discovered, as he says, " a real wholehearted Englishman ". He adds a sentence which all travellers emerging from uncivilized countries will appreciate :

" Seeing me ill, he benevolently offered me his bed. Never shall I forget the luxuriant pleasure I enjoyed in feeling myself again on a good English couch, after six months' sleeping on the ground."

But, in spite of all this luxuriant comfort, the malarial poison still prevailed. He had arrived at the end of May, but in August he suffered a serious relapse which, as he writes, reduced him to a mere skeleton. While he lay prostrate, his Zambesian men kept themselves well supplied by gathering firewood from the forests and helping to unload a ship which came bringing coal for the British cruisers lying in the harbour to control the export of slaves.

In spite of all control and regulation, that export trade continued, and Livingstone tells us that his friendly Commissioner Mr. Gabriel, in 1847, saw thirty-seven slave-ships waiting in the harbour for their human freight under the protection of the guns in the fort, and the Government received a capitation fee for each slave, just as they did fifty years later. He says that, by recently agreeing to suppression of the trade (I think in 1842), the Portuguese Government had sacrificed a large proportion of their revenue, but he adds that the intentions of the Government, however good, were not carried out because the pay of the officials in Angola was so small that the temptation to engage in the lucrative commerce in human beings was irresistible. Fifty years later the case was the same. The regulations for the enlistment and employment of the " serviçaes " were fairly good, but no one thought of observing them.

Almost prostrate with malaria and rheumatism, Livingstone remained for several weeks in the comfort of Mr. Gabriel's home. Meantime a small squadron of three British cruisers or gunboats had arrived, and the officers showed him and his Zambesians every possible kindness. They offered him a passage home in one of the ships. The fame of his arrival on the coast had reached London. What the enthusiasm for the great traveller's exploit rapidly became may be judged by the record of what his reception in Great Britain actually was when at last he reached home two years later—the private interviews with Queen Victoria and the Prince Consort, a specially minted gold medal (the highest honour that could be granted by the Royal Geographical Society), the Freedom of the Cities of London, Edinburgh, Glasgow, and Dublin, receptions of honour at the Universities, vast meetings arranged by the London Missionary Society, banquets, complimentary speeches, and all the public forms that British admiration for a heroic character loves to take. And there were his wife and family too, separated from him since 1852. All were waiting to receive him at home, and here in Loanda lay the British warship offering to take him securely and comfortably to London.

It may be said that honours and receptions would not have appealed to him. In comparison with his passion for exploration, all the gold medals, banquets, Freedoms of Cities, and interviews with royalties would have appeared trivial as passing shadows. I suppose that was true. But when I remember what he says he never forgot—the luxuriant pleasure he enjoyed in feeling himself again on a good English couch after six months' sleeping on the ground; when I think of that frail body worn to a skeleton by malaria, dysentery, and rheumatism; and when I read his own record of the perils he had faced in the last eight or nine months—perils of soaking wet, wretched food, and hostile savages—then indeed I

"DAILY SELF-SURPAST"

am overwhelmed at the heroism of his immediate decision. Upon his heart lay his promise to his Makololo and other Zambesians. He had promised that nothing should happen to them which did not happen to himself. He knew that it was impossible for them to return home without his authority and guidance. They would be killed by the Chibokwe or other savages on the way; or else they would be captured and sold as slaves. He had given his word, and would fulfil the pledge.

He arrived in Loanda, as we have seen, on the 31st of May, 1854, and on the 20th of September he quietly turned back to lead his twenty-seven men to their homes in Linyanti and the Barotse region. In all the great history of our country, I have found no action more ennobling or more enviable.

He has left us an account of the outburst of joy among the natives when he arrived with his men at Libonta on the Zambesi—such demonstrations of joy, he says, as he had never witnessed before. It was July the 27th, 1855:

> "The women came forth to meet us, making their curious dancing gestures, and loud lulliloos. Some carried a mat and stick in imitation of a spear and shield. Others rushed forward and kissed the hands and cheeks of the different persons of their acquaintance among us. We were looked upon as men risen from the dead, and the most skilful of their diviners had pronounced us to have perished long ago.—The men gave us two fine oxen for slaughter, and the women supplied us abundantly with milk, meal, and butter.—Our progress down the Barotse valley was just like this. Every village gave us an ox, and sometimes two.—We returned to the Makololo as poor as we set out. Yet no distrust was shown, and my poverty did not lessen my influence."

What City banquets or University honours could

"DAILY SELF-SURPAST"

equal that? He reached his old quarters at Linyanti on the 11th of September, 1855, having left it on the 11th of November, 1853. Only a few weeks later—on the 3rd of November—he set out upon his next great journey of exploration, moving down the Zambesi, past the Victoria Falls, which he then named, and so out to Quilimane on the Indian Ocean, opposite Madagascar.

Such were the memories that filled my mind as I contemplated the shrivelled and enfeebled ghost of that indomitable spirit almost visible at my side while the Portuguese slave-ship lay completing its human cargo in the port of Loanda. It was comfortable to think that in about six weeks I should probably be at home in London again, but all the time I was remembering that trustworthy British heart who here, at the height of a great achievement, had taken no account of comfort or fame, but to redeem his promise to a handful of unknown and ignorant savages turned back upon the harsh and perilous track he had so lately traversed.

SCENE XV

THE RED SULTAN

How, being in Macedonia, I witnessed the misrule of Abdul Hamid, and in the Bosphorus followed his subsequent fate

IN the early autumn of 1929 I was invited by the St. Barnabas Pilgrimages (for St. Barnabas was the Son of Consolation) to accompany a party of two-hundred-and-forty pilgrims who wished to visit the graves of their beloved relatives or friends in Italy, Greece, and the Dardanelles. I was asked to talk about ancient Greece and Greek architecture, about the fighting around Salonika in the Great War, because I had been present there; and, for the same reason, to describe the Dardanelles campaign and conduct any who wished over the scenes of conflict at Helles, Anzac, and Suvla Bay. I did all this as well as I could, and to myself the interest of climbing over the cliffs and gullies of the tragic Peninsula was overwhelming.

On our return journey in the Italian ship, I came again to Constantinople, the gate of east and west. I had been there already since the Young Turk revolution and since the Great War, but still I was astonished at the changes brought about since my first visit more than twenty years before. Gone was the Galata bridge of boats; bare the space where Dervishes had danced; gone the families of dogs, who, their friends said, would buy meat for the gift of a coin, build nests of newspapers for their young, and divide the whole city into separate regions, like Montagues and Capulets. The crimson fez was now replaced by the second-hand cap of the British workman, the peak worn on one side so as to allow the forehead to touch the ground in religious obeisance. Except for one or two old widows, women walked the streets unveiled, shameless as Europeans. Beauty and Oriental romance had departed, and only three of the lovely city's characteristics appeared to remain as I knew them long ago:—the itching palm of officials, symbolized by the thumb of the right hand gently rubbed against the fingers; the peculiar business of those who lurked outside the fashionable hotels advertising curious amenities to foreigners; and the hamals or porters still as of old staggering blindly along the streets bent double under immense loads—wardrobes, pianos, huge iron or earthenware stoves. The trade is limited to an hereditary caste, and one can only hope the babies are born like young cuckoos with backs ready shaped for their future duty.

But where was the Sultan, the Khalif of the Faithful, the very heart and centre of Islam? How vast was the change since first, thirty-two years before, I went out to the vain but heroic attempt of Greeks to defy the Sultan's armies and deliver Crete from his oppression! How great since at his command all Armenians—five thousand of them at least it was said—were bludgeoned to death on the streets of this very city, and the women carried off to harems! And how great the change again since 1903, when he let loose his regulars and bandits upon the Bulgar villagers of Macedonia, where I counted over one hundred and twenty villages destroyed by fire, and so was able to testify how the inhabitants were slaughtered, ravished, or driven up into the snow-covered mountains. Why he endured the shame of granting permission to a foreigner to pass among the fires and ruins of that miserable country at the time of its worst misery, I could not understand. I suppose he felt the " long arm of England ", but to us in these later days the whole episode seems strange, almost unimaginable. By the Sultan's orders, Hussein Hilmi Pasha, sitting in the Konak of Monastir and vainly supposing he was giving peace to the whole country by issuing his commands, provided me with an escort of ten Turkish soldiers and a neat little Turkish officer, who every evening squatted down beside a wall and, holding a piece of paper stretched on his left hand, as was the Turkish manner, wrote in Turkish a summary of where I had been, what seen, and as far as possible what said or thought. The sheet of paper was then sent off every day to the Sultan crouching in Yildiz Kiosk, and I suppose he read the document and then consigned it to the mass of the *djornals* or daily reports of his spies from every quarter of the empire. Multitudes of those *djornals*, all apparently noted and filed, were found stored in great sacks at the revolution of 1909.

I often pictured the Sultan living in his Star Pavilion, and, like other people, I compared him to a poisonous spider in the centre of his web. There he squatted, engaged upon intrigues with all the Great Powers in turn—Russia, Austria, England, and latterly with Germany, on terms of mutual interest. For all desired what he possessed, namely Salonika, the route to Baghdad, and the City herself. The intrigues were intricate, but equally intricate were the

THE RED SULTAN

means of preserving his own life—the walls of his rooms covered with mirrors to reveal the movements of a possible assassin, the secret houses scattered over the gardens, the upper rooms changed nightly for sleeping and isolated by ladders which he drew up after him like drawbridges, the swarm of black eunuchs, the fifteen hundred girls and women of the harem, his nominal concubines, the official murderer and his assistants, entrusted with the duty of torturing or drowning suspects, and the mixed Albanian and Arab guards in the great yellow barracks.

Once, in 1907, with the assistance of a sinister Englishman, who was the spy of the Sultan and the Young Turk Party combined, I gained entrance to the outer courts of Yildiz itself, and sat among the debtors and other parasites for whom thousands (at least eight thousand, it was said) of midday meals were daily prepared in the Sultan's kitchens, and carried out on trays, as I saw. An old Hindu doctor who sat with me was twenty-seven months in arrears of pay, but he received his daily dinner; for it would be inhuman to allow debtors seated at an Emperor's gate to die of starvation. The various beasts and unnumbered birds that roved about the park or fluttered in cages against the walls were daily fed in the same way. But for the Sultan himself, every meal was cooked in a secret chamber, as it were in a safe, wrapped up in a sealed napkin, and carried to some devious room, where the Sultan broke the seal. Jewels and gold of great value were at that time hidden inside mattresses and pillows or under floors in the various little domiciles and harems, but the place was also choked up with useless furniture, musical instruments, and cheap clocks. Never was such a chaos of " old junk " unloaded as when Yildiz Kiosk was at last cleared out!

THE RED SULTAN

Once a week, on Friday, the descendant of the Prophet and sacred head of Islam enjoyed one hour of terrified freedom. It was the Selamlik, when religious routine ordained that he should be driven in a little carriage with white horses out from the walls of Yildiz to the Hamidieh Mosque. Fear added speed—an unpleasant speed for the mob of fat eunuchs, fat Pashas, and other officials whom duty and love of life incited to keep pace with the carriage along its brief but dangerous course. A shout from the troops, a muttered service in the mosque, and back His Majesty was hurried to the soothing security of the familiar walls. A smallish man he seemed, his thin body shrunken together like a starveling bird's, his short beard white but dyed with henna at the point into reddish brown, and from each side of the nose, hooked like an eagle's beak, the deep-set eyes glowered with terror ill-concealed. After the Selamliks so tremulously performed while I was in the courts of Yildiz in the winter of 1907, the Sultan had still two years to reign, his fears increasing while the revolution of Young Turks and the Committee of Union-and-Progress simmered. In 1908 it boiled over, and in April, 1909, he was entrained to Salonika with his jester, sufficient baggage, and a few of his women—" only seven ", as he justly complained, out of the hundred-and-fifty whom he had been accustomed to have around him. Since he complained, fifteen more were sent after him as a solatium.

Three years he was maintained in Salonika, looking over the great harbour to the curving heights of Mount Olympus, covered with snow, where Zeus and other gods once lived. But the Greeks in the first Balkan War, 1912, absorbed Salonika, and the unhappy Sultan was returned to the great City, and lodged in the Beylerbey palace overlooking the Bosphorus. There, during the gathering turmoil of the next two years, he remained in the quietude of impotence, except that now and then he sent messages of good advice to his younger brother Reshid, now ruling as Sultan in his place. And, certainly, Reshid as Mohammed V needed all the good advice that experience in murder and intrigue could give. For as a brother too near the throne he had lived a prisoner in a neighbouring palace, occupied with the pleasing pursuits of literature and contemplation, far from the storms that now began to whirl around him. In 1913 Shevket and Nazim were murdered. Next year the *Goeben* and *Breslau*, having by miracle escaped the British fleet in their flight from Sicily, appeared off the Golden Horn, and the Kaiser's policy of winning the Turks by visiting the Red Sultan in state, presenting the beautiful City with a memorial fountain of singular ugliness, and entering Jerusalem through a breach specially prepared, was justified and fulfilled.

Then was heard the boom of great guns echoing up the Dardanelles and across the Sea of Marmora. It was thought for certain that the British fleet would force the Narrows and arrive. All the rich and powerful began hastily to pack up and send their wealth and families across the brief passage of sea to the safety of Asia. When, in 1929, I walked along the shore in front of the deserted palace, a scene upon a stormy background of fourteen years before rose to my mind.

It was evening, and an old man, dressed in a fez and a tightly buttoned black coat, leant forward from a window gazing down the deep-flowing channel into the sunset of a peaceful April day. Faintly grey and blue against the dying light, a few thin lines were visible, like unlit candles before a fire. They were the minarets of Stamboul, and looking at them the old man remained long silent. Upon the edge of a wooden chair not far apart, his jester sat with bowed head, eyes fixed on the ground, hands laid flat across his chest, and awaited the befitting time to speak.

"It is getting long ago—six years ago," said the old man, rousing himself with a deep-drawn breath.

The jester rose, touched his heart, mouth, and forehead quickly with his right hand in reverence, and said, "Time, your Majesty, is the dog which barks us all to Hell. Or some of us, I suppose," he added, " he barks into Paradise."

"It was out of Paradise that Time barked me then," the old man remarked, with a bitter smile.

"Sire," replied the jester, seating himself upon the carpet at the old man's feet, " let me tell you a tale. There was once a great King who dwelt in a tent of stars. The tent stood upon a low hill, looking over sea and land, and in a setting of sea and land shone the fairest jewel of all cities. The King had gradually adorned and extended the tent itself till to strangers coming from the farthest parts of the earth and peering through the gates was revealed a City of God. In the midst of a shaded park rose a marble palace containing chambers of every size, that looked, as a star looks, to all points of heaven, and protected the majestic inmate from summer heat and winter cold. A marble corridor led to another palace of equal splendour, partitioned into a hundred halls and sleeping-rooms, the hope of children's children. There dwelt the world's loveliest women, bright as constellations, and in such number that no man could tell their names or distinguish the beauty of one from another's. For every year the Princes of the Empire sent as a gift the fairest virgins of their land, if perchance they might find favour in the sight of the King. Gigantic eunuchs from Ethiopia watched over them, clad in purple uniforms faced with gold, and in their service were employed young girls and grown women of every hue, carefully trained as slaves from early childhood in special arts, whether to make music, or to dance, or cook, or work upon the loom.

" The Princes also sent horses as gifts, and in long rows of marble stalls, two hundred steeds, each with an Arab groom, proudly neighed and champed the golden corn. The palace and the harem were crammed with the offerings presented in humility and admiration by Frankish potentates, who vainly strove to rival the glory of the King. Here were instruments which, at the touch of a silver spring, created pictures more closely counterfeiting reality than the art of the most cunning limner could contrive. Here were flower-shaped trumpets which, on the turning of a handle, reproduced the barbaric discords of Frankish music as upon a field of battle; and here were clocks and watches studded with diamonds, which the King could set to tell what time he pleased, indifferent to the sun. But the most flattering gift was offered by the Teutonic Emperor, who, with an Imperial train of nobles, arrived to do obeisance. For in the midst of the great city's most beautiful square, he caused his country's cleverest architects to erect the finest fountain they could design as a memorial of the visit, and as an evidence that the Infidel's most elaborated art must appear monstrous in hideousness contrasted with the King's.

" Other noble buildings did the Tent of Stars contain within the circuit of its walls—an armoury for the forging and adornment of beautiful swords and guns, a workshop for the manufacture of the Royal porcelain, and innumerable halls and ante-chambers where suppliants stood for months, and even years, humbly petitioning for grace, and daily fed by meals carried to them on separate trays in the hands of a thousand slaves from the King's own kitchen. Also, around the gleaming palaces extended flowering gardens and grassy parks, where the King could ride a white Arab in every direction or in unending circles. There the King loved to watch the prismatic colours on the necks of pigeons, and to feed the soft-nosed fallow-deer from his hand. For, like God himself, he was merciful, was compassionate."

" O my son, O joy of my liver," sighed the old man, suddenly interrupting the brilliant picture of past years, " remind me not of happiness."

" Nevertheless," continued the jester, " that great King had little joy in all his splendour, nor did gifts or riches or the tenderest women bring relief to his incessant cares. From dawn till evening he sat upon a silken divan, with trusted secretaries around him, while he controlled the welfare of fifty million souls. All day long and far into the darkness the trembling wires brought him news from every quarter of his boundless heritage. Petitions and complaints from suffering or disobedient subjects came ; false accusations from distant senates, who took upon themselves the prerogatives of rival monarchs ; shameless demands from Infidel ambassadors, who in the beautiful City's very midst intrigued perpetually to tear his realm asunder. To all these troublesome serpents answer had to be given. One enemy to the Believer's peace must be set against another, and upon the King's own head the cares of all the Faithful world were gathered. Even the few moments of rest brought no pleasure. So bitter is the envious malignity of the wicked that continually they seek to destroy the just man, whose upright life reproaches them. For fear lest death should terminate the benefactions of his extended reign, that righteous King could eat only from sealed napkins, and had to climb for sleep through a trapdoor in the ceiling, up which he dragged the ladder after him. Consider what evil the loveliest slave-girl might do upon the King as he lay beside her in the night. Judge then, O Commander of the Faithful, whether your lot be not happy in comparison with that mighty King's."

There was a silence, and then the old man said, " O my soul, O my lamb, your words are true. Even such was I in the days when God was with me. Why, then, did the Unbeliever exult at my ruin and applaud the triumph of the apostates who called themselves the Young and proclaimed that their watchword was peace ? "

" They tell me the world is full of strife," he presently continued : " From every side come rumours of war, and the clouds drop blood mingled with the rain. In the thirty years of my glory, all for the cause of peace and justice I stamped upon ten thousand rebellious subjects as a peasant stamps upon vermin, and for the exercise of that Imperial right—a right they freely exercise themselves—the Infidels, greedy for my lands, called me the Red, the Unspeakable, the Damned. They spoke of my ' fell Satanic orgies '. They threatened to drive me, bag and baggage, back to Asia. Which of them is now so merciful as I was then ? Which of them has hands as white ? "

" Sire," replied the jester, " God is just as well as merciful. The Infidels are killing more of each other every week than you executed of your iniquitous subjects in thirty years. I feel their souls whirring past me to Hell every hour, and at Satan's gate they crowd so thick that the devils cannot give them entrance or sort out for which furnace each is fitted. The Feast of Bairam is now approaching—the Feast of Sacrifice to commemorate the willing offer of himself to death by Ishmael, father of all wandering Moslems—not poor home-keeping Isaac, as the Hebrews vainly teach. And truly it is a great Feast of Sacrifice which the Infidels are now celebrating for their generation !"

" Is, then, the Infidel's talk of brotherly love more deadly than Islam's sword ? " asked the old man, bitterly.

" Sire," answered the jester, " as wise men say, the speaker is one, the listener is another. Not all men obey their Prophet as we of the Faithful obey ours. Therefore all the Infidel world is set upon slaughter, and the time has come spoken of by our Holy Prophet in his Scripture, where, in the Chapter called ' Of the Infallible ' the prophecy is written :

> ' When the trumpet shall be blown with one blast, and the earth shall be borne away and the mountains too, and both shall be crushed with one crushing, in that day shall the inevitable happen, and the heavens on that day shall be cleft asunder, from that day shall they wane, and the angels upon the sides thereof, and above them on that day shall eight bear the throne of the Lord.'

" Remember also what the Prophet prophesied in the Chapter called ' The Folding Up ', how he said :

> ' When the sun is folded up, and when the stars do fall, and when the mountains are moved, and when the she-camels ten months gone with young shall be neglected, and when the beasts shall be crowded together with fear,

and when the seas shall surge up, and when souls shall be paired with bodies, and when the child who was buried alive shall be asked for what sin she was slain, and when the pages shall be spread out, and when the heaven shall be flayed, and when Hell shall be set ablaze, and when Paradise shall be brought nigh, the soul shall know what it has produced.' " [1]

" O my son ! O my lamb ! " cried the old man, " what terrible sound is that I hear ? They are coming ! They are coming ! The Infidels have passed the Straits ! They are at the entrance to the City ! They hurl large shells among the mosques ! For me they are searching. They always hated me. They are coming to kill me now. For every minute of threescore years and ten I have escaped death, and to-night death is coming. What is so terrible as death ? "

" Yet men say," said the jester, " that where there is life there is sorrow."

" When death is quick, they say, you feel nothing," cried the old man, " but they lie. The shock that stops life—the crash of the bullet in the brain, the stab of the long, cold dagger piercing the heart between the ribs, the slice of the axe through the neck, the stifling of breath when someone kicks away the stool and the noose runs tight—do you not feel that ? One moment I am alive, I am well, I can talk and eat. Next moment life is going—going—and it is no use to struggle. Thought stops, breath stops, I can see and hear no more. One second, and I am nothing for ever."

" Your Majesty is pleased to overlook the joys of Paradise," said the jester. " The joys of the Prophet's

[1] *The Qur'ân*, Part II, translated by E. H. Palmer (The Sacred Books of the East, edited by Max Müller, Vol. ix).

Paradise are not to be compared with the blessedness of your Majesty's happy reign, but for a great and merciful King they are assured."

"Let me live! Only let me live!" the old man whimpered. 'I am not old. Many men have lived twenty or even thirty years longer than I have. They say that when you are really old, death comes like sleep. Nothing is so terrible as death. That was why I showed myself merciful in my power. What other Sultan ever kept his own brother alive for thirty years? Did I not give him a fine palace to live in, and gardens where he could walk with but few to watch over his safety? Did I not feed him on pigeon's milk, sending him delicate food every day from my own table? Did I not grant him such women as he desired, and books to read, and music to delight his soul? His were all the joys of Paradise, and he was alive and well. He had life—life, the one thing needful, the one thing that can never be restored! And now my own brother turns against me. He will let them take my life. The shock of death will strike me down."

"Sire," said the jester, "even in your blessed reign men have died. To them their life was sweet, but they contrived to die, and what is so common can hardly be intolerable."

"Have I not watched over my people?" the old man continued. "Have I not toiled? What pleasure have I given myself, though the right to every pleasure was mine? When have I been drunk with wine as the Infidels are drunken? What excess of delight have I taken with the women who were sent to me every year? They departed to their chambers, and I saw them no more. Week by week I risked my life to worship God. From dawn to evening I have laboured, taking no rest. Whatever passed in my Empire I knew, and where treachery thrust out its head, my sword was ready.

"But the Powers of the Infidel stood waiting. Like vultures round a dying sheep they stood waiting round the dominions of the Faithful. Now and then one snatched a living piece of our flesh and devoured it as though it were carrion, while the others screamed with gluttonous fury, fighting with wings and claws."

"Sire," said the jester, "you have proved to the world how Christians love one another."

"I have not lived without glory!" cried the old man, rising in his seat. "From east to west the moon of Islam shines brighter than before. The sons of Islam are gathering side by side. I see the brown peoples of Asia, I see the black peoples of African deserts and forests. They pledge their faith on the Sacred Book. They issue out again to the conquest of the world, and it was I who gathered the might of Islam into one hand. I swept away the princes, the governors, the ministers and the agents who divided the power of Islam and squandered our riches. I gave the word and they were not. I stored up wealth for the great day when the holy sword of Islam shall again be drawn."

"Others, too, have stored up wealth, Sire," said the jester, "and if only I could lay my hand on it, Islam would be more secure, and I less hungry."

"I held the City of the world," the old man went on; "I kept the breath of life moving throughout the Empire when all said it must perish. For thirty years my brain alone outmatched the diplomats of all the Embassies. Emperors have been proud to enter my palaces. Kings have called me venerable. The Powers of Europe will not let me die. They are coming to protect me. An Emperor with an invincible army is coming. He will not let me die!"

"The Emperor is proud," said the jester, "and in the book of the Prophet it is written, 'Hell is the resort of such as are big with pride.'"

The booming of distant guns was renewed, and it sounded nearer.

"Europe will not endure it," the old man whined, crouching down again upon the divan. "The Powers will intervene. They always intervene. They are coming to set me free, for I alone can govern this people. I am the only chance of peace. They know it. I have worshipped God. I never harmed an honourable soul. They themselves say I am merciful. They will not let me die. I have done each of them a service in turn. I shall not die. My power will be returned to me—my power and my life."

But the jester, speaking darkly, replied: "As the Lord said to the angels at the Creation of the world, I know what you do not."

The booming of heavy guns redoubled. The old man covered his ears with his hands and stared before him.

There was a knocking at the door. He started up, crying, "They will murder me before I can be saved! It is death! Death! And I shall die! Oh, give me yet a little time—a little time for life, a little time for repentance. All the saints are given a little time for repentance. My hour has not come. I am Abdul Hamid, the Sultan, the Khalif, the seed of the Prophet. They have not come to murder me!"

A stately, middle-aged woman entered the door.

"Sire, your word is law," she said in deep salutation, with her hands across her breasts. "I have orders to pack Your Majesty's essential belongings for a journey. Which cloak would Your Majesty prefer for protection against the evening air as we cross the passage of the Strait?"

They crossed that night with due allowance of money, clothing, and women. The little party made its way through the desolate lands of Asia till they came to the ancient city of Magnesia, about thirty miles north-east of Smyrna. There the Red Sultan dwelt at ease for three more years, and there, in February, 1918, at the good old age of eighty, he died in peace, as most men die.

SCENE XVI

ON THE OCEAN WAVE

How, in passing the icebergs off Newfoundland, I beheld the drowning of Mr. Jones

IN July, 1920, I was returning from my first visit to Canada. Our ship was the *Metagama*, named after some Red Indian chief, and we proceeded slowly from Montreal down the broad and shallow St. Lawrence. Late in the evening we passed under the great railway bridge to Quebec, and then came the beautiful city itself, sparkling with lights, high above us on the historic bluffs. That night for the first time I saw the perpetual miracle of the northern lights—a low, broad arc of brilliant shafts, spreading upwards from some unseen centre below the horizon, continually changing colour and varying in intensity of radiance. All a glorious miracle to me, though I suppose electricians understand it well. The sky was clear, and the north star stood exactly over the middle of the arc. The wonder began about eleven, and was visible till after midnight. The passengers did not appear interested, for most of them had seen the miracle before.

I had hoped to pass out into the ocean through the Belle Isle straits so as to see just a glimpse of the stern coast of Labrador, but the icebergs were coming south under the summer heat, and Captain Turnbull refused to take the risk. He chose the longer passage —two-hundred-and-eighty miles longer—south of Newfoundland, and even then we ran into thick fog and cold. All day the siren sounded at intervals, chiefly to warn the fishing fleets, and at night it sounded double every ten minutes to show that our engines were stopped and we lay drifting. For three nights the engines were stopped, and the cold was bitter ; for icebergs surrounded us, though they were invisible in the fog. I was told how once, in this very ship, the Captain had just caught a glimpse of a great iceberg right in front of him. Should he try to skim round it on the port side, or drive the bow straight into the frozen mass ? Hardly three seconds were given to decide, and he drove right on, headlong into the ice. His bows were battered in. Huge blocks of ice fell on the decks. I was shown a photograph of them as they had fallen. By reversing engines and moving slowly stern-first, he brought his ship safe to St. John's. It was one of those moments when the heroic mind is called upon to decide by the instinct born of courage and unconscious experience long stored up. The experience was a flash of memory. Below the iceberg a ledge or base of hidden ice might be projecting. Unseen as a torpedo, it might rip open the ship's side. Just in this way a hidden base of ice had ripped open the *Titanic* eight years before.

That night I saw a vision of the *Titanic* herself—the proud new ship, the finest that ever sailed from the yards of Belfast, where I had watched her building. She had sailed on a Wednesday morning in April, and now it was ten-twenty-five on Sunday evening : a dark night but clear, all the stars shining. There was an almost imperceptible shock, and over one-thousand-six-hundred people had but two and a half hours to live—just about the time between dinner and the final taste of supper, the seventh meal of the day. Tell a healthy man, comfortable after dinner and full of vitality, that he will die before bedtime, and what will he do or think as the minutes rush by?

"I say, we've bumped into something!" said someone coming into the smoking saloon.

"Guess it's a whale," said one of the card-players. "Reminds me of our trip to Norway when we almost saw a polar bear."

"Your trip to the Zoo, you mean," answered his partner. "Did you say no trumps?"

"I certainly did feel a kind of a shock," said one of those men who always stand watching a game, but never play. "I had to steady my whisky-and-soda."

"A whisky-and-soda often wants steadying at this time of night, Mr. Jones," said the funny man of the players.

"Well, if you don't believe me, come and see," replied the first speaker. "A steward told me there's a lot of ice fallen on the deck."

"Yes," said the funny man, "that's how they stock the refrigerator. Smart man, our skipper!"

"I'll come and have a look," said Mr. Jones, glad of an opportunity of being seen with a distinguished passenger, whom he had noticed walking up and down the deck with a millionaire.

Certainly he could see lumps of ice lying on the deck—small bits that might have been thrown up from little blocks upon the surface when the bows were cutting the water at so high a speed.

"Rather a narrow squeak," he ventured to observe to his dignified companion.

"Looks like it," the other answered; "but it's

beastly cold out here. I'm going to turn in. Good night."

Mr. Jones felt hurt at his abruptness, but was comforted on returning to the smoking-saloon when a man of American fame asked him why the engines had stopped.

"They say we've carried away a propeller," he answered, with nautical pride.

"Rot!" said the funny man; "The skipper always stops once every voyage, just to show he can do it if he likes."

"Then we shan't make a beat this time," yawned a passenger who had just come up in his dressing-gown. "I'll go below and do a bit of readin'. *Buried Alive*—do you know it?—good book, very! Just the thing to go to sleep on." And the bridge went on.

But in five minutes he opened the door of the smoking-saloon again, looking quite different. For over his dressing-gown he now had a queer thing buckled round his chest.

"I say, you fellows!" he cried in a loud voice. "I don't want to stop the game, but the stewards are shouting for all passengers to come on deck in their lifebelts."

"That's what's called fire-drill," said the funny man. "We always get fire-drill on Sundays now, instead of church-parade. Keeps the liver going, you know. Want it on board ship. Not enough ecker, and too much to eat. Never had a better dinner than to-night."

"Nor I," said his partner, laying out dummy; "not since a dinner I had in Cairo last October. Kept the menu, by George! Will show it you in the morning if you remind me."

There was a disturbing noise of shuffling and tramping overhead. Now that the engines had stopped, everything could be heard very distinctly, as when a train stops and you hear church bells in the distance. There were shouts, orders, and a rattle of chains.

"It sounds as if we were going to cast anchor," observed Mr. Jones, but no one noticed the remark. Women's voices were heard, and strange shapes began to hurry past the tinted windows.

"This is beginning to look serious," said one of the bridge-players, getting up.

"Rot!" said his partner; "finish the game! I've got the hand of my life. When it's done, we'll remember our childhood's hymns and go to bed like angels."

"Are you aware," said the funny man, with mock solemnity; "are you aware, I say, that this ship cost one and three-quarter million pounds to build, and is insured for a solid million pounds? God will think twice before damning a vessel of that quality. You recognize the quotation?"

With shaking hand, Mr. Jones gulped down the rest of his whisky, and followed the others out through the door.

A large white object was swinging slowly down between the top-deck rail and the stars. He could hear the creaking of new ropes as they strained through the sockets. Suddenly he realized that they were lowering a boat. In boys' books they always did lower boats at a moment of crisis, and all but one of them, containing the hero and heroine, always sank. But the ship was quite steady, and it was absurd to think of danger. Probably a pilot was being put off to reconnoitre if there was more ice ahead, or an engineer was being sent round to look at the damaged propeller. None the less, he noticed that many passengers had lifebelts on, and he thought he had better go down to his cabin to fetch his. As he went towards the hatchway, a sailor took him by the arm and said, " Beg pardon, sir, only women allowed on this deck."

" Sorry," he answered, " very sorry, I'm sure," feeling as though he had entered a ladies' compartment by mistake. " I'm just going below."

Then he remembered the joking cries of " Women and children first ! Throw them all overboard to save the ship ! " whenever the wash of a passing steamer made waves at happy old picnics on the river. His heart sank.

Pushing on down what he called the staircase through a confused half-dressed and questioning crowd of ladies, he met his steward in the gangway, and boldly asked him why a boat was being lowered.

" Merely as a precautionary measure, sir," the steward answered, as one accustomed to the conversation of the best circles ; " slight abrasure reported on the vessel's external plates, sir," and the steward hurried into the cabin with hot water for the passenger who had the berth above Mr. Jones.

He was a gentleman whom Mr. Jones disliked for his foreign ways, but honoured for his reputed wealth. He had gone to bed early, but was now putting on his evening clothes again and preparing to shave.

" I should wait till morning, if I were you," said Mr. Jones, whom the steward's comfortable words had rendered genial.

" If I go die, I go die like English gentleman," said the foreigner with his irritating accent, and when the steward had laid out his black tie and *smokère* again, he gave him a sovereign as a tip. " In case I not see you on landing. Good man you. Verr' good man," he added.

"Die!" thought Mr. Jones, and his knees shook so that he had to sit on the edge of his berth while the steward fastened on his lifebelt. The idea was absurd.

"There's no calculable danger, sir," the steward insisted; "this here vessel's practically unsinkable. You haven't no cause to be nervous."

"I'm not in the least nervous," said Mr. Jones, standing up and handing the steward a trembling five-pound note, in the joy of his heart. Die! The idea was absurd.

Pulling on an overcoat, he walked down the gangway and up the staircase again. Everything was just as usual, except that he seemed to be walking a little downhill. But that did not matter. The ship was quite steady. The lights were burning. He could hear the gentle throbbing of the dynamos. All of a sudden the band began to play.

"That's a good idea," thought Mr. Jones. "Nothing like music to restore confidence. That will at once end the momentary panic."

He was glad to think he had kept so cool when many others had certainly seemed a little flurried. In passing, he looked into the dining saloon. No one was there, but the chairs and tables all stood in order, waiting for the breakfast things to be laid in the morning. The whole saloon shone with various coloured woods, glass, and elaborate decorations.

"She really is a splendid ship," he thought; "no wonder they took care to make her practically unsinkable, and insured her for a million."

He went up to a higher deck and looked over the side. By the ship's light he could see a lot of darkish things upon the black water, and he knew they must be the boats. "Rather a mistake to make such a fuss, isn't it?" he observed to a man who was leaning over the rail at his side. The man made no answer.

"She's practically unsinkable, you know," Mr. Jones added, confidently. But still the man said nothing. He only kept his eyes fixed on one of the boats.

Turning to another man beside him, Mr. Jones, with a kind of challenge in his voice, repeated, "She's practically unsinkable!"

"Depends what you mean by practically," answered the other, shortly.

"I mean she can't sink!" cried Mr. Jones. "She's built in watertight compartments or bulkheads or something. They tell me she's practically unsinkable."

"Dangerous word, practically," said the other. "So's virtually." And he moved away.

"There's the last boat putting off," muttered someone.

"But they'll all be called back directly," said another; "I've heard we are to go ahead stern-first, under half-steam."

"No place for yours truly," Mr. Jones heard the funny man say. "When we get back to no-place-like-home, we must agitate for 'One Man one Boat'. I'll raise the question in Parliament. One bloody Man one bloody Vote, as the rustic said of Manhood Suffrage. It'll sweep the country like a Reform Bill!" No one laughed, and Mr. Jones heard him singing as he strolled away, "But I'll go down with the ship I love!"

For himself, Mr. Jones banished all thought of fear. "Unsinkable! Going astern under half-steam!" he kept repeating to reassure himself. The crew and all the passengers were quieter now that the boats had all gone. Men were walking about like himself, to keep warm. A few married couples were standing close together in shaded corners. The ship remained perfectly steady. The lights shone. The band played. The postal clerks were busy with the mail-bags. Mr. Jones thought of the squash-racquet court; then of the Winter Garden, "Like the Riviera"; then of the splendid suite of rooms costing eight hundred pounds for the voyage. It was obviously ridiculous to suppose that there could be danger on a ship like that! You might as well think of danger at the Ritz! Besides, he had absolute confidence in the Captain. Everyone had. So he stood beside the band, listening to their merry ragtime tunes.

At the end of one tune, he wondered what time it was and, remembering he had left his watch in the cabin, he thought he might as well go and fetch it. As he went, he saw by a ship's clock that it was a quarter-past-two. He was surprised to find it so late. In three hours daylight would be coming again.

But what was the matter with the gangway? The carpet was all wet. There was a sort of pool at one end, and it rippled gently to and fro as the ship swayed with the sea. He would get his feet wet going into the cabin, and he turned to go back up the hatch. He began to run, but he could hardly climb the stairs now. It was like climbing a mountain-side. He had to cling on with his hands and climb like a monkey. At last he reached a deck. The band was still playing. It sounded like some hymn-tune now. But the deck was slowly tilting up. It was difficult to stand on it without clutching to a railing. The music-stands were slipping away and rolling down to the scuppers. Leaning against the base of a funnel, some of the musicians continued the hymn. The conductor still beat time with his fiddle-bow. The deck tilted up more and more steeply.

"I'm going to die ! I'm going to die ! " groaned Mr. Jones, clinging to an iron bar. He was now lying flat against the deck, and it rose till he was almost upright, his feet dangling in air. Slowly the whole ship slid a little forwards, and he heard a great cry.

People came sliding over him and splashed below. He felt cold water in his dress-shoes ; then under his dress-clothes. It was horribly cold.

Letting go of the bar, he clutched at a black thing that seemed to be floating on a surface.

" Sorry, sir, no more accommodation here," said the voice of his steward.

Mr. Jones answered, " All right, William," and quietly let go.

He felt himself being driven with tremendous force downwards, and always downwards. He was spun round and round. He felt a lot of things knocking against him in the water—people and harder things.

He thought of his pleasant little home in the suburbs, and he saw the sun shining on the apple-blossom while his pretty daughters put up the tennis net, and his wife read a telegram. " Now I mustn't breathe," he thought ; " if I hold my breath I shall float up to the top all right."

Then he knew he was sitting in his office chair, singing the same hymn that the band had played. Then he was being taken to bathe by his mother on the sands at Ramsgate at the edge of the waves. The bathing had always been the only shadow on the bright days of the holiday—the happiest days of his life. But she ducked him in, so that the water came right over his head. He felt the horrid taste of it in his mouth and at the back of his nose.

"Oh, mother, mother, lift me out!" he cried. And he heard her answer, "Don't cry, darling! Don't cry! It'll soon be over."

But somehow he had grown so heavy that she couldn't lift him out, and Mr. Jones heard no more, but went whirling down and down into darkness through fathoms of salt water. And down with him went sixteen-hundred-and-thirty-five other men and women, with all their wealth and jewels, with the wreckage of luxury, and the corpse of the greatest ship that ever sailed.

"There go all your pretty nighties!" said a lady to her companion in one of the boats that were saved. For so in moments of overwhelming horror sanity is preserved.

SCENE XVII

DISSOLVING VIEWS

How, in travelling over the sites of the Great War at various times, I witnessed scenes in which I had then been present

WHEN I was brought to London as a boy, one of my treats was to be taken to the " Dissolving Views " at the ancient Polytechnic in Upper Regent Street, where one might also be dropped into a watery deep in a diving bell. " Dissolving Views " were something like a modern cinema, but the figures did not move or speak, and the scenes did not run along in succession but melted each into the next as dream melts into dream. So it is with me when I look into the dark backward of the Great War and recall the scenes I witnessed as correspondent of the *Manchester Guardian*, the *Daily News*, the *Daily Chronicle*, and the *Daily Telegraph*, sometimes separate, but more often combined.

In memory I see the war as the baseless fabric of a vision, an insubstantial pageant faded, scene melting into scene, each almost incredible, and yet in turn visible to me as present reality. Horrible most of the scenes inevitably are. Nothing—nothing at all—is too horrible for war. In every war the most effective way of killing the enemy will certainly be used, and no rules of mitigation laid down by International Conferences or Peace Societies will ever make the slightest difference when the killing begins. But at the moment of action the sense of horror is dulled by excitement, by fear, by self-preservation, by discipline, or by the necessity of hurrying forward to the next horrible event. It is afterwards, as now after twenty or sixteen years, that the horror is realized and seems incredible.

So whenever I visit Berlin again it seems incredible that when I was there in the first five days of August, 1914, the Kaiser himself, still living in 1934 twenty years afterwards, was dashing to and fro from Palace to War Office in his motor that sounded the four Imperial notes. There were the infantry parading in their new field-grey uniforms, in place of the " Prussian blue " that I had known for thirty years. There were the Uhlans swinging on to their fine horses, with lances and sabres, bags of rations and fodder, all the crowd cheering them forward to almost certain death. There were the wildly excited citizens, men, women, and especially girls, marching up and down " Unter den Linden," shouting " *Die Wacht am Rhein* " hour after hour without a pause. There was I being dragged from the Hotel Adlon by two military policemen, who held a revolver at each of my ears, ready to shoot me like a dog, as they repeatedly assured me, but in reality saving me from the far more bloodthirsty assaults of the crowd armed with fists, umbrellas, and sticks, though I had never given any of them cause for personal animosity. Next day a shelter in our Embassy was offered me by Sir Edward Goschen, and early on the 6th a seat in his special train to the safety of Holland, while at every station all the population that could sound a musical instrument stood at the carriage window blasting " *Deut-*

schland, Deutschland über Alles," into the ear of our Ambassador, who sat immovable as an eagle among sparrows.

The scene dissolves into a vision that haunts Boulogne whenever I land there now. It is the disembarkation of the " Old Contemptibles," which I witnessed in the middle of August. Owing to Haldane's foresight and genius, I suppose no such perfect army ever landed on a foreign shore—men trained to perfection, equipment faultless, guns moving as though alive, and beautiful horses with their shining coats and intelligent, patient eyes, all to be marched off to Mons and the great retirement, from which so many would not return. And at Calais I still see the host of Belgian villagers trailing away with children and the customary refugee bundles of bedding, food, and birdcages into the unknown. Or I again see the slated spire of the old church, so often the very symbol of France to me, and inside I hear a strange service in which at intervals for the space of an hour old men and girls stretched out both arms, crying " *Sauve la France ! Sauve la France !* "

And then I see Dunkirk for the first time, and the roads through burning and ruined villages to Dixmude, a largish town then in flames and crashing down under ceaseless shell-fire, the streets strewn with window-glass that crackled as I walked, and in one large house near the entrance bridge a primitive dressing station, where Belgian surgeons cut and bandaged and handed out the " sitting-cases " or " lying-down-cases " for Lady Dorothy Feilding and me to drive back to Hector Munro's little hospital in Furnes, where we discharged some already dead. From Dunkirk too I drove to the pleasant " seaside resort " of Westende falling to pieces under crashing shells that fell unsuitably into charming bedrooms, billiard-rooms, restaurants, and bathing-machines constructed for so different a fate.

But the most definite vision of Dunkirk came to me in the early autumn of 1931, as I was crossing from Tilbury by the pleasant route to the Black Forest through famous places along the French frontier. The boat was running quietly towards a brilliant sunrise and the coast was already visible. Well-known friends were with me, and everything promised pleasure in the peace of unknown hills and woods marked here and there by old German villages, beautiful in their exact construction for warmth, shelter, and storage. But in place of sunlit sea and the expectation of quiet days, I saw a black destroyer rushing past us at thirty knots, and not far in front were four other destroyers circling round a three-funnel cruiser obviously in trouble. She was the *Hermes*, struck twice at an interval of half an hour by a submarine's torpedoes, and sinking by the stern. I was then helping a Quaker Ambulance Unit, and the thirty of us stood by ready to man the boats; but by the time we reached the spot the destroyers had rescued all the crew except fifteen who were killed while asleep by the explosions.

Seeing one of them floating about on the surface, a Quaker boy (now the headmaster of the famous Quaker Bootham's School at York), gallantly dived from the top deck and hauled him to a boat, but he was already dead. A naked officer, seemingly drowned or killed by exposure, was put in my charge to do what I could with. I laid him on the cushions in the saloon, and worked at him for half an hour, chafing and pummelling and rolling him to and fro, without the least knowledge of scientific treatment.

Then to my amazement he began to sigh and groan and pour out the sea-water he had swallowed, crying aloud and cursing horribly in the extreme anguish of returning life, so that I wondered whether death and oblivion would not have been happier. Yet I was delighted when we returned to Dover and I put him ashore alive. He was an officer of Marines, but I did not hear his name, and he never knew whose unskilled labour brought him back from darkness to see the sun. I saw the *Hermes* slowly sinking stern first and hanging for a time with her bows above water; then turning a somersault, so that the keel of the bows remained visible for half an hour, and sailors thought her masts touched the bottom. It was a vision of October the 31st, 1914, which I thus beheld nineteen years later.

My next dissolving view of the Great War revealed itself on September the 3rd, 1928. I had been invited by the St. Barnabas Pilgrimages (as I told in a previous scene) to guide about two-hundred-and-forty Pilgrims to the scenes in the Dardanelles and Salonika campaigns where fathers, sons, husbands, or lovers had fallen and were buried. I do not myself feel any consolation in gazing upon the grave of some beloved man or woman, but to view the actual scene where a beloved person looked for the last time upon the earth and died, is much, is something. Besides, there were a few among us who had not come as Pilgrims to lament the dead but, like myself, to revisit places which they had known in the war, whether at the three occupied points on the Dardanelles peninsula, or around Lake Doiran facing Bulgarian armies far up country from Salonika. Day by day I did my best to explain to all who cared to listen the objects and results of the landings at Helles, Anzac, and Suvla,

DISSOLVING VIEWS

and, with the few who were willing to climb those steep cliffs and make their way through the prickly scrub that covered the dark hills, I then beheld with intense interest the positions I had once known as held by one side or the other in the tragic drama of April to December, 1915.

So it came that on that September day in 1928 I stood alone on the summit of the Chunuk Bair range, which had been the main objective of the night attack from Anzac on August 6th, 1915. I had left the few who cared to scramble with me up the Aghyl Dere (an almost impassable dry water-course) to its junction with the similar Chainak Dere. They had remained on the little open patch of formerly cultivated stubble called by us " The Farm ", where General A. H. Baldwin and his 38th Brigade were destroyed in hand-to-hand fighting on August the 10th. Anxious first to reach the top on which so many disappointed hopes had once been set, I climbed on alone, and from there could view the whole scene of that gallant failure.

As I looked down upon the Anzac side of the range which I had climbed, I realized again the appalling difficulties of a night attack confronting the scattered columns of Anzacs, British, and Gurkhas who attempted it on the night of August 6th to 7th, 1915. I could again imagine the desperate struggle of all those men thrown into an unexplored region of dry and tortuous water-courses, unexpected cliffs and ravines, complicated by almost impenetrable spiky bush, threatening inextricable error to any wanderer who attempted to pass even by daylight and in peace. What, then, must have been the perplexity of armed and heavily burdened men threading those unknown wilds in total darkness, haunted by the expectation of deadly fire at every turn of the ravines, from the blackness of every thicket and the edge of every cliff? Turning half-left, I could trace the length of Rhododendron Ridge up to " The Apex ", the highest point which we held to the end, and only a short distance farther up I could see the bit of summit where Colonel W. G. Malone had climbed with his own Wellington Battalion and some of the 7th Gloucestershires. I could even make out the site of Quinn's Post along the line of various summits far away on my left—Quinn's Post always so dangerous a position, and always kept so clean and tidy by Malone, who there assured me that " the whole art of war consisted in the exercise of the domestic virtues ". But on that summit above the Apex no domestic virtues availed. Malone himself and nearly all his men were swept out of life by the concentrated fire of shell and rifle.

Just below my feet on the front of Chunuk Bair I could see the cleft or " chimney " extending far down the face into which the Turks had flung their dead, to lie there rotting for many weeks, as I saw them lie. Walking along to my right I passed over a similar point to Chunuk, but lesser (it was " Hill Q ") and so came to the steep ravine or precipitous break which, looking from Suvla, I had thought completely cut off Koja Chemen Tepe (Hill 971), the highest point of the range, from the other summit. But here I made the discovery that the Turks had avoided the ravine by making a bit of road, capable of guns, round the farther end of it, so that I was able without difficulty to climb to the top of the dominating Hill 971 itself. And on returning I made another discovery, which indeed I had hoped for and expected. I climbed down and along the front of the range between Hill Q and Chunuk, and not much more than fifty yards below the summit I found what I was hoping to find. There I could trace a long but shallow trench, much grown over, and at intervals almost obliterated.

That was undoubtedly the trench hastily dug by Major Cecil Allanson's gallant party of 6th Gurkhas and two companies of South Lancashires when they had climbed up there from " The Farm " during the night of August the 8th. They numbered about four hundred in all, and there they lay till a quarter-past five on the morning of the 9th. At four-thirty the whole crest of Chunuk and Hill Q were heavily bombarded by our cruisers, monitors, and guns upon the shore. Striking the sky-line of a summit, such a bombardment flings up spouts of black smoke and huge fragments, spreading fan-shape like the explosions of volcanoes, but it is powerless against entrenchments on the reverse slope. At five-sixteen the bombardment was switched off, and the guns were silent. That was the pre-ordained moment for the assault. Up the few yards of rocks and grass the Gurkhas and Lancastrians clambered. As they rose over the top, the Turks rushed upon them hand to hand. Men and officers fell together. Major Allanson was wounded. But the conflict was brief. The surviving Turks suddenly turned and fled for life down the steep slope leading to their shelters in the gullies below.

For a moment Major Allanson and the remains of his four hundred paused for breath. They were standing on the saddle between Hill Q and Chunuk Bair, and the dead lay thick around them. But far below, straight in front, lit by the risen sun, like a white serpent sliding between the purple shores, ran the sea, the Narrows, the Dardanelles, the one aim and object of all these battles and sudden deaths. Never since Xenophon's Ten Thousand cried " The sea !

The sea ! " had sight been more welcome to a soldier's eye. There went the ships. There were the Turkish transports bringing new troops over from Asia. There ran the white road to Maidos. There the Krithia road. Motor lorries moved along it carrying shells and supplies to Achi Baba. It was the supreme moment in the war. Only hold that summit and victory was ours ! Peace would come again, and the most brilliant strategic conception in the war would be justified.

It was a moment of supreme exultation. Gurkhas and Lancastrians raced and leapt down the reverse slope, pursuing the Turks, and firing as they ran. Allanson, though wounded, raced with his men. Suddenly, before they had gone a hundred yards, crash into the midst of them fell five or six large shells and exploded. Where the shells came from will be a matter of controversy till the war itself is forgotten, but to me it seems almost certain that our own howitzers and mortars stationed near No. 2 Post along the shore were obeying orders to shell the reverse slopes immediately after five-sixteen, and those were, in fact, the only guns that could touch a reverse slope. Naval or monitor shells would either strike the crest or speed over the Straits and explode in Asia. Whatever the cause, the effect was irretrievable. Startled and alarmed, the relics of Allanson's men scrambled back over the summit and into this little trench again. Allanson with a small group stood firm till the Turks, noticing the check, swarmed up with overwhelming reinforcements, and the brightest hope of the campaign faded away. Baldwin's brigade, which ought to have supported Allanson's party, was at the same moment just starting from " The Farm " far below, and was itself doomed to approaching destruction.

DISSOLVING VIEWS

Visible to me, standing on Chunuk Bair that September day in 1928, was the Suvla scene whence Stopford's divisions should have supported the whole of the main attack from Anzac, but on that morning of crisis (August the 9th) all was delay and confusion there. The expected support never came from that quarter, and I who had been stationed as a witness there had nothing to witness but inertia, mistaken or neglected orders, useless deaths, the exhaustion of heat and thirst and a chaos from which no help could come either to the men struggling upon the mountain range or to the service of the war.

From my mountain top I could see the semicircular curve of Suvla Bay from Biyuk Kemikli or Suvla Point to Nibrunesi Point, and inland from the bay stretched the almost circular Salt Lake, nearly dry but gleaming with a deposit of white salt from occasional floodings of the sea. Rather nearer to me I could make out the hills, once so familiar that next day I conducted a few of my party along the now open flats beside the shore where exposed trenches once ran from Anzac to Suvla. With my party I now walked easily up the gravelly space that from its shape gave its name to Scimitar Hill, the scene of our last great effort to drive the Turks off the central range of the peninsula. For this attempt Sir Ian brought round the celebrated 29th Division, and from the Hill called " Chocolate " close in front of it, I saw the famous battalions striving to push up that open " blaze " of gravel or to penetrate through prickly and even flaming bushes on either side. Time after time they strove, and were always driven back under the terrible Turkish fire from the top. It was all in vain, for by this time Mustapha Kemal, now renowned as " The Ghazi," was in command. The opportunity when, on Sunday the 8th, the 6th East Yorks had actually occupied that vital point, was gone for ever. This final effort came on August the 21st, a fortnight too late. It cost us about five thousand casualties, and on the top of that fatal Scimitar-shaped blaze of gravel I now found bones scattered about, thirteen years after they had died. They may all have been Turkish bones. British cemeteries have been laid out with great care at various points on the peninsula. But after thirteen years there is no distinction between the bones of Moslems and Christians.

As I was there again after so many years I could not help walking back a little way to " Chocolate Hill " for old acquaintance' sake. I had stood there beside a machine-gun among the waiting reinforcements in the afternoon of that misty 21st of August, witnessing the terrible contests on Scimitar Hill. Bullets and shells were whining and crashing stormily around us there also, and quite suddenly I was felled like an ox by a shell or fragment which cut a neat crescent on the top of my skull, and drenched my shirt and breeches with blood. Beyond the stunning blow, like the stroke of a huge hammer, I was hardly conscious of pain, and after being bandaged on the reverse side of the hill to check the bleeding and the lumps of pinkish jelly which kept oozing out, and which I feared might be all the brains I possessed, within an hour I was back at my former position and there remained till darkness fell and the terrific and disastrous day was over. Then I walked the four miles or so to the dressing station by the shore, and when a sympathetic surgeon told me my skull was fractured and he must insert a silver plate, I gave him the information that my skull was impenetrable to all but reason. And so it proved, for, except for a renewed dressing every day for a fortnight, I went about my business as usual. On my return after those thirteen years to the dark backward of that time, I found my former position on Chocolate Hill almost unaltered, though the trenches were crumbling and overgrown. No traces of my blood were visible!

Let us omit the next three years of the war, crowded though they were with visions of a dark backward to which time was adding the varied scenes actually passing before me. Let us omit Mityleni, haunted by Sappho, who lives immortalized by two pages of scattered fragments of verse ; and omit Salonika, where one could meet the shade of Alexander, and of Roman legions tramping the great road to Constantinople, and of insignificant St. Paul evolving doctrinal Christianity, and of the builders who designed the three Byzantine churches, and of devastating Turks half paralysing the beautiful city as certain wasps half paralyse a caterpillar so that their grubs may devour it at leisure. Let us omit Egypt, too, the long and narrow coffin of immemorial death. Thickly crowded with visions of the past and of the passing present were all those scenes that I beheld during the years of the war. But let us go back again to the familiar land of France.

In old days, moving along the solid ground, I always found a peculiar charm in that customary journey from Calais or Boulogne to Paris. No matter how often I had passed that way, every French station, every village, every farm, almost every house was a new delight. So was that watery region full of deep ponds fringed with sedge and brown willow wands, among which fishers sat contentedly all day long watching their floats in vain. But the chief delight was to look out for the approach to Abbeville, to see the great towers of St. Wulfran's Church, if only for a minute; or perhaps to drop a train and walk through the town itself to see the clear river Somme gliding under ancient walls and look up at the flamboyant west front, over-decorated, no doubt, but still so nobly lavish of its richness—so lavish compared with the interior, which is almost as unadorned as a chapel in Scotland. In the war, only a few miles away, I found the sister church of St. Riquier, designed, I suppose, by the same builders, with west front even more flamboyant and over-decorated, but with interior far more beautiful. I could imagine no reason for the difference, except perhaps that Abbeville had so often been destroyed by fire that at last the builders thought further elaboration a waste of energy.

And next along the line came Amiens. The cathedral is still visible from the train as it slows down through the public gardens, and the east end and flèche are still visible for a moment between the gasworks as it leaves the station. But in the old days there was a longish interval for lunch, and an active lover of beauty could almost run to the west front itself and yet return in time to clamber up the high steps into a carriage as the train moved off. Indeed the exertion was worth some risk, and even some hunger.

The days of the happy tourist alive to beauty have gone. Abbeville and Amiens have far different visions of memory hovering around them now. Passing Abbeville, I see once more the Châteaux of Rollancourt and Vauchelles, where we correspondents were stationed in the last years of the war. And in passing Amiens again, I see the station shattered, the main streets in ruins, the glass in the cathedral removed, the elaborate carvings on the west front (showing in sculpture the whole history of the Jewish scriptures, including the prophetic poems) all protected with sandbags like an entrenchment—all but the large representation of the Last Judgment above the main west door, the culmination of the Christian Sculptures. And in the height of the roof I see two ominous holes where shells had penetrated, though without much damage, except that the shrine of St. John was broken. But whether it contains the relic of St. John the Baptist or of St. John the Beloved Disciple has for some centuries been disputed.

The cathedral certainly needed all possible protection at the beginning of the war and again in its last year. As all visitors know, Amiens commands the line communicating the Channel ports with Paris, and it is the junction for other lines. In the early summer of 1918, the German guns were advanced to within shelling distance of the city, and German troops occupied most of the plain of Santerre, lying just south of the Somme and the ridge between Corbie and Peronne. Corbie itself, with its large two-towered and ruined church, stands only some seven miles away, near the junction of the Ancre with the Somme, names of rivers now terribly familiar. Upon that ridge overlooking the Santerre plain I was present on the day which marked the beginning of the war's end.

It was three-thirty in the morning of August the 8th, 1918. Starting at 2 a.m. from Rollancourt I had driven with our famous censor C. E. Montague and my fellow-correspondent Beach-Thomas, had skirted Amiens and Corbie, and so climbed the ridge on foot and waited there for the appointed hour of 4 a.m. Though it was high summer, a thick white mist lay over the whole country. As dawn approached a dim light glimmered through it, but one could not see more than fifty or a hundred yards. We ought to have been able to look right down to the Somme, fringed with reedy pools, and across the river to the undulating plain, once so fertile but now marked only by the names of ruined and deserted villages—Hamel, Rosières, Chaulne, Villers-Bretonneux, scene of Australian heroism, and Mondidier, where the French line began. But none of this was visible, and not a sound arose as we stood waiting in the obscurity. Holding our watches we saw the hands move on towards four o'clock, bringing death to so many who were waiting or sleeping below us. As the hands touched four, the crash and boom of a hundred batteries burst from the invisible guns, and hundreds of shells screamed and burst in deadly fragments among the trenches and dug-outs of surprised and bewildered Germans, enveloped like ourselves in the thick white mist. A similar mist had helped their terrible advance against our 5th Army in the previous March.

Montague and I walked for a mile or two along the top of the ridge towards Bray as far as " Welcome Wood ", where we had come under heavy shell fire only a day or two before. But the sun was not yet strong enough to clear the mist, and I saw only dark lines moving along the plain below, no doubt our infantry, interspersed with large black objects, probably tanks. It was disappointing, for a kind of " instinct " told me that day was to be the cardinal point on which the dark portal of the war would open for our advance. Instinct was only a number of collected reasonings subconsciously at work, but it told me right. It appeared to be confirmed when we met whole companies of disarmed German prisoners marching towards us down the road. Thousands of

German prisoners had been taken before, but the sight of these companies that misty morning filled me with hope. We stood indeed at the turning hinge of the war, and Ludendorff in his memoirs described that 8th of August as his " Black Day ". Surprise, too rarely secured in this war, is the surest way to victory, and in going over the Santerre plain in the sunlight of next day I found all the evidences of surprise—officers' breakfasts laid ready on the tables in their dug-outs, letters and little possessions of the men abandoned in haste, and, strewn on the ground, the bodies of those who had no time to stand and fire, or even to run away. On August the 15th, a week after our victory, I attended a great service in Amiens Cathedral to celebrate the Virgin's Assumption and to render thanks for the preservation of the supremely beautiful building.

Two other scenes naturally rise before me whenever I now pass through that haunted corner of North-east France and the Flemish borders. In both, as on August the 8th, C. E. Montague was with me, and to be with him at any point of the war was always a special delight. All our censors were first-rate men at their business. There were four of them in the closing years of the war, all under command of Major Neville Lytton, an artist well known in Paris, and the only one among us who possessed the enormous advantage of speaking French so as to be interesting to a Frenchman. As I said in an earlier chapter, the man who did most work and organized best was Captain C. R. Cadge, a solicitor from Norwich, who, like the rest, had been too badly wounded to serve in the fighting line. But C. E. Montague had every quality of nature and knowledge that could attract me. From Balliol he had passed straight into the service of C. P. Scott, the famous editor of the *Manchester Guardian*, and there had won the highest position a journalist can win as leader-writer and dramatic and literary critic. He was a perfect master of our language, and his knowledge of our literature was almost overwhelming. He was rather ashamed of it, and he laughs at his gift of exact quotation in " My Friend the Swan ", one of the excellent scenes in his *Fiery Particles*, which also contains " Honours Easy ", the best satire on officers greedy for ribbons. I told him once that I saw the apt quotation sticking in his throat but checked for fear of boring me. His books are well known—*A Hind let Loose, The Right Place, Rough Justice*, and *Disenchantment*, the best criticism written on the war.

But, though his ironic humour and imaginative gifts were a perpetual pleasure to me whenever I had the fortune to have him with me as " accompanying officer ", that pleasure was equalled for my own special work by his extraordinary sense of country and direction. I have thought myself almost as good as a horse or a dog at that faculty, but Montague could beat any mule or collie. He knew exactly where the watersheds lay, and what was the course of every river and stream. Perhaps it was his long experience as a mountaineer and Alpine climber that guided him, though he never spoke of such adventures. Indeed, if modesty can be a fault, he was just too modest for the world. But, like myself, the world lost heavily when this incomparable man died on Whit-Sunday, 1928, after two brief years of quiet literary work in an old farmhouse at Burford, not far from Oxford. When he was retiring from his splendid service on the *Manchester Guardian*, he wrote to me : " Shall I confess —writing in my beloved M.G. had become, in a way, too habitual—too much in danger of becoming easy. Isn't there a lot in old Pater's notion that 'failure in life is to form habits'?" The thought and the motive are characteristic of the man. And indeed it may have been partly for this fear of forming habits that, while also indignant at the German invasion of Belgium, he dyed his white hair as black as possible and recruited as a private in the " Sports Battalion " at the beginning of the war. We have heard from *The Prisoner of Chillon* and other records that black hair may turn white from fear in a single night ; but in Montague's case courage caused the reverse to happen, as I once said at a *Manchester Guardian* dinner in his honour.

Each evening it was the custom for a correspondent to suggest to his " accompanying officer " where to drive out next day, and so I see myself on August the 24th going with Montague to the battered site of Mesnil, a village overhanging the valley of the Ancre, opposite the ill-omened heights of Thiepval. We made our way down to the stream through sticks of trees that once were a wood, and were still strewn with fragments of man. Montague, in his sensitive way, looked at me sideways to see if I noticed them. I did notice them, but after what we had lived through, the expression of horror failed. We crossed the Ancre and its swamps on a few boards, and began to climb the opposite hill, up which the Germans had just retreated, though they held the line of the summit, on which we could see the base of a windmill and a few shattered houses that Montague told me was Pozière, standing on the famous road from Albert to Bapaume. As we went up, British soldiers came swarming out of Thiepval wood on our left, and from pits and ravines around us small groups of Germans rose, holding up their hands in appeal and throwing away their rifles at our command. We formed a batch of seven two deep, and marched them back over the river to the charge of the authorities at Mesnil. As we were both unarmed that might seem risky, but the poor fellows were only anxious to be captured. Conversing with them as we went, I found that all were under nineteen and were dead sick of the war. One told me regretfully that his mother had a nice little house near Frankfurt-am-Oder, and always kept a comfortable bed with clean sheets ready waiting for his return, but here he had been for months, coated in mud, sleeping in filth among rats, and covered with lice. Millions of men on both sides could have joined in lamenting that monstrous contrast.

The other scene that I witnessed with Montague fell on Armistice Day, November the 11th, 1918. Our little group of correspondents was then stationed at Lille. Starting at dawn by the gate of the Vauban fortifications, he and I rushed through Orchies and a big forest to the deserted city of Valenciennes, and, turning sharp left, followed the canal, scene of heroic disaster four years before. The emotional cheering, laughter and tears of the returning refugees as we ran through them was strangely infectious, as joy is usually more infectious than sorrow. In a suburb of Mons we drove through thin woods and public gardens where German corpses still lay unburied, unfortunate men killed just a few hours too soon. Then we ran right into Mons, and stopped before the Town Hall in the beautiful old market-place. A Canadian Brigade and a squadron of the old 5th Lancers (the Irish) were drawn up in the square. The appointed hour of eleven o'clock struck from the belfry. The British and Belgian National Anthems were played. The chimes attempted " God Save the King " and " Tipperary ", which to foreign minds was its rival throughout the war. All the people shouted, sang, and wept. The greatest war in history was over, and I had seen it end in Mons. So far as war-correspondence goes, it was my biggest exploit, and Montague shared my satisfaction. But my editor thought nothing of it. Sitting in Fleet Street beside the 'bus and Tube, how could he realize the distance from Lille to Mons, or any other magnitude of space ? Besides, he wanted slush and tosh by the column, and no wonder he was disappointed.

Then comes the final dissolving view of the war. On September the 23rd, 1931, I was in Cologne as a passing visitor, driven home by such a fall in the value of the sterling that I lost six marks in every pound. Looking out upon the Rhine, I saw a vision of myself more than fifty years ago eagerly spelling out the first great scenes of " Faust ", especially the " Prologue in Heaven ", and so excited by admiration that I read nearly all night. And then, by way of contrast, I saw a small group of men gathered at the entrance of the great Kaiser Bridge, where railway, road and foot-path pass between heavy bronze statues of recently departed Emperors on horseback. I was standing there with my colleagues, a distinguished number, including Perry Robinson, Percival Phillips, Philip Gibbs, Beach-Thomas, Cecil Roberts, and Lacon Watson, who had lately joined us. It was December the 16th, 1918, and at nine-fifteen Field-Marshal Haig appeared, accompanied by a small personal staff.

I had watched Haig's progress for more than twenty years, ever since my old colleague, Charlie Williams, who had seen fifteen campaigns, pointed him out to me at an Aldershot Field-Day as the future Commander-in-Chief—an astonishing instance of foresight, just forestalled by the same prophecy made by Colonel G. F. R. Henderson at the Staff College. Of course Haig was a Scot and retained the definite Scottish qualities, but he was brought up at an English public school and at Oxford. I now could observe more closely the characteristic face—the forehead low but broad, the chin and jaws square and resolute, the blue, colour-blind eyes, calm and unilluminated by passion or excitement ; and the rather tall and powerful figure, kept trim by riding, daily exercises, and the careful diet of one who fears old age and incapacity more than any other fate. He was as usual dressed with the careful exactness which he brought to all his work, and with which he strove to endue the General Staff and the whole spirit of the army as reorganized by Lord Haldane, for whom he retained a loyal admiration when Haldane was shamefully dismissed by Asquith owing to the clamour of Tories and the mob. One might call an imperturbable calm his finest quality. At a sign of undue excitement he would say, " Don't fuss ". Outwardly cool and aloof from boyhood, he never gained an army's personal affection such as Napoleon, or Sir John Moore, or Roberts could command. But as became a Scot, he was conscious of an underlying spiritual influence in all he attempted, and one of his favourite sayings was, " It is the spirit that quickeneth." Endurance and persistence were the military virtues with which he inspired the army, and Napoleon accounted those qualities far more valuable than courage. As I looked at his unyielding figure in that moment of triumph upon Cologne bridge, I recalled his famous order issued in the moment of national peril only in the previous April :

"Every position must be held to the last man : there must be no retirement. With our backs to the wall, and believing in the justice of our cause, each one of us must fight to the end."

While we correspondents and our censors stood at attention before him, he began haltingly to address us. He was one of those men who inspire confidence in our English people by their inability to speak. Outside Ladysmith after his failure at Spion Kop, Buller made to his troops an incomprehensible speech which roused them to such enthusiasm that they gladly followed him to his next disaster. If Kitchener had been a fluent orator, he would never have raised the thousands of his New Army, but we all thought him a rock of defence, and rocks are dumb. Men of that kind act by a sort of instinct or inspiration, which they could not explain, just as from the beginning of the arts it has been supposed that artists and poets work under the influence of some unconscious and inexplicable power of which they can give no account in words. Even in the Houses of Parliament rhetoric counts for less and less, and in one House it has faded away. So on the Kaiser Bridge Haig followed his British nature and made no attempt at a speech. He just thanked us for our services, and then in more definite words added the significant sentence that the ensuing peace must on no account be a peace of vengeance. If only the vengeful rhetoricians who were soon to gather in Versailles had laid those words to heart, how different the condition of the world for the next fifteen years would have been! Thus having spoken, or failed to speak, he handed to each of us mature and experienced correspondents a little Union Jack nailed to a stick of firewood, and sent us away happy as good children at a school treat.

The dissolving views fade away. The war was over so far as the killing of men went, and I was left in Cologne for many weeks watching the killing of women and children by the British blockade, prolonged for months after the Armistice. I have been told that the blockade killed more Germans than the war, and that may well have been so, for the condition of the women, the children, and the infants was beyond conception horrible. Among the working classes the children were thin as sticks, and the infants shapeless and boneless. The mothers had no milk, and the French had requisitioned vast numbers of cows. Happily a deadly form of influenza was quickly reducing a population exhausted by hardship and a starving diet.

One gleam of consolation may illuminate this dismal side of victory. It came when Field-Marshal Plumer, commanding the Army of the Rhine, wrote to the Ministers in London that the blockade must be called off, for he could no longer restrain his troops from giving away their rations to the starving people.

Thus, in successive scenes at which I have myself been present, I have attempted in the chapters of this book to reveal glimpses into the dark backward and abysm of time as they rose before my mind like visions. Such glimpses into the backward of mankind's prolonged history, or of our brief personal life, may be seen by everyone who lives, and at any time of the day or night. They make the shifting cloud-scenery of all human memories whether for joy or sorrow, for peace or war, for hope or disaster, and I can claim no private gift or advantage in my perception of them as they rise before my inward sight—except perhaps that my course of life has given me the advantage of moving in varied scenes behind which great events in the mysterious course of time have lain hid or been revealed.

Note.—My own personal experiences given in this last chapter and one or two of the earlier are described more fully in my autobiography, *Changes and Chances, More Changes More Chances*, and *Last Changes Last Chances*.

INDEX

Abbeville, 116
Abdul Hamid, Sultan, 224 ff.
Abyssinian Church, 81
Actium, 59 ff.
Adam and Eve, ix
" A. E." (George Russell), viii
Æneid, The (reference to), 11
Agincourt (Azincourt), 113 ff.
Albanians, the, 58, 85, 86
Albert, Prince Consort, 219
Alexander, 260
Allanson, Major Cecil, 256–7
Amiens, 116, 261–2, 264
Amphitheatre, 101
Antony, 59, 63 ff.
Apuleius, 70
Armenians, the, 49, 223
Armistice Day, 267
Arnold, Matthew, 197
Arta, 58, 69
Artaxerxes, 36, 39
Asquith, H. H., 269
Athens, 26 ff.
Auerstädt, Battle of, 177 ff.
Augereau, Marshal, 174 ff., 182

Babylon, 14 ff.
Baghdad, 14, 23, 41
Baldwin, General A. H., 254, 257
Balkan Races, 87
Balmerino, Lord, 153
Balue, Cardinal, 132
Beach-Thomas, William, 110, 262, 268

Benguella, 204 ff.
Bernadotte, 174, 176, 178
Bertier, 174
Black Prince, the, 114, 115
Blessington, Lady, 196
Blücher, 173, 177
Bourchier, James, 86, 185
Brion, Friederike, 181
Brooke, Rupert, 197
Brunswick, Duke of, 173 ff.
Buller, Sir Redvers, 270
Bunyan, 209
Burns, Robert, 159
Byron, 53, 187 ff.

Cader Idris, 161
Cadge, Captain C. R., 110, 264
Cæsar, 65, 67
Caucasus, 24, 48
Chalybes, 53
Charlie, Prince, 152 ff.
Cheirosophus, 44, 47, 51
Chinon, 123 ff.
Chrestěna, 56
Christian Martyrs, 102 ff.
Christiane Vulpius, 180–2
Clairmont, Claire, 196
Clearchus, 35, 38, 41
Cleopatra, 59, 64, 65, 67
Commines, Philip de, 133
Constantine, Emperor, 88, 107
Constantine, King, 185
Constantinople, 222
Crete, 185–7
Cromwell, Oliver, 142

273

INDEX

Cumberland, Duke of, 154, 158–9
Cunaxa, 37, 56
Cyrus, 33, 34, 36, 39

Dante (*Inferno*), 81
Dardanelles, 222, 227, 253 ff.
Das, Madhu Sudan, 77
Davout, 174 ff., 178
Diocletian, 88 ff.
Dolgelly, 161 ff.
D'Orsay, Count, 196
Druids, the, 164–5, 168–9
Durham, Edith, 85, 86

Eckermann, 183
Edward III, 113, 115
Elcho, Lord, 153
Epictetus, 69
Euripides, 29
Evans, Sir Arthur, 185

Feilding, Lady Dorothy, 251
Frederick-William III, 173, 177

Gabriel, British Commissioner, 217–18
Gargantua, 123 ff.
Garibaldi, 195
George V, 112
Gibbs, Philip, 110, 268
Gneisenau, 173
Goethe, 177, 180 ff., 191, 193
Goschen, Sir Edward, 250–1

Haig, Field-Marshal, 268–70
Haldane, Lord, 251, 269
Hamilton, General Sir Ian, 258
Hampden, John, 142
Harfleur, 114
Henderson, Colonel G. F. R., 269
Henry II, 127, 131
Henry V, 111, 113
Hermes, the, 252–3

Hilmi Pasha, 224
Hohenlohe, Prince, 174 ff.

Iliad, The, 4 ff.
Italy, 98

Jeans, Sir James, xi
Jena, Battle of, 174 ff.
Jena, University of, 170 ff.
Jerusalem, 72 ff.
Jesus Christ, 75 ff., 108
Jews, the, 74
Joan of Arc, 121, 127, 131
Johnson, Samuel (*quoted*), ix

Kaiser William II, 227, 229, 236, 250
Kemal, Mustapha, 258
Kitchener, Lord, 270
Koran, The, 232–3
Kurds, the, 47, 48, 49

Lannes, Marshal, 173 ff., 182
Leonardo, 134
Livingstone, David, 210 ff.
Loanda, 203 ff.
Lodovico, Il Moro, 133 ff.
Loire, River, 122
Ludendorff, 264
Lysander, 31
Lytton, Major Neville, 110, 264

Macedonia, 223
Maisoncelle, 113, 117, 120
Makololo, the, 212 ff.
Malone, Colonel W. G., 255
Mantinea, 57
Marvell, Andrew, 139 ff.
Masefield, John, 111
Mashíko, 213
Massingham, H. W., 185
Maximian, 89, 99, 107
Menon, 41
Meredith, George, xi
Metagama, the, 238

INDEX

Milton, John, 137 ff., 182
Mithras, 105
Moffat, 214
Montague, C. E., 110, 262 ff.
Moore, Tom, 189, 194, 195
Munro, Dr. Hector, 251
Murat, 175, 176, 178, 179–80
Murray, Lord George, 154, 155, 158

Napoleon, 172 ff., 269
Nebuchadnezzar, 17 ff.
Nevinson, John, 148
Nevinsons of Newby, 147 ff.
Newby, 147 ff.
Newfoundland, 238
Newstead Abbey, 184 ff.
Ney, Marshal, 174–5, 182
Nicopolis, 59, 69
Nietzsche, 182

Octavia, 67
Octavian (Augustus), 63 ff.

Palestine, 72 ff.
Palmyra, 13
Parry, William, 199
Phillips, Percival, 110, 268
Pilate, 79
Plumer, Field-Marshal, 271
Polytechnic, the, 249
Pretender, the Young, *see* Charlie, Prince
Principé, 204 ff.
Prisca, ex-Empress, 92
Proxenus, 33, 39, 41, 43

Quaker Ambulance, 252

Rabelais, 123 ff.
Rawlinson, General Sir Henry, 121
Rawstorne, 209
Reshid, Mohammed V, 227
Roberts, Cecil, 268

Robinson, Perry, 110, 268
Rollancourt, Château, 109, 261, 262
Rüchel, 174
Russell, Herbert, 110

St. Barnabas Pilgrimages, 222, 253
St. Paul, 260
Salŏna, 94 ff.
"Samson," 165 ff.
San Thomé, 204 ff.
Sappho, 260
Scharnhorst, 173, 177
Schiller, 180
Scillus, 56
Scott, C. P., 265
Scott, Walter, 193
Sects, various Christian, 82, 83
Shelley, 194, 196
Slavery, 205 ff.
Socrates, 28 ff., 67
Somme, River, 116
Soult, Marshal, 174–5
Spalato (Split), 87 ff.
Stein, Charlotte von, 180
Suli, 53
Swift, Jonathan, ix

Taocians, 52
Theches, Mount, 54
Thélème, Abbey of, 127 ff.
Theodora, Saint, Empress, 70
Thrasybulus, 32
Tissaphernes, 40, 45
Titanic, the, 239 ff.
Trebizond, 25, 55
Trelawny, 196, 199
Tripoli, 85
Trojan Women, The (references to), 10, 11

Union-and-Progress, Committee of, 226

INDEX

Valmy, 177
Vassos, Colonel, 185
Venizelos, 184, 187-8
Victoria, Queen, 219
Vierzehn Heiligen, 172, 175, 176, 178-9
Virgil, 125

Wade, Marshal, 153, 154
Watson, Lacon, 268

Weimar, 179 ff.
Williams, Charlie, 268

Xenophon, 26 ff., 66, 256

Yeats, W. B., 112
Yildiz Kiosk, 224, 225, 228-30
Young Turks, the, 222, 226

Zenobia, 13